Binary
Options

Founded in 1807, John Wiley & Sons is the oldest independent publishing company in the United States. With offices in North America, Europe, Australia and Asia, Wiley is globally committed to developing and marketing print and electronic products and services for our customers' professional and personal knowledge and understanding.

The Wiley Trading series features books by traders who have survived the market's ever changing temperament and have prospered—some by reinventing systems, others by getting back to basics. Whether a novice trader, professional or somewhere in-between, these books will provide the advice and strategies needed to prosper today and well into the future.

For a list of available titles, visit our Web site at www.WileyFinance.com.

Binary Options

Strategies for
Directional and
Volatility Trading

ALEX NEKRITIN

WILEY

John Wiley & Sons, Inc.

Published by John Wiley & Sons, Inc., Hoboken, New Jersey.

Published simultaneously in Canada.

For general information on our other products and services or for technical support, please contact our Customer Care Department within the United States at (800) 762-2974, outside the United States at (317) 572-3993 or fax (317) 572-4002.

Wiley publishes in a variety of print and electronic formats and by print-on-demand. Some material included with standard print versions of this book may not be included in e-books or in print-on-demand. If this book refers to media such as a CD or DVD that is not included in the version you purchased, you may download this material at http://booksupport.wiley.com. For more information about Wiley products, visit www.wiley.com.

Library of Congress Cataloging-in-Publication Data:

Nekritin, Alex, 1980–
   Binary options : strategies for directional and volatility trading / Alex Nekritin.
      p. cm.—(Wiley trading series)
   Includes index.
   ISBN 978-1-118-40724-0 (cloth); ISBN 978-1-118-41777-5 (ebk);
   ISBN 978-1-118-52868-6 (ebk); ISBN 978-1-118-42182-6 (ebk)
   1. Options (Finance) 2. Futures. I. Title.
   HG6024.A3N448 2013
   332.64'53—dc23
                                            2012032301

Printed in the United States of America

10 9 8 7 6 5 4 3 2 1

This book is dedicated to my parents, Nina and Boris Nekritin.
Thanks for all your unconditional love and support.
Without you, none of this would have been possible.

Contents

Foreword

Binary options are a relatively new and unique way to take part in the financial markets. Over the past decade they have become popular instruments in Europe and Asia, and more recently, over the past few years, have not only gained acceptance, but have seen widespread growth in the United States, particularly within the retail trading community.

One may ask, "Why, with all of the investment vehicles available, stocks, futures, forex, options, exchange-traded funds, and so on, would I want to take a look at another contract type?" This is a legitimate question.

One of the main reasons traders may look to a contract like a binary option is risk control. Any seasoned trader in any market knows that profitability on any given trade is secondary, but risk management on every trade is mandatory and of the utmost concern. This is particularly true when participating in leveraged markets such as futures and currencies, where one mistake can not only result in large losses, but in some cases, losses that exceed the amount of capital in the trader's account. This can create an ugly scenario for any trader—the dreaded margin call. If you're not familiar with this concept, just think of the reaction of Randolph and Mortimer Duke at the end of the movie *Trading Places* and you may have a good idea of the devastating effect a margin call can have.

In the case of a binary option, whether I am buying or selling, my risk is always limited and 100 percent defined up front, before the order is submitted. What this means is that a trader can very closely manage the risk on every trade. No matter what happens in the world while the trade is on—geopolitical tensions, central bank announcements, natural disasters, whatever the case—the investor cannot lose more than is put up for the trade. No worries of margin calls or being margined out, and more importantly, no chance of your broker calling you up and telling you that you have to deposit more funds—funds that you may not have.

Another reason to consider binary options is simply cost. Many of you reading this may have wanted to speculate in the financial markets. You may have been standing at the gas pump and thought, "I knew oil was going up." Or perhaps you were reading the newspaper, saw something that caught your eye, and said, "I think stocks are going up tomorrow." Unfortunately for many, the cost of placing a trade in the traditional markets may just be too great. Whether it be because of large margin requirements, or the risk of trading a single contract alone is just too great, you've been shut out of the trading community.

If that is the case, binary options, because of the low barrier to entry, may offer you the opportunity to participate in markets you otherwise wouldn't have access to. Most importantly, you can now take part in these markets while protecting yourself through the limited risk nature of these contracts. Additionally, if you are a seasoned trader, you may look to binary options as an alternative vehicle, giving you opportunity to trade in situations you otherwise wouldn't take in the more traditional markets.

You may be saying to yourself, this sounds really good, but if it is so good, why isn't everyone doing this?

Well, one reason is that trading, in any market, is not easy. It is a skill and, like any skill, takes time to develop. It is a path that one should start down slowly, and trading, in and of itself, is a never-ending process of learning and trying to improve.

Another reason binary options have not become a household name is simply that as a relatively new trading vehicle, there has been a severe lack of quality material on the subject. Some information has been available; however, it often took a great deal of digging to find it, and when one did, it could be difficult to piece it all together and assemble into a sensible format.

Thankfully, with the publication of Alex's work on binary options, this hindrance has become a thing of the past. The following pages in this book provide a clear, concise guide to trading binary options. In a way, it is hard for me to call this just a "book." It is in fact a complete user manual, providing a step-by-step guide to trading binary options. Starting with the very basics and moving all the way through to advanced strategies, it offers what will undoubtedly be a very valuable reference for traders of all levels.

Whether you've never placed a binary options trade—or, for that matter, a trade in any market—this course will give you a solid foundation from which to enter the market with a full understanding of mechanics, price movement, and, most important, risk.

Even if you're an experienced binary options trader, this work will likely provide new ideas and strategies to enhance your current trading methodology. Even though I have studied binary options for several years, the material covered here gave me new concepts to explore and opened my eyes to looking at familiar concepts in a whole new light.

I hope you enjoy this work as much as I do and wish you much success in all your endeavors.

Dan Cook
September 2012

Preface

Exchange-traded binary options are fixed-risk/fixed-reward instruments that are fairly simple to trade. They are distinctly different from regular vanilla put/call options and they absolutely should *not* be confused with over-the-counter binary options. In this guide, we will cover what sets exchange-traded binary options apart and explain to you in great detail how they work.

Please read this guide very carefully and follow along with the examples provided. The text is deliberately packed with a ton of examples, some of which may seem repetitive to you. The idea behind this is that once you go through enough examples, you will be able to grasp the concept. In order to solidify the concepts even further, you can visit www .traderschoiceoptions.com for more trade examples and even quizzes. Once you are clear on the concept, you may find binary options to be simple to implement. You will also see that they have certain unique and clear advantages that provide for potentially great trading opportunities.

This guide is beneficial for beginner, intermediate, and advanced traders who are not familiar with binary options.

If you are a beginner, all concepts are diligently explained, and you will find a detailed glossary to cover all trading-related terms that you may or may not be familiar with. You certainly don't need to be a mathematics genius to trade binary options. The only type of math really involved is basic addition and subtraction. You really need to understand the concept, and the rest will be easy, fun, and potentially rewarding—although, as with all types of trading, there are always risks.

If you are an intermediate or an advanced trader, you should be able to pick up the theory behind binary options pretty quickly. You may still want to take a look at the basic sections of this guide, as the concepts that we introduce build on one another. You should put a great deal of focus on the sections that explain the theory and practice behind binary options. Once you go through a number of examples and learn the key attributes of binary options, you will see how they have certain unique features that, if used correctly, can provide you with many great trading opportunities. By using this guide with a demo trading account, you should be well on your way to taking advantage of this great trading instrument.

After completing this intro course, you may want to take a look at our strategy guide at www.traderschoiceoptions.com to give you some interesting trading strategies and systems that you can use with binary options.

The course is broken down into sections, and each section builds on the previous one. The best way to approach this guide is to read it in order.

PART 1: INTRO TO BINARY OPTIONS

Here, you will learn the basics, like: What are binary options? Where are they traded? What instruments are they traded on? How safe is your money when you are trading them? How do they differ from other kinds of options?

PART 2: BINARY OPTIONS THEORY

Here, you will learn the theory behind binary options and how you can use them to speculate on the markets. Among other aspects, you will cover margin/collateral, expiration times, the mechanics of strike prices, and how to read a binary option chain. Once you are clear on the concepts, you can follow our trade examples to make sure that you understand the logic behind binary options trades.

PART 3: TRADING BINARY OPTIONS

Here, you will learn how to actually trade binary options. You will learn how to read price quotes and order tickets and how to enter and exit positions. You will learn the transaction costs associated with binary options trading and will walk through placing a trade. Once you are clear on these concepts, you can go through more trade examples to make sure that you are ready to start trading binary options.

PART 4: BINARY OPTION TRADING STRATEGIES

Here, you will learn some directional and volatility trading strategies with binary options using both technical and fundamental analysis. With directional trading, you can simply speculate on the underlying asset's price to move in one direction or another.

The great factor of volatility trading strategies is that you can speculate on the underlying asset to stay within a certain range or go outside of a range by expiration. This allows you a lot more options and flexibility in your trading strategies. In order to trade volatility vanilla put/call options, trading accounts require relatively high deposits; however, binary options open up the world of volatility trading to you with only a $100 deposit for every contract traded.

PART 5: CREATING YOUR BINARY OPTIONS STRATEGY

Here, you will learn all about how binary options can be extremely beneficial for setting up a trading system. Binary options can help mitigate the effects of emotion and make calculating potential risks and rewards very straightforward. In addition, this section will teach you about some of the basic trading strategies that you can use with binary options. Long, short, range-bound, breakout-bound—the list goes on and on. The advantages of trading binaries are endless.

PART 6: MANAGING YOUR BINARY OPTIONS ACCOUNT

Here, you will learn that, as with any trading account, there is a large amount of work involved with a binary options account. However, it doesn't have to be very difficult or stressful if you follow our guidelines to control your risk and protect your gains. This section will teach you about many aspects of risk management as they pertain to binary options. Before you start trading, be sure to study this section.

PART 7: PROFITING WITH VOLATILITY

Here, you will learn about one of the most potentially profitable ways to trade binary options: premium collection. This allows you to make money off of instruments doing what they often already do: staying where they are. By using our descriptions of both the basics and the complexities of premium collection, you can set up a trading system that is reliable, robust, and successful.

So strap yourself in and get ready to learn about a new trading instrument that can provide you with endless possibilities and great opportunity.

Acknowledgments

First of all, I want to thank my father, Boris Nekritin, for getting me in the trading game many years ago. Without him, I would never have accomplished even one tenth of what I have accomplished, and I certainly would never have been able to write this book. There are many other people who deserve acknowledgment; the list includes but is not limited to the following: Dan Antonuccio, for pretty much managing all of my projects and, as usual, putting everything together to turn my ideas into reality; Eddie Kwong, who is a great friend and one of the most connected guys I know in the trading industry, for putting me in touch with Wiley and teaching me a ton about the business; Dan Cook, who is the real expert in binaries, for patiently answering all of my complex questions about the product; Abe Cofnas, who is one of the most knowledgeable and enthusiastic traders I have met, for getting me excited about binary options in the first place; Patrick Tobin and Even Nelson, who were a lot of help with the writing and many of the images in the book; the team at Wiley—Evan Burton, Meg Freeborn, and Simone Black—for believing in the idea and making the book a reality. Of course, my parents Nina and Boris Nekritin for unconditional love and support in everything I do. And last, but certainly not least, my fiancée, Kendra, for helping me stay focused with her love and support.

PART I

Introduction to Binary Options

T his section will provide you with an overview and discussion of the main benefits of binary option trading.

What You Will Learn:

- What are binary options?
- How do binary options differ from traditional options?
- Which underlying instruments are binary options available to trade on?
- Where can you trade binary options?
- What are the benefits of trading binary options?
- What makes binary options unique compared to other instruments and options?

When you complete this section you should have a basic understanding of what binary options are and be familiar with their main advantages.

CHAPTER 1

What Are Binary Options?

B inary options are also known as digital options or all-or-nothing options. They are derivative instruments that can be considered a yes-or-no proposition—either the event happens or it does not.

Binary options are considered binary because there are only two potential outcomes at expiration: 0 or 100; 0 and 100 refer to the settlement value of a binary option and could be viewed in dollars. At expiration, if you are incorrect, you do not make anything ($0), and if you are correct, you make up to $100. The next section will go into further detail on the settlement value of binary options.

ON WHAT ASSET CLASSES ARE BINARY OPTIONS AVAILABLE?

Binary options are available on four different asset classes. These include stock index futures, commodity futures, spot forex, and economic data releases. This section will explain the basics of what each of the asset classes are and how they work.

Before we explain the different futures asset classes, it is important to first understand what futures are. A future is a contract that says that the buyer or seller will purchase or sell a specific asset for a specific price at a specific time in the future. Investors trade futures contracts to speculate for profit and to hedge their assets. One of the benefits of trading futures is that traders don't have to physically buy a certain commodity in order to speculate on its price movements. They can simply enter their trade with a smaller amount of cash on margin.

Futures contracts are traded on an exchange, and their price typically moves with the price of the underlying asset. Since traders are speculating on a future price of an asset, the futures price can be slightly higher or lower than the spot price.

All futures contracts have specific expiration dates that vary by the asset class on which the futures contract is based.

Let's look at an example of speculating with futures contracts:

Let's say the price of physical gold is currently $1000 per oz. and you believe the price is going to increase. Instead of buying physical gold, you can buy gold futures on margin for $1050 per oz. Let's assume that after one month physical gold has gone up to $1200 per oz. and gold futures contracts are trading at $1210. You can exit your position and lock in a profit of $160. This profit is calculated by subtracting the futures purchase price from the futures sale ($1210 per oz.) or $1210 – $1050 = $160.

For a trader, using futures on margin is a lot more convenient than actually buying and holding physical goods.

To see real time futures quotes, simply visit www.traderschoiceoptions .net.

Stock Index Futures

Stock index futures are futures contracts based on a variety of global and domestic stock indexes. They can be used to speculate on the price direction of a stock market index, or hedge (protect) against a sudden price decrease of a portfolio of stocks.

Traders use futures to speculate on stock indexes so that they don't have to buy or sell every single stock in an index. Futures allow traders to buy an entire index on margin, which is much more convenient.

Stock index futures contracts are traded only for a certain period of time, typically one quarter of the calendar year. This means that the price of a futures contract is good only until the expiration date, on which the particular futures contract can no longer be traded.

Let's take a look at a binary option trade on a stock index future:

Let's say that Standard & Poor's (S&P) futures are currently trading at 1000 and you think that the S&P futures are going to decline to 995 later today. You can sell one daily US 500 (S&P 500) binary options contract with a strike price of 1000 that will expire at the end of the day. With this binary option an assumption is made that at the end of the day the futures price will be below 1000. At the end of the day the S&P 500 futures are trading at 990 and your binary options contract has expired. Because you were correct in your assumption, your binary option contract yields a profit. The mechanics of binary options contracts will be covered in subsequent sections of this guide.

Binary options are available on the following stock index futures:

- *Wall Street 30 (Dow Futures)*. Futures based on the Dow Jones Industrial Average (DJIA). The DJIA is a stock index of the 30 largest publicly traded stocks on the New York Stock Exchange (NYSE).
- *US 500 (S&P 500 futures)*. Futures based on the S&P 500, an index made up of 500 large publicly traded companies that trade on either the NYSE or the Nasdaq.
- *US Tech 100 (Nasdaq Futures)*. Futures based on the Nasdaq 100 index. The Nasdaq 100 is an index composed of the 100 largest, most actively traded U.S. companies listed on the Nasdaq stock exchange. The Nasdaq is a stock exchange that is traditionally where many high-tech stocks are traded.
- *US SmallCap 2000 (Russell 2000 futures)*. Futures based on the Russell 2000 index. The Russell 2000 is an index measuring the performance of 2,000 "small-cap" publicly traded companies. Small-cap refers to the number of outstanding (owned) shares of a company, and in this case the companies are small.
- *FTSE (Liffe FTSE 100 futures)*. Futures based on the FTSE 100 index. The FTSE 100 index is an index of blue-chip (large companies) stocks on the London Stock Exchange.
- *Germany 30 (Eurex Dax futures)*. Futures based on the DAX 30 index. The DAX 30 is an index of the 30 largest German companies traded on the Frankfurt Stock Exchange.
- *Japan 225 (Nikkei 225 futures)*. Futures based on the Nikkei 225 index. The Nikkei 225 index is made up of Japan's top 225 companies on the Tokyo Stock Exchange.
- *Korea 200 (KOSPI 200 futures)*. Futures based on the KOSPI 200 index, which is made up of the 200 largest companies on the Korean Exchange.

Commodity Futures

Commodities are physical goods, such as oil, corn, or gold. Commodity futures are a financial instrument that can be used to speculate or hedge on various physical commodities.

Commodity futures are usually priced slightly higher than the spot commodity in order to account for the convenience that the futures offer to the trader. Commodity futures are exchange traded and typically change along with the price of the underlying.

Let's take a look at a binary option trade on a commodity future:

Let's say that gold futures are currently trading at $1000 per oz. and you think the gold futures are going to reach $1100 later today. You can buy one daily gold binary option contract with a strike price of 1100. With this binary option an assumption is made that at the end of the day the futures price will be above 1100. At the end of the day the gold futures are trading at 1100 and your binary options contract yields a profit.

Binary options are available on the following commodity futures:

- *Crude oil futures.* Futures contracts based on current price if you were to buy or sell physical crude oil. Crude oil is the commodity that is used to produce heating oil and gasoline. Crude oil futures have contracts that expire each calendar month.
- *Natural gas futures.* Futures contracts based on the current price if you were to buy or sell actual natural gas. Natural gas is used to heat homes. Natural gas futures have contracts that expire each calendar month.
- *Gold futures.* Futures contracts based on the current price if you were to buy or sell physical gold. Physical gold is used to make jewelry and is also used in manufacturing. Gold futures have contracts that expire in February, April, June, August, and December.
- *Silver futures.* Futures contracts based on current price if you were to buy or sell physical silver. Physical silver is used to make jewelry and is also used in manufacturing. Silver futures have contracts that expire in March, May, July, September, and December.
- *Copper futures.* Futures contracts based on the current price if you were to buy or sell physical copper. Physical copper is used in electronics, manufacturing, and architecture. Copper futures have contracts that expire in March, May, July, September, and December.
- *Corn futures.* Futures contracts based on the current price if you were to buy or sell physical corn. For the most part, the corn on which these futures are based is used to feed livestock. Corn futures have contracts that expire in March, May, July, September, and December.
- *Soybean futures.* Futures contracts based on the current price if you were to buy or sell physical soybeans. Soybeans are turned into cooking oil and flour, and can be used to feed livestock. Soybean futures have contracts that expire in January, March, May, July, August, September, and November.

You can find many great websites to view charts of various futures contracts and also streaming quotes. www.barchart.com is an excellent free charting website that will display delayed price charts of almost every different asset class, from stocks to commodity futures.

www.forexpros.com/ is an excellent resource that allows you to view free streaming quotes for almost every asset class including stocks and futures.

Spot Forex

Before going into examples of binary options on spot markets, you should be clear on what a spot market is. The spot market or cash market is a public financial market in which financial instruments such as currency and bonds, or commodities like gold and silver, are traded. The spot market is called the "cash market" or "physical market" because prices are settled in cash on the spot at current market prices. In essence, the spot market could be considered a market where goods are traded based on the price in the market right now and are bought and sold immediately.

Spot forex is the abbreviation for the foreign exchange or currency market. The forex market is considered a spot market. A spot market is any market that deals in the current price of a financial instrument. Retail spot forex is traded via forex dealing firms and banks.

One way to look at forex trading is that you are effectively speculating on the economies of various countries.

Currencies are always quoted in pairs, such as GBP/USD or USD/JPY. The reason they are quoted in pairs is that in every foreign exchange transaction you are simultaneously buying one currency and selling the other. Here is an example of a foreign exchange rate for the British pound versus the U.S. dollar: GBP/USD = 1.7500.

To see real time forex quotes, visit www.traderschoiceoptions.net. See Exhibit 1.1.

The currency listed to the left of the slash ("/") is known as the base currency (in this example, the British pound), while the one on the right is called the quote currency (in this example, the U.S. dollar).

When buying, the exchange rate tells you how much you have to pay in units of the quote currency to buy one unit of the base currency. In the

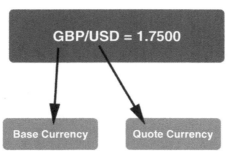

EXHIBIT 1.1   Advantages and Disadvantages of Binary Options

preceding example, you have to pay 1.7500 U.S. dollars to buy one British pound.

When selling, the exchange rate tells you how many units of the quote currency you get for selling one unit of the base currency. In the example, you will receive 1.7500 U.S. dollars when you sell one British pound.

Let's look at an example of a binary options trade on spot forex:

Let's say that the EUR/USD is currently trading at 1.3000. You think the euro is going to depreciate (go down) in value relative to the U.S. dollar and will decline to 1.2800 later today. You decide that you want to take a position on the EUR/USD by selling one daily EUR/USD binary option contract with a strike price of 1.3000. With this binary option an assumption is made that at the end of the day the EUR/USD will be trading below 1.3000. At the end of the day the EUR/USD is trading at 1.2800. Because you were correct in your assumption, your binary option contract yields a profit.

Binary options are available on the following currency pairs:

- *AUD/USD.* The exchange rate between the Australian dollar and U.S. dollar.
- *EUR/USD.* The exchange rate between the euro and U.S. dollar.
- *EUR/JPY.* The exchange rate between the euro and Japanese yen.
- *GBP/JPY.* The exchange rate between the British pound and Japanese yen.
- *GBP/USD.* The exchange rate between the British pound and U.S. dollar.
- *USD/CAD.* The exchange rate between the U.S. dollar and Canadian dollar.
- *USD/CHF.* The exchange rate between the U.S. dollar and Swiss franc.
- *USD/JPY.* The exchange rate between the U.S. dollar and Japanese yen.

Economic Data Releases

Binary options contracts are also available on key economic data releases. Before we go into examples of binary options on economic events, we should first discuss what we mean by "economic events" and, more important, what an economic event is.

What are economic events? Throughout the year the U.S. government issues various reports that detail the overall health of the U.S. economy. These reports are released by departments of the U.S. government and revolve around several components to the U.S. economy. Some of these components are consumer spending (whether or not people are buying goods), jobless claims (the number of current unemployed individuals), labor reports (whether companies are hiring), and interest rates (the interest rates banks charge for loans).

www.forexfactory.com is a great resource to learn more about economic events.

Let's take a look at a binary options trade on an economic event:

Let's say that you are interested in taking a position on the jobless claims report that will be coming out on Thursday. You think that fewer people have filed for unemployment benefits and that the job market as a whole has been improving. Last week 352,000 new unemployment claims were filed, and you feel that this week the number will be less. You sell one jobless claims binary option with a strike price of 352,000.

With this binary option the assumption is made that on Thursday the jobless claims number will be less than 352,000. The jobless claims report is issued and according to the report there were 340,000 new unemployment claims. You were correct in assuming that the jobless claims would be less than 352,000 and therefore your binary option expires for a profit.

You are able to trade binary options on the following economic data releases:

- *Federal funds rate.* U.S. banks are obligated to maintain certain levels of reserve funds at all times. These reserves are either held with the Federal Reserve Bank (the central bank for the United States) or in cash located in their vaults. Sometimes when a bank issues a loan it depletes part of this required reserve. When this occurs the bank must borrow funds from another bank with a surplus. The federal funds rate is the interest rate at which these banks lend funds to each other. The federal funds target rate is determined by a meeting of the members of the Federal Open Market Committee, the committee in charge of the U.S. government's money supply and interest rates. The federal funds rate is released once a month.
- *Jobless claims.* This is a report that is issued by the U.S. Department of Labor on Thursday of each week. The jobless claims report tracks how many individuals have filed for new unemployment benefits during the past week. Jobless claims are an important way to gauge the U.S. job market. More people filing for unemployment is an indication that there are fewer jobs. Fewer people filing for unemployment is an indication that there are more jobs.
- *Nonfarm payrolls.* This is a report issued by the U.S. Bureau of Labor Statistics on the first Friday of each month. This report was created to describe the total number of U.S. employees, excluding government employees, nonprofit employees, and farm employees. This report also estimates the average weekly earnings of all employees, excluding those outlined above. This report essentially looks at whether businesses are hiring people or not.

You can get a breakdown of all upcoming releases with all details on our companion site, www.traderschoiceoptions.net.

BINARY OPTIONS VS. CBOE (VANILLA) PUT/CALL OPTIONS

Traditional options are derivative instruments that are exchange traded. An option gives the owner the right to buy or sell the underlying instrument at a particular price. Options are traded on various instruments such as individual stocks, futures, currencies, and indexes.

There are two basic types of options: a call option and a put option. When you buy or sell an option, you enter into a contract that has an expiration date. Just like with binary options, traders can buy and sell them any time before expiration.

Here is how the two types of contracts work:

- *Call option.* A call option gives the owner the right to purchase the underlying instrument at a particular price (known as the strike price) any time before expiration. As an options trader you would buy a call option if you think the price of the underlying instrument will go up. If the underlying instrument goes up in price, then the owner can purchase the instrument at the lower strike price and sell it on the open market to lock in a profit. If the underlying instrument does not go up in price above the options strike price, then the option will expire worthless.

   Exhibit 1.2 depicts the profit and loss of a long vanilla call trade. The x-axis represents the price of the underlying at expiration. The y-axis represents profit and loss.

   If you believe that the underlying instrument will not reach a certain strike price, you can sell a call option. When you do this you receive the options premium, but in return you have an obligation to sell the underlying at a particular price. If the underlying stays below the price, no one will want to buy the underlying from you at the strike price and you will simply get to keep the premium you collected. However, if the underlying instrument goes up in price above the strike price, you will be obligated to sell it to the owner of the option at the lower strike price. Therefore, you will incur the loss of the difference between the market price of the underlying and the strike price of the call option.

- *Put option.* A put option gives the owner the right to sell the underlying instrument at an agreed-upon price (the option's strike price) any

Profit ↑

Strike Price

Price at
Expiration

Maximum Risk = Premium

Loss ▼   Loss = Premium (if price <= strike price upon expiration)

EXHIBIT 1.2   P&L Graph of a Long Call

time before expiration. As an options trader you buy a put option if you think the price of the underlying instrument will go down. If the underlying instrument goes down in price below the strike price, you could buy the instrument at market value and sell it at the strike price, thus locking in your profit.

Exhibit 1.3 depicts the profit and loss on a long vanilla put trade. The x-axis represents the price of the underlying at expiration. The y-axis represents profit and loss.

If you believe that the underlying instrument will not drop below the strike price, then you can sell a put option. When you sell the put option you will collect the price of the option. In return you now have the obligation to buy the underlying at the strike price. If the underlying stays above the strike price, you simply collect the premium. However, if the underlying drops below the strike price, you will have to buy the underlying at a price that is higher than its market price, thus incurring a loss of the difference between the strike price and the market price.

Most options are not exercised at the expiration date and are simply bought and sold prior to expiration. Options on indexes are never exercised; they are simply settled in cash. Option trading is a zero-sum game, meaning for every winner there is a loser. By trading regular options, traders can create a plethora of strategies to suit their style and requirements. There are, however, some issues associated with trading regular options.

One key issue is that when you sell the option you have to put up margin and you theoretically have unlimited risk. This way you can lose more

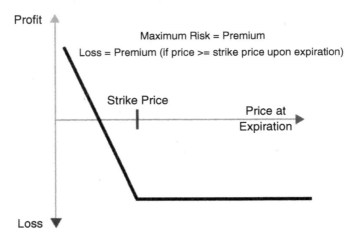

EXHIBIT 1.3   P&L Graph of a Long Put

than you put in. For example, let's assume that you sell a put option on a particular stock and the stock drops significantly in a short period of time. As a seller of a put option, you are obligated to buy this stock at the strike price. Since the stock dropped significantly, you may end up taking a huge loss on your trade in a very short amount of time. This is because your trade was not collateralized but taken on margin and the percent losses can be enormous.

The exchange and option clearinghouses take this into consideration and require that traders put up a lot of money as margin when selling options and have a certain level of experience since the use of margin can make this type of trading very risky. Therefore, it's not always easy to fully take advantage of all the features that put and call options can provide.

Just like traditional put/call options, binary options have an underlying asset, that is, stock indexes, foreign currency, and futures. Binary options also have a strike price and an expiration time. Just like traditional index options, binary options cannot be exercised; they are all cash settled at expiration. Binaries can be traded in and out of at any time before expiration.

Binaries are similar to traditional options but with six key differences:

1. *They have a fixed risk and fixed reward.* This means your maximum risk and reward are always known and capped. If you hold a binary option until expiration, you will either get $0 and lose your entire investment or get $100 per contract. Unlike vanilla put/call options, there is nothing in between. However, please keep in mind that you may always trade in and out of binary options contracts.

2. *Binary options have no puts or calls.* They simply have price conditions for the underlying. (This will be covered in greater detail in the subsequent sections of this text.)

3. *Binary options are fully collateralized so that you can never lose more than you put into a trade.* With binary options you can implement directional and volatility trades and spreads without any debit balance or margin call risk.

4. *Low collateral requirement.* With binary options you can get into long and short trades with minimal collateral; thus, you can customize your trading strategies without having to put up large margin requirements.

5. *Unique behavior as expiration approaches.* Since binary options can be priced only at $0 or $100 at expiration, their premiums behave completely differently from traditional put/call options as expiration approaches. (This phenomenon and ways to take advantage of it will be discussed in greater detail later on in this text.)

6. *Expiration times.* Traditional put/call options usually have monthly and weekly expirations. Binary options have weekly, daily, and intraday expiration times, which provide for different trading opportunities.

ADVANTAGES/DISADVANTAGES OF BINARY OPTIONS

The main advantage of trading binary options is their fixed risk and fixed reward. When you enter a binary options trade you know your maximum profit and maximum loss up front. With a binary options contract you can never lose more than $100 on any one contract. On the other side of the coin, you can never win more than $100 on any contract.

Binary options have relatively small contract sizes, which are always based on $100. They are available on multiple instruments and require less initial investment than traditional options. This way you can trade commodities markets and economic events all from a simple online platform with a low deposit.

Once you understand the concept of binary options, you should find them fairly easy to trade since you are simply speculating on a particular outcome to occur or not occur by a particular time with a fixed risk and a fixed payout.

There are also several disadvantages associated with trading binary options. The obvious one is limited upside. Also, the market is not yet as big as with vanilla options, so sometimes there are not as many strike prices, expiration times, or contracts available with binaries.

Exhibit 1.4 details the advantages and disadvantages of binary options.

EXHIBIT 1.4 Advantages and Disadvantages of Binary Options

Advantages	Disadvantages
Fixed risk	Fixed reward—maximum potential return of $100 per contract
Small contract sizes	Market not as large as traditional options market
	Potentially fewer strike prices available
Easily available on multiple instruments	
More expiration times available	

REASONS TO TRADE BINARY OPTIONS

There are a few key reasons you may want to trade binary options:

- *Simple.* Easy-to-understand "yes"/"no" propositions.
- *Intuitive pricing.* At any point the price of a binary is simply the market's perception of the percentage likelihood of the contract's settling as a "yes." This works out naturally based on the way binary options are priced, and it will be covered in much greater detail later in this text.
- *Very small contract size.* At expiration each lot settles at $100 for a "yes" or $0 for a "no." The maximum collateral required is always less than $100 per contract, often much less. You can never lose more than your collateral.
- *Strictly limited risk.* At no point can the contracts be priced outside the range $0 to $100, regardless of the volatility in the underlying market. You always know your absolute worst-case risk for any position you take, regardless of whether you are going long or short the contract.
- *Multiple markets.* With binary options you can speculate on a wide range of markets and asset classes all from an online platform with a low minimum deposit. Additionally, you can actually use binary options to speculate on the outcome of various economic data releases, which would normally be fairly difficult for a retail trader without the use of binary options.
- *Option's price behavior at expiration.* Due to their binary nature, the behavior of a binary option as it approaches expiration greatly differs from any other trading instrument. If used properly, this behavior may be exploited for some very interesting trading strategies.
- *Binary options markets are open right up until the moment of expiration.* This allows you to place orders to enter and exit a given

binary position multiple times as the market moves. Even though the contracts have an "all-or-nothing" payout, you are not restricted to an "all-or-nothing" trading strategy since you can trade in and out of your contract at any time before expiration.

To sum it up, with binary options you can easily trade volatility (as opposed to just direction) on multiple instruments with limited risk and a relatively low investment.

KEY POINTS: PART 1

To take a quiz on this section, simply visit our companion education site, www.traderschoiceoptions.net.

- Binary options, also known as digital options or all-or-nothing options, are a type of options derivative that can be considered a yes-or-no proposition—the event either happens or it does not.
- They have a fixed risk and fixed reward. The most you can lose on each contract is your collateral, and the most you can win is $100.
- You can never lose more than you put into a binary option trade.
- You can use binary options to trade both volatility and direction.
- Binary options have daily, weekly, and hourly expirations.
- Binary options have certain unique characteristics that are unavailable with CBOE vanilla put/call options.
- Binary options are available to trade on the following underlying instruments:
  - Stock index futures
  - Commodities futures
  - Spot currency
  - Economic data releases
- There are several advantages to trading binary options:
  - Simple
  - Intuitive pricing
  - Small contract size
  - Strictly limited risk
  - Trade multiple markets
  - Unique price behavior at expiration
  - Market open right up until the moment of expiration

PART II

Binary Options Theory

This section will provide you with a basic understanding of how binary option trades work.

What You Will Learn:

- What is the theory behind binary options?
- What are the components of a binary option?
- How do binary option strike prices work?
- When do binary options expire?
- How do you take a long binary option?
- How do you take a short binary option?
- How are binary options priced?
- How do you read a binary option chain?

When you complete this section you should clearly understand the logic behind binary option trades.

CHAPTER 2

What Does Binary Mean?

Binary options are considered binary because there are only two potential outcomes at expiration: 0 or 100. At expiration, the condition you are speculating on can be simply *true* or *false*. For example, if you are trading binary options on the Standard & Poor's (S&P) futures, the price of the underlying will either be trading above the strike price (true) or below the strike price (false) at expiration. Binary options will always settle at 0 if false and 100 if true.

As a binary options trader you can profit from either a true or false scenario. This is because you can buy or sell the binary option contract, depending on where you feel the underlying instrument is heading. You can also use binary options to profit from volatility. This means that you can use binary options to forecast market ranges and breakouts without having to predict direction.

For example, if you see a strong support level on a certain underlying instrument, you can use binary options to speculate on the underlying's *not* going below that level. Notice how you do *not* have to forecast where the underlying will go. You are simply forecasting where it will not go. Unlike with many other instruments, you can do this with a relatively low deposit amount.

COMPONENTS TO A BINARY OPTION

There are three main components to a binary option. This section covers these components in great detail.

The key components are:

- Strike price
- Expiration
- Premium/Price

Strike Price

When trading binary options, a strike price is simply a price condition that you are speculating on. With binary options you are speculating if this condition is going to be true or false when the option expires. Each underlying instrument has multiple price conditions that you can speculate on. Each condition is notated as follows: "underlying name > strike price/expiration date time."

For example, an option for speculating on the price condition of whether the S&P futures will be above or below 1200 by 4:15 P.M. would look as follows: "US 500 (march) > 1200 4:15pm." Throughout the text, strike prices may be referred to with a shorthand "> 1200" or simply 1200.

If you believe that the S&P futures will be above 1200 at 4:15 P.M., you would buy the "> 1200" strike price option. If the S&P futures end up above the strike price, you win, and if they end up below, you lose.

If you believe that the futures will be below 1200 at 4:15 P.M., you would sell the "> 1200" option. If the S&P futures end up below the strike price, you win; if they end up above the strike price, you lose.

Each underlying instrument has multiple strike prices that you can speculate on. All of the strike prices that traders can speculate on are available on what is known as an option chain.

Exhibit 2.1 is an example of an option chain for US 500 binary options. The first column displays all of the available US 500 binary option strike prices. The second column displays the expiration date and time of each binary option contract. The third column displays the current bid (price to sell) and ask (price to buy).

Typically, there will be strike prices available at 2 times the average range for an underlying instrument, both above and below its market price. For example, if the S&P 500 futures have an average daily range of 5 points and they are trading at 1200, then there will be strike prices available for 10 points—5 above and 5 below. Daily strike prices will usually be available in increments of 2, and weekly option strike prices will have larger increments. For this specific example, you should see strike prices up to 1248 and down to 1104 for the daily options.

For weekly options you will see strike prices at 2 times the average weekly range. Most underlying instruments move in a wider range during a week than they do during a day. Therefore, you should see more strike prices available for weekly options than you would for daily options. For

Contract			Exp		Bid Size	Bid		Offer Size
US 500 (Dec) >1248.5		1	02-D	2	500	35.00	3	500
US 500 (Dec) >1236.5			02-DEC-11		500	55.50	59.50	500
US 500 (Dec) >1224.5			02-DEC-11		500	73.00	77.00	500
US 500 (Dec) >1212.5			02-DEC-11		500	85.00	88.50	500
US 500 (Dec) >1200.5			02-DEC-11		500	92.00	95.50	500
US 500 (Dec) >1188.5			02-DEC-11		50	95.50	99.00	50
US 500 (Dec) >1176.5			02-DEC-11		50	97.00	-	-
US 500 (Dec) >1164.5			02-DEC-11		50	97.00	-	-
US 500 (Dec) >1152.5			02-DEC-11		50	97.00	-	-
US 500 (Dec) >1140.5			02-DEC-11		50	97.00	-	-
US 500 (Dec) >1128.5			02-DEC-11		50	97.00	-	-
US 500 (Dec) >1116.5			02-DEC-11		50	97.00	-	-
US 500 (Dec) >1104.5			02-DEC-11		50	97.00	-	-

EXHIBIT 2.1 Option Chain

example, on a weekly option chain for S&P futures with a market price of 1200, you may see options all the way up to 1220 and down to 1180, while on a daily option chain for the same underlying instrument with the same market price, you may only see strike prices from 1190 to 1210.

There are traders trading each of the strike prices for a particular underlying instrument. Option premiums change as time passes, as does the price of the underlying moves. Just like vanilla put/call options, binary options can be in-the-money, at-the-money, and out-of-the-money. Since there are no puts, these definitions change, depending on whether you are taking a long or short position.

Expiration

As you will shortly learn, when trading binary options contracts you are speculating for a certain price condition to be true or false by a certain expiration time. For example, if S&P futures are trading at 1295 when you enter your trade, you can speculate that the price of S&P futures will or will not be above 1300 by the end of the day.

With binary options you are able to trade contracts based on several expiration models:

- *Intraday.* With intraday binaries you are able to choose several binary options contracts that expire throughout the day. With intraday binary options you can choose from binaries that expire at 11 A.M., 12 P.M., 2 P.M., and 4:15 P.M. EST. These options expire within a trading day.
- *Daily.* Daily binary options expire daily at 4:15 P.M. EST Monday through Friday.
- *Weekly.* Weekly binary options expire every Friday at different times, depending on the underlying asset.

Different expiration times give you the opportunity to trade on price movements over different time frames, from the very short term to one week in the future. Just like with vanilla put/call options, the further away the expiration date, the more time value an options contract will have. Please keep in mind that you can trade in and out of any binary options contract at any time up until expiration.

LONG TRADING

Long In-the-Money

A binary option is considered in-the-money on a long trade if the strike price is below the current market price. For example, if the S&P futures were trading at 1200, an 1180 option would be considered in-the-money.

When buying an in-the-money binary option you are speculating that the underlying will not drop below a certain price. It does not matter to you whether it goes up or down as long as it does not drop below the strike price.

In Exhibit 2.2, the y-axis represents the available strike prices. The dark grey dashed line represents the market price of the underlying (S&P futures) and the light grey dashed line represents the binary option contract.

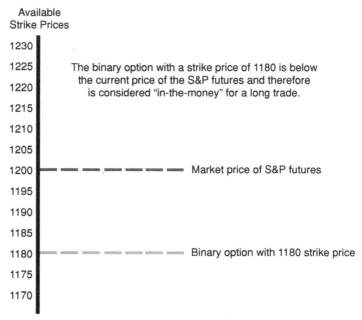

EXHIBIT 2.2   Long In-the-Money Binary Option

Long Out-of-the-Money

A binary option is considered out-of-the-money on a long trade if the strike price is above the current market price. For example, if the S&P futures are trading at 1200, a 1220 option would be considered out-of-the-money.

When buying an out-of-the-money option, you are speculating that the underlying will move up by a certain amount. When buying an out-of-the-money option, you have better payout odds than you do with an at-the-money or in-the-money option.

In Exhibit 2.3, the y-axis represents the available strike prices. The dark grey dashed line represents the market price of the underlying (S&P futures), and the light grey dashed line represents the binary option contract.

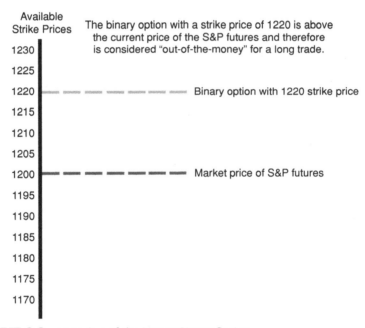

EXHIBIT 2.3   Long Out-of-the-Money Binary Option

Long At-the-Money

A binary option is considered at-the-money when the strike price and underlying price are the same. When buying an at-the-money option, you are simply speculating that the underlying instrument will go up and don't care by how much. For example, if the market price of the underlying is 1200, the price of the binary option that you would buy is also 1200.

In Exhibit 2.4, the y-axis represents the available strike prices. The dark grey dashed line represents the market price of the underlying (S&P futures), and the light grey dashed line represents the binary option contract.

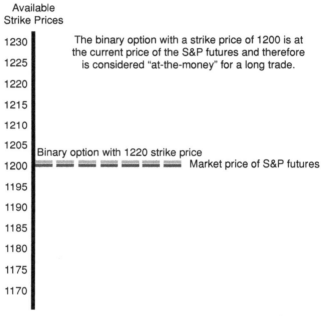

EXHIBIT 2.4   Long At-the-Money Binary Option

SHORT TRADING

Short In-the-Money

On a short trade, a binary option is considered in-the-money when the strike price is above the underlying price. When selling an in-the-money option, you are speculating that the underlying will not reach a strike price. You don't care if it goes up or down as long as it is not above the strike price at expiration. For example, if the S&P futures are trading at 1200, a 1210 option is considered in-the-money.

In Exhibit 2.5, the y-axis represents the available strike prices. The dark grey dashed line represents the market price of the underlying (S&P futures), and the light grey dashed line represents the binary option contract.

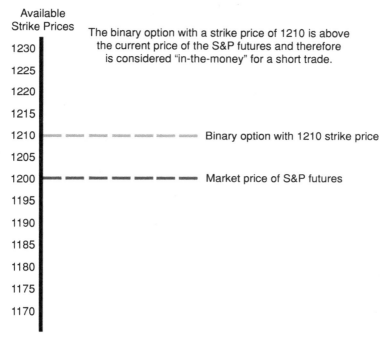

EXHIBIT 2.5 Short In-the-Money Binary Option

Short Out-of-the-Money

On a short trade, a binary option is considered out-of-the money when the strike price is below the price of the underlying. When selling an out-of-the-money binary option, you are hoping that the underlying will drop by a certain amount. The reason you would sell an out-of-the-money option instead of an in-the-money or an at-the-money option is that the out-of-the-money options offers higher payout odds.

In Exhibit 2.6, the y-axis represents the available strike prices. The dark grey dashed line represents the market price of the underlying (S&P futures), and the light grey dashed line represents the binary option contract.

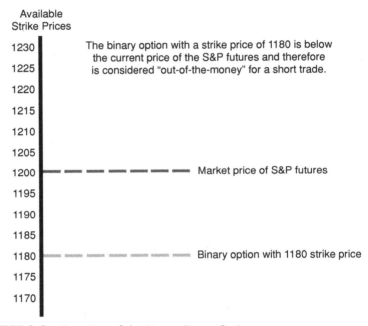

EXHIBIT 2.6   Short Out-of-the-Money Binary Option

Short At-the-Money

Just like with a long trade, a binary option is considered at-the-money when the strike price and the market price of the underlying are the same. The reason you would sell an at-the-money binary option is that you want to speculate on the underlying's simply going down and don't care by how much. For example, if the market price of S&P futures is 1200, you would sell the 1200 option.

In Exhibit 2.7, the y-axis represents the available strike prices. The dark grey dashed line represents the market price of the underlying (S&P futures), and the light grey dashed line represents the binary option contract.

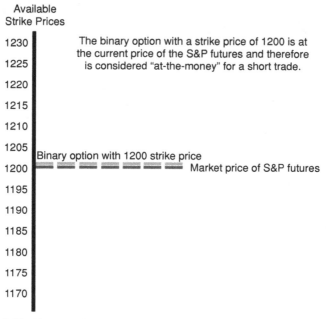

EXHIBIT 2.7   Short At-the-Money Binary Option

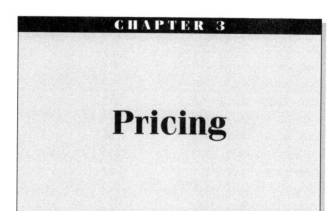

Pricing

Since a binary option can be settled at expiration only at $0 or $100, the price of the option will fluctuate between $0 and $100 until expiration. The price will fluctuate as a result of market transactions made by traders.

Just like all markets, the participants will make bids and offers to each other in order to trade each strike price of the options contract until expiration. There are a number of components that will be taken into consideration by market participants in order to determine the price of a binary option contract. Two key components are the strike price of the option and the time remaining until expiration.

STRIKE PRICE

As you learned earlier, the strike price represents a specific price condition for the underlying instrument. Each instrument will have multiple strike prices. For example, if the Standard & Poor's (S&P) futures are trading at 1200, there may be strike prices for 20 points up and 20 points down.

Exhibit 3.1 displays an option chain of the US 500 binary options strike prices.

Typically, there are strike prices available for two times the average daily range for each underlying security, both above and below its market price at any given time the market is open.

Contract	Bid	Offer
Daily US 500 (Mar) > 1221	2.1	5
Daily US 500 (Mar) > 1218	2.1	5
Daily US 500 (Mar) > 1215	4.9	7.8
Daily US 500 (Mar) > 1212	9.7	12.7
Daily US 500 (Mar) > 1209	17	20
Daily US 500 (Mar) > 1206	26	29
Daily US 500 (Mar) > 1203	36.1	40.1
Daily US 500 (Mar) > 1200	48.1	51.6
Daily US 500 (Mar) > 1197	60.1	63.1
Daily US 500 (Mar) > 1194	71.2	73.9
Daily US 500 (Mar) > 1191	79.9	83.4
Daily US 500 (Mar) > 1188	87.4	90.4
Daily US 500 (Mar) > 1185	92.3	95.3
Daily US 500 (Mar) > 1182	95.4	98.4
Daily US 500 (Mar) > 1179	96.4	99.4

12 hours until expiration, futures trading at 1200

EXHIBIT 3.1   Option Chain

When traders purchase a certain strike price, they want the underlying instrument to be above that strike price at expiration so that they can receive the $100 settlement. Conversely, when traders sell a certain strike price, they want the underlying instrument to be below that price at expiration so that they can receive their $100 settlement. This will be explained in greater detail in the subsequent sections.

TIME VALUE

Time value simply represents the amount of time until expiration. An out-of-the-money option with more time until expiration has a higher chance of being settled in-the-money for a trader than an option with less time until expiration. For example, a 10-point move on the S&P futures is more likely to happen over one week than in one day.

Exhibit 3.2 depicts how an option's time value decreases as the contract nears expiration. The y-axis represents the time value of an option. The x-axis represents the amount of time until the option contract expires.

Time value is taken into consideration by traders, as their chances of winning are higher if they own an option that has more time until expiration. Therefore, they are willing to pay more money for the options

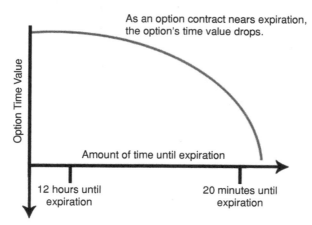

As an option contract nears expiration, the option's time value drops.

Option Time Value

Amount of time until expiration

12 hours until expiration

20 minutes until expiration

EXHIBIT 3.2 Image Representing an Option's Time Value

with longer duration. For example, if the S&P futures are trading at 1200, a 1210 weekly option will be more expensive than a 1210 daily option, which will subsequently be more expensive than a 1210 hourly option.

Exhibit 3.3 depicts a trader's willingness to pay more for options with a longer time until expiration. The longer the time until expiration, the better the odds the event will occur, and therefore the option will be priced higher.

Because you can trade in and out of binary options up until expiration, their time value will change as expiration approaches. This is known as time decay. As traders deem an option to be unlikely to expire in-the-money, they will want to sell it, which drives its price down toward $0.

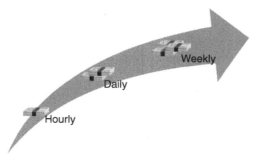

Weekly

Daily

Hourly

EXHIBIT 3.3 Image Representing an Option's Price Relative to Time until Expiration

EXHIBIT 3.4 Behavior of a Binary Option's Contract Value as Expiration
Approaches

As Expiration Approaches ...	Contract Value Is:
Underlying market price is lower than strike price	Decreasing to 0
Underlying market price is higher than strike price	Increasing to 100

However, as traders perceive an option likely to expire in-the-money, they will want to buy it and thus drive its price up toward $100.

To summarize time decay, as expiration approaches, if the underlying market price remains below the strike price, the contract value will continuously decrease to 0. If, however, the underlying market price remains above the strike price, the contract value will increase to 100.

Exhibit 3.4 shows the contract value of a binary option as its expiration approaches.

PRICE AS A NATURAL MARKET CONSENSUS

Another way of looking at binary options pricing is: The more likely a price event for an underlying entity is to occur at expiration, the closer the price of the option is going to be to $100. Conversely, the less likely an event is to occur, the closer the price will be to $0. Every point on a binary options contract is worth $1.

The logic behind this is as follows: If a price event is perceived to be very likely to occur at expiration, then all market participants are going to want to bet on its happening. Therefore, they will all want to buy the option that signifies the price event, so price of this option will head toward $100, which is its maximum value.

Conversely, if a price event is unlikely to occur at expiration, market participants are not going to want to purchase the option. The participants that are holding it are going to want to sell it to preserve at least some of their investment. For this reason, the price of the options is going to head toward $0.

Using this same logic, if the market participants perceive there to be a 50-50 chance of an event's occurring, the option that will signify this event will be around $50.

Exhibit 3.5 shows how price behaves based on the view of market participants. For example, let's assume that the S&P futures are trading at 1200 with four days until expiration:

EXHIBIT 3.5   Market Participant View of an Event Occurring and the Effect This Has on a Binary Option's Strike Price

Market Participant View of Event Occurring	Binary Option Price
More likely	Price increases toward $100
50-50 chance	Price is roughly $50
Less likely	Price decreases toward $0

- A strike price of 1300 with one day until expiration would be most likely worth $0 since it is so highly unlikely that the S&P futures will jump 100 points before expiration.
- A strike price of 1100 will most likely be trading at $100 since it is very likely that the S&P futures will not drop below 100 points by expiration.
- A strike price of 1200 will most likely be worth around $50. The reason for this is that there is roughly a 50-50 chance that the S&P futures will end up below or above that strike price since 1200 is the market price. Traders have roughly a 50 percent chance of success on the trade; therefore, they will need at least a 2-to-1 payout to enter it. Since the payout at expiration is $100, the options price will be roughly $50.
- A strike price of 1210 will be under $50 since there is a less than 50 percent chance that the S&P futures will end up above 1210 and traders will need better odds to enter the trade. To get better odds, the option will need to be priced under $50 since the payout is $100 at expiration.

Of course, time until expiration plays a critical role here also. If there is a very short amount of time until expiration and it's unlikely that the underlying will reach the strike price, the option price will head toward $0.

If there is still some time left until expiration and traders believe that the price may reach 1210 by then, they would be willing to pay something for the option contract. This amount will be below $50 and depends on the time until expiration and other factors that may affect the perception of the market participants.

As you can see, the price of a binary option naturally can be viewed as the consensus of market participants of where the underlying is going to go by expiration.

Exhibit 3.6 is an example of what a binary option chain (of the US 500 binary options) may look like 12 hours until expiration.

Contract	Bid	Offer
Daily US 500 (Mar) > 1268	2.1	5
Daily US 500 (Mar) > 1265	4.9	7.8
Daily US 500 (Mar) > 1262	9.7	12.7
Daily US 500 (Mar) > 1259	17	20
Daily US 500 (Mar) > 1256	26	29
Daily US 500 (Mar) > 1253	36.1	40.1
Daily US 500 (Mar) > 1250	48.1	51.6
Daily US 500 (Mar) > 1247	60.1	63.1
Daily US 500 (Mar) > 1244	71.2	73.9
Daily US 500 (Mar) > 1241	79.9	83.4
Daily US 500 (Mar) > 1238	87.4	90.4
Daily US 500 (Mar) > 1235	92.3	95.3
Daily US 500 (Mar) > 1232	95.4	98.4

12 hours to expiration, futures trading at 1250

EXHIBIT 3.6   Option Chain with 12 Hours until Expiration

Exhibit 3.7 is an example of what a binary option chain of the US 500 binary options may look like 20 to 30 minutes until expiration.

As market participants make trades on each of the strike prices, the bid and ask price of the option contracts change.

Contract	Bid	Offer
Daily US 500 (Mar) > 1268	-	3.0
Daily US 500 (Mar) > 1265	-	3.0
Daily US 500 (Mar) > 1262	-	7.0
Daily US 500 (Mar) > 1259	-	7.0
Daily US 500 (Mar) > 1256	-	7.0
Daily US 500 (Mar) > 1253	54.00	66.00
Daily US 500 (Mar) > 1250	56.00	60.00
Daily US 500 (Mar) > 1247	70.00	80.00
Daily US 500 (Mar) > 1244	97.00	-
Daily US 500 (Mar) > 1241	97.00	-
Daily US 500 (Mar) > 1238	97.00	-
Daily US 500 (Mar) > 1235	97.00	-
Daily US 500 (Mar) > 1232	97.00	-

20 minutes to expiration, futures trading at 1250

EXHIBIT 3.7   Option Chain with 20 Minutes until Expiration

Let's look at some more examples here:

If the S&P futures are trading at $1280 on Monday and you are looking to enter trades for binary options that will expire on Friday:

- A $1230 option is likely to be priced very close to $100 since the market participants will find it likely for the S&P futures to stay above $1230 at expiration.
- A $1350 option is likely to be priced very close to $0 since market participants will find it unlikely that the S&P futures will move up this much in such a short period of time.
- A $1280 option will be priced at around $50 since market participants see a roughly 50 percent change for the S&P futures to end up above $1280.

READING A BINARY OPTIONS CHAIN

Just like regular vanilla options, binary options have option chains. These chains show you all the possible conditions that you can speculate on. In other words, you can bet on the price of the underlying to be above or below a wide range of prices. Typically, strike prices are available roughly two times the average daily range for daily options and two times the average weekly range for weekly options. To see an actual option chain, you can download a demo at www.traderschoiceoptions.net.

The higher the probability of a condition to occur by expiration, the less your payout odds are on your trade. For example, if you are to forecast the underlying's going up 50 points by expiration, you may have to put up only $5 to win $100. However, if you speculate for the underlying simply not to drop by 50 points until expiration, you may have to bet $95 to win just $5. Of course, in the second example you are much more likely to win than you are in the first example, which is why the odds available to you are much lower. Please keep in mind that we are using arbitrary numbers in these examples. They are not an actual reflection of what any underlying would be doing, and they are not connected to any option chain.

Exhibit 3.8 illustrates the payout odds based on the probability of a move. Exhibit 3.9 is an example of an option chain of the US 500 binary options strike prices with 12 hours until expiration.

In Exhibit 3.9, the S&P futures (US 500) are trading at around 1225. If you want to speculate that the US 500 is going to close above 1297.5 by expiration, you can purchase your option at the ask price of $6.5. The price of the option is relatively cheap since, historically, it is fairly unlikely that the S&P futures will jump up above the strike price by expiration.

EXHIBIT 3.8	Table Depicting the Probability of a Condition's Being True and the Payout Odds Associated with It	

Probability of Condition to be True	Type of Trade	Payout Odds
Lower	Out-of-the-money	Higher Example: Put up $15/contract to win $85/contract
Close to 50-50	At-the-money	Close to even Example: Put up $51/contract to win $49/contract
Higher	In-the-money	Lower Example: Put up $70/contract to win $30/contract

Exhibit 3.10 is the profit-and-loss (P&L) graph of going long the 1297.5 binary option. The x-axis depicts the price of the underlying asset, and the y-axis depicts profit and loss. The 1297.5 binary option is considered out-of-the-money. The chances of the S&P futures moving 72 points and closing above 1297 are very small, and therefore the payout is high.

Since the S&P futures are trading at 1225.5 during the snapshot of the option chain, the 1225.5 option has an ask price of 55.5 and a bid price of 51. The reason for this is that the strike price and the price of the underlying are very close to each other. When this occurs, there is a roughly 50 percent chance that the underlying will go above or below its actual price by expiration and therefore the binary options price gives you roughly 1-to-1 odds, meaning you bet $55.5 to win $44.5 for a reward to risk ratio of .802:1 (44.5/55.5).

US 500 (Mar) >1321.5 (4:15PM)		16-DEC-11	-	-	3.00
US 500 (Mar) >1309.5 (4:15PM)		16-DEC-11	50	1.00	4.50
US 500 (Mar) >1297.5 (4:15PM)		16-DEC-11	500	3.00	6.50
US 500 (Mar) >1285.5 (4:15PM)		16-DEC-11	500	6.50	10.50
US 500 (Mar) >1273.5 (4:15PM)		16-DEC-11	500	12.00	15.50
US 500 (Mar) >1261.5 (4:15PM)		16-DEC-11	500	19.50	23.00
US 500 (Mar) >1249.5 (4:15PM)		16-DEC-11	500	28.50	32.50
US 500 (Mar) >1237.5 (4:15PM)		16-DEC-11	500	39.50	43.50
US 500 (Mar) >1225.5 (4:15PM)		16-DEC-11	500	51.00	55.50
US 500 (Mar) >1213.5 (4:15PM)		16-DEC-11	500	62.00	66.00
US 500 (Mar) >1201.5 (4:15PM)		16-DEC-11	500	71.00	75.00
US 500 (Mar) >1189.5 (4:15PM)		16-DEC-11	500	78.50	82.50
US 500 (Mar) >1177.5 (4:15PM)		16-DEC-11	500	64.00	88.00

EXHIBIT 3.9 Binary Option Chain (To see a live option chain, you can download a FREE demo at www.traderschoiceoptions.net)

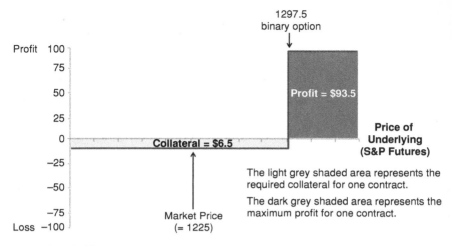

EXHIBIT 3.10 Payout Odds of a Large, Less Likely Move (out-of-the-money)

Exhibit 3.11 is the P&L graph of going long the 1225.5 binary option. The x-axis depicts the price of the underlying asset and the y-axis depicts profit and loss. There is roughly a 50 percent likelihood of the S&P futures closing above 1225.5 and therefore the payout reflects this.

If you believe that the underlying will not go down significantly, you can purchase the 1177.5 strike price for $88. When you make this purchase,

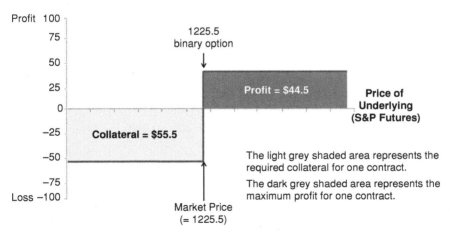

EXHIBIT 3.11 Payout Odds of a Smaller, More Likely Move (at-the-money)

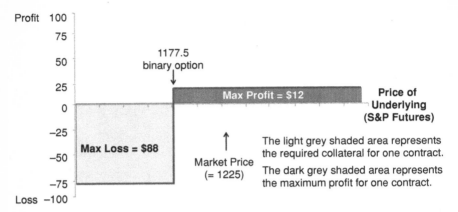

EXHIBIT 3.12   Payout Odds of a Larger, Less Likely Move (in-the-money)

as long as S&P futures do not drop by 47.5 points to 1177.5, the option will settle at $100 and you will turn your $88 into $100, meaning you bet $88 to win $12 for a reward to risk ratio of .136:1 (12/88).

Exhibit 3.12 depicts the profit and loss of going long the US 500 binary option with a strike price of 1177.5. In this example, the 1177.5 binary option is in-the-money, and the chance of the S&P futures going down 47.5 points is relatively small; therefore, the payout is much less than the previous examples. The x-axis depicts the price of the underlying asset and the y-axis depicts profit and loss.

 ## KEY POINTS: PART 2

To take a quiz on this section, simply visit our companion education site, www.traderschoiceoptions.net.

- Binary options are considered binary because there are only two potential outcomes at expiration: 0 or 100. At expiration, the condition you are speculating on can be simply either TRUE (100) or FALSE (0).

- There are three main components to a binary option:
  - Strike price
  - Expiration
  - Premium/Price of the binary option

- When trading binary options, a strike price is simply a price condition that you are speculating on. With binary options you are speculating if this condition is going to be true or false when the option expires.

- Binary options have several expiration times:
  - Intraday: Intraday binary options expire daily at 11 A.M., 12 P.M., 2 P.M., and 4:15 P.M. New York time (EST).
  - Daily: Daily binary options expire daily at 4:15 P.M. New York time (EST).
  - Weekly: Weekly binary options expire every Friday at varying times depending on the underlying asset.
- On a long trade, a binary option is considered in-the-money if the strike price is below the market price of the underlying.
- On a long trade, a binary option is considered out-of-the-money if the strike price is above the market price of the underlying.
- On a short trade, a binary option is considered in-the-money when the strike price is above the market price of the underlying.
- On a short trade, a binary option is considered out-of-the-money when the strike price is below the market price of the underlying.
- On either a long or short trade, a binary option is considered at-the-money when the strike price and the market price of the underlying are the same.
- Because a binary option can be settled at expiration only at $0 or $100, the price of the option will fluctuate between $0 and $100 up until expiration.
- As expiration approaches, if the underlying market price of the binary remains below the strike price, the contract value will continuously decrease to 0. If, however, the underlying market price remains above the strike price, the contract value will increase to 100.
- Typically, strike prices are available roughly two times the average daily range for daily options and two times the average weekly range for weekly options.
- Binary options chains show you all the possible conditions that you can speculate on.
- The higher the probability of a condition's occurring by expiration, the less your payout odds (return on collateral) are on your trade.

PART III

Trading Binary Options

This section will provide you with an explanation of how binary option trading works.

What You Will Learn:

- How are binary option trades collateralized?
- How are binary option trades settled at expiration?
- What are the commissions and fees associated with trading binary options?
- How do you enter a binary option trade?
- How do you properly exit a binary option trade?

When you complete this section you should understand how to trade using binary options.

CHAPTER 4

Binary Options Contract Collateral

MARGIN AND DEBIT RISK OF VANILLA OPTIONS AND FUTURES

Unlike vanilla put/call options, binary options are fully collateralized. This means that regardless of whether you are buying or selling an option, you cannot lose more than you put up per contract on the trade.

When trading commodity or stock index futures without the use of binary options, the trader is trading on margin. When trading on margin, you are using a small amount of money to control a larger amount of an asset class. This means that if you are trading futures or options on futures, you can lose more than you put into the trade. In plain and simple terms, that can be scary, especially if you are holding positions overnight.

Trading volatility is trying to speculate on the magnitude of a price movement of the underlying asset within a certain time frame. When trading volatility, you are not trying to forecast market direction but simply the size of the move. In simple terms, you are speculating whether an underlying will stay within a certain range or trade outside of a certain range by expiration.

If you use vanilla put/call options to speculate on market ranges, you will be trading on margin. This means if the underlying makes a drastic move outside of the range that you predicted, you may lose more than you put into the trade.

One great factor of trading binary options is that your trades are fully collateralized. This means that you can never lose more than you put into the trade. Traders find this advantageous since they can use binary options to speculate on both price direction and volatility of stock indexes, commodities, forex, and economic data releases without having to worry about debit balance risk.

At the same time, the fact that binary options are derivative instruments means that you are able to take advantage of large price movements by putting up only a relatively small premium. In other words, you don't need to put up nearly as much money to trade with binary options as you would to trade the actual underlying instrument.

COLLATERAL EXPLAINED

Binary options have relatively small contract sizes. For every contract that you trade, you simply need to put up collateral (margin) of up to $100. The amount you put up depends on whether you are buying or selling an option, how far your contract is from the strike price, and the option's expiration date.

In short, you are fully collateralized when trading binary options. This means that you can never lose more than you put up on a trade. This section will examine how this concept works more deeply.

Exhibit 4.1 illustrates that a binary option can never be worth more than $100 or less than $0.

EXHIBIT 4.1 The Lowest Possible Price and the Highest Possible Price for a Binary Option

BINARY OPTIONS EXPIRATION VALUES

In order to explain how binary option trades are collateralized, you first need to be clear on what happens to binary options at expiration:

- If the underlying instrument closes or is trading above the options strike price at expiration, the value of the option will go to $100 per contract.

- If the underlying instrument closes or is trading below a strike price at expiration, the value of the option will be $0 per contract.

Exhibit 4.2 depicts the value of binary option contracts at expiration. If at expiration the underlying asset is above the binary option's strike price, the contract will be worth $100. If at expiration the underlying asset is below the binary option's strike price, the contract will be worth $0.

EXHIBIT 4.2 Possible Expiration Values for Binary Options Contracts

Underlying Asset	Value at Expiration
Above option strike price	$100
Below option strike price	$0

Because collateral is always equal to your maximum potential *loss* on a binary option trade, this section will clearly show you what will happen if you *lose* on your trades. Don't get too depressed—you can win on your binary option trades also!

Once you are clear on how binary options are priced at expiration, you are ready to learn how to calculate the maximum loss and thus collateral on binary option trades.

For long trades, figuring out collateral is a very straightforward process. For short trades it is slightly trickier, but once you understand the basic principle, you should be able to grasp the concept fairly easily.

COLLATERALIZING A LONG TRADE

When you make a long trade, you are paying a premium hoping that the underlying instrument will trade or close above your options strike price at expiration. If the underlying does close above the strike price, your revenue will be $100. And your profit will be the $100 revenue minus the premium that you paid for the option.

However, if the underlying is below your strike price at expiration, you will lose the entire premium that you paid. Therefore, your maximum loss and thus collateral for every contract on a long trade is simply the premium of the option. So when you enter a long trade, you simply pay the option premium for every contract that you purchase.

Following are a few examples of how a long binary options position may be collateralized. Let's use the binary options chain to examine how this will work. Assume that the Standard & Poor's (S&P) futures is the underlying and is trading at 1250 at the time the transaction is entered into.

Contract	Bid	Offer
Daily US 500 (Mar) > 1268	2.1	5
Daily US 500 (Mar) > 1265	4.9	7.8
Daily US 500 (Mar) > 1262	9.7	12.7
Daily US 500 (Mar) > 1259	17	20
Daily US 500 (Mar) > 1256	26	29
Daily US 500 (Mar) > 1253	36.1	40.1
Daily US 500 (Mar) > 1250	48.1	51.6
Daily US 500 (Mar) > 1247	60.1	63.1
Daily US 500 (Mar) > 1244	71.2	73.9
Daily US 500 (Mar) > 1241	79.9	83.4
Daily US 500 (Mar) > 1238	87.4	90.4
Daily US 500 (Mar) > 1235	92.3	95.3
Daily US 500 (Mar) > 1232	95.4	98.4

12 hours to expiration, futures trading at 1250

EXHIBIT 4.3   A Binary Option Chain

Exhibit 4.3 is an image of an option chain of the US 500 binary options strike prices with 12 hours until expiration.

As you look at these examples, please keep in mind that you can get in and out of your trade at any time before expiration. This will be covered in greater detail in the subsequent sections of this text.

In-the-Money Long Collateral Example

Rationale   The S&P futures are currently trading at 1250. You assume that the S&P futures will be above 1244 at expiration.

Entry Breakdown   You buy 10 contracts of US 500 binary options with a strike price of 1244 and an ask price of $73.9 per contract. The required collateral to place this trade is $739, and the maximum you stand to lose is also $739.

Exhibit 4.4 depicts the required collateral for going long 10 contracts of the 1244 US 500 binary option. The x-axis represents the price of the underlying and the y-axis represents profit and loss (P&L). In this example, the collateral is represented as the shaded area and would be the maximum loss for this trade.

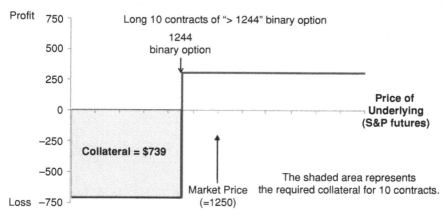

EXHIBIT 4.4 P&L Graph of a Long Binary Option Trade

Summary Exhibit 4.5 contains all of the data points for this trade.

EXHIBIT 4.5 Data Points for Long Binary Option Trade

Trade	Figure	Calculation
Underlying asset	S&P futures	
Market price	1250	
Expiration	1 day	
Strike price	1244	
Long/Short	Long (buy)	
Size	10 contracts	
Entry price	Ask price of $73.9/contract	
Max loss	$739	Ask price × number of contracts = max loss $73.9 × 10 = $739
Collateral	$739	Max loss = collateral

Out-of-the-Money Long Collateral Example

Rationale If you believe that the S&P futures will go up in price, you may want to purchase a 1259 out-of-the-money option.

Entry Breakdown You buy one contract of US 500 binary options with a strike price of 1259 and an ask price of $20 per contract. The required collateral to place this trade is $20 since it is the maximum you stand to lose.

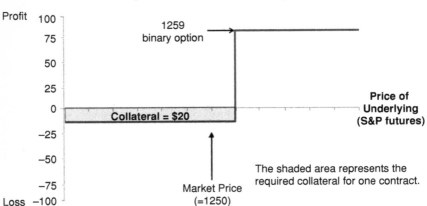

EXHIBIT 4.6   P&L Graph for an Out-of-the-Money Binary Option Trade

Exhibit 4.6 depicts the required collateral for going long one contract of the 1259 US 500 binary option. The x-axis represents the price of the underlying and the y-axis represents profit and loss. In this example, the collateral is represented as the shaded area and would be the maximum loss for this trade.

Summary   Exhibit 4.7 contains all of the data points for this trade.

EXHIBIT 4.7   Data Points for Out-of-the-Money Binary Option Trade

Trade	Figure	Calculation
Underlying asset	S&P futures	
Market price	1250	
Expiration	1 day	
Strike price	1259	
Long/Short	Long (buy)	
Size	1 contract	
Entry price	Ask price of $20/contract	
Max Loss	$20	Ask price × number of contracts = max loss $20 × 1 = $20
Collateral	$20	Collateral = max loss

At-the-Money Long Trade Collateral Example

Rationale If you believe that the S&P futures will go up in price, but not a lot, you may want to purchase a 1250 at-the-money option. The 1250 contract will be priced at $51.6.

Entry Breakdown Once again, the ask price of the options times the number of contracts you trade is the collateral that you put up on the trade. This way, if you are trading five contracts, your total collateral will be equal to $51.6 (price) × 5 (number of contracts) or $258.

Exhibit 4.8 depicts the required collateral for going long five contracts of the 1250 US 500 binary option. The x-axis represents the price of the underlying and the y-axis represents profit and loss. In this example, the collateral is represented as the shaded area and would be the maximum loss for this trade.

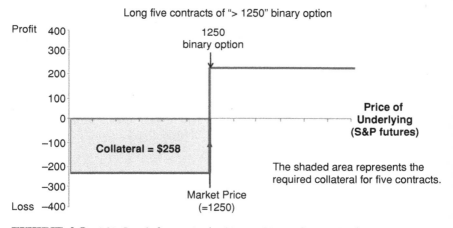

EXHIBIT 4.8 P&L Graph for an At-the-Money Binary Option Trade

Summary Exhibit 4.9 contains all of the data points for this trade.

EXHIBIT 4.9 Data Points for At-the-Money Binary Option Trade

Trade	Figure	Calculation
Underlying asset	S&P futures	
Market price	1250	
Binary option	US 500	
Expiration	1 day	
Strike price	1250	

(Continued)

EXHIBIT 4.9 (Continued)

Trade	Figure	Calculation
Long/Short	Long (buy)	
Size	5 contracts	
Entry price	Ask price of $51.6/contract	
Max loss	$258	Ask price × number of contracts = max loss $51.6 × 5 = $258
Collateral	$258	Collateral = max loss

COLLATERALIZING A SHORT BINARY OPTIONS TRADE

In order understand how to collateralize short binary options trades, you have to be clear on two items:

1. You should be clear on the basic concept that you have to put up your maximum potential loss when collateralizing any binary option trade.
2. You have to understand why someone would want to sell a binary option and the mechanics of selling a binary option.

Let's carefully look at what happens when you enter a binary options short position to explain how the trade will be collateralized.

THE MECHANICS OF A BINARY OPTIONS SHORT TRADE

The reason you are entering a binary options short position is that you are speculating that the underlying instrument will be below a certain price condition at expiration.

There are two reasons why an underlying instrument may end up below a certain strike price at expiration. The first reason is that the underlying instrument may end up below a certain strike if it goes down in price.

For example, if the S&P futures are trading at 1250 and you think they will drop below 1240, you can sell the 1241 strike price. If the futures close below 1241 at expiration, you will win. If they close above 1241 at expiration, you will lose.

In Exhibit 4.10 the y-axis represents available strike prices. The dark grey dashed line represents the market price of the S&P 500 futures, and the light grey dashed line represents the 1241 binary option.

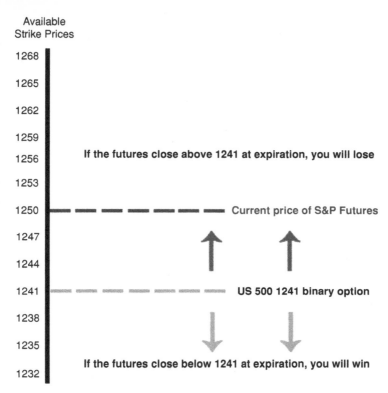

Available
Strike Prices

1268	
1265	
1262	
1259	
1256	**If the futures close above 1241 at expiration, you will lose**
1253	
1250	— — — — — — Current price of S&P Futures
1247	
1244	
1241	‑ ‑ ‑ ‑ ‑ ‑ ‑ **US 500 1241 binary option**
1238	
1235	
1232	**If the futures close below 1241 at expiration, you will win**

EXHIBIT 4.10   Underlying Instrument Going Below a Binary Options Strike Price at Expiration

The second reason is that the underlying instrument may end up below a certain strike price if it simply does not reach it. It may go up, it may go down, it may stay where it is, but as long as it does not reach your strike price at expiration, you will win on your binary options trade.

For example, if the S&P futures are trading at 1250 and you don't think that they will reach 1260 by expiration, you may want to sell the 1262 option. If the S&P futures close below 1262 at expiration, you will win. However, if the S&P futures go up and settle above 1262, you will lose.

In Exhibit 4.11 the y-axis represents available strike prices. The dark grey dashed line represents the market price of the S&P 500 futures and the light grey dashed line represents the 1262 binary option.

The idea is that you will want to sell the contract to collect the premium. The premium is simply the price of the contract. In short, when you

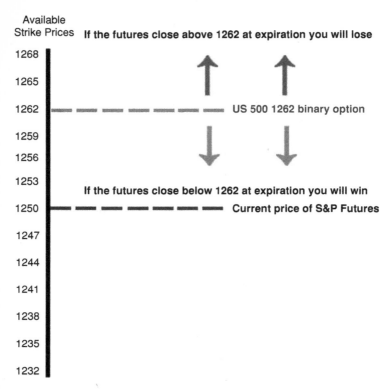

EXHIBIT 4.11   Underlying Instrument Below the Strike Price of a Binary Option

sell a binary options contract and the underlying ends up below a strike price at expiration, you will get to keep the entire premium that you sold the option for. If it ends up above the strike price at expiration, you will lose your collateral.

Let's look at the option chain in Exhibit 4.12 to explain this concept.

Exhibit 4.12 is an image of an option chain of the US 500 binary options strike prices with 12 hours until expiration.

Let's assume that the S&P futures are trading at 1250 and you think that they will go below 1244 by expiration. In order to make this speculation with binary options, you would want to sell the 1244 strike price. If you do this and you are correct, you will earn the premium of $71.2 (the bid price for the > 1244 option). However, if you are incorrect and the S&P futures stay above the 1244 strike price, then the value of the option at expiration would go up to $100 and you would lose $28.8 per contract.

Contract	Bid	Offer
Daily US 500 (Mar) > 1268	2.1	5
Daily US 500 (Mar) > 1265	4.9	7.8
Daily US 500 (Mar) > 1262	9.7	12.7
Daily US 500 (Mar) > 1259	17	20
Daily US 500 (Mar) > 1256	26	29
Daily US 500 (Mar) > 1253	36.1	40.1
Daily US 500 (Mar) > 1250	48.1	51.6
Daily US 500 (Mar) > 1247	60.1	63.1
Daily US 500 (Mar) > 1244	71.2	73.9
Daily US 500 (Mar) > 1241	79.9	83.4
Daily US 500 (Mar) > 1238	87.4	90.4
Daily US 500 (Mar) > 1235	92.3	95.3
Daily US 500 (Mar) > 1232	95.4	98.4

12 hours to expiration, futures trading at 1250

EXHIBIT 4.12   Option Chain

However, unlike vanilla put/call options, you don't simply collect the premium when you enter your trade. Instead, you put up your maximum loss when you initiate the trade. In order to fully collateralize a short binary options trade, you put up your maximum loss, which is $100 minus the contract premium. In Exhibit 4.12 this works out as follows: $100 max settlement value minus $71.2 (option bid price) = $28.8 collateral.

The formula for short trade collateral is:

$$\$100 - \text{Option Premium} = \text{Short Trade Collateral}$$

In this example, the most you can lose on your trade is $28.8 per contract, and therefore $28.8 per contract is what you have to put up to enter the trade. If you are correct, you get $100 revenue per contract, which makes your profit equivalent to the option's premium. A $100 cash inflow at the point of sale minus the $28.8 collateral that you put up to enter the trade equates to $71.2 (your option's premium).

Now let's take a look at some short collateral examples to solidify the concept. Once again, let's use the same option chain and assume that the S&P futures are trading at 1250 when you are entering your trades. Just as with long trades, you can trade in and out of your short binary options positions at any time before expiration. You will learn how this works in the subsequent sections of this text.

Exhibit 4.13 is an image of an option chain of the US 500 binary options strike prices with 12 hours until expiration.

Contract	Bid	Offer
Daily US 500 (Mar) > 1268	2.1	5
Daily US 500 (Mar) > 1265	4.9	7.8
Daily US 500 (Mar) > 1262	9.7	12.7
Daily US 500 (Mar) > 1259	17	20
Daily US 500 (Mar) > 1256	26	29
Daily US 500 (Mar) > 1253	36.1	40.1
Daily US 500 (Mar) > 1250	48.1	51.6
Daily US 500 (Mar) > 1247	60.1	63.1
Daily US 500 (Mar) > 1244	71.2	73.9
Daily US 500 (Mar) > 1241	79.9	83.4
Daily US 500 (Mar) > 1238	87.4	90.4
Daily US 500 (Mar) > 1235	92.3	95.3
Daily US 500 (Mar) > 1232	95.4	98.4

12 hours to expiration, futures trading at 1250

EXHIBIT 4.13 Binary Option Chain

Out-of-the-Money Short Collateral Example

Rationale If you believe that S&P futures will go down, you can sell the 1244 contract. Let's assume that you decide to sell 10 "> 1244" contracts. The premium of the 1244 contract is $71.2 per contract (the bid price).

Entry Breakdown If you hold the contract until expiration and the S&P futures close above 1244, the value of each contract will be $100. Therefore, your maximum loss per contract is $100 minus the option premium of $71.2. This equates to $28.8.

Because your maximum loss is always your collateral, you will have to put up $28.8 per contract in collateral when you sell the "> 1244" option. On 10 contracts this equals $288.

Exhibit 4.14 depicts the required collateral for going short 10 contracts of the 1244 US 500 binary option. The x-axis represents the price of the underlying, and the y-axis represents the trader's profit and loss. In this example the collateral is represented as the shaded area and would be the maximum loss for this trade.

Summary   Exhibit 4.15 contains all of the data points for this trade.

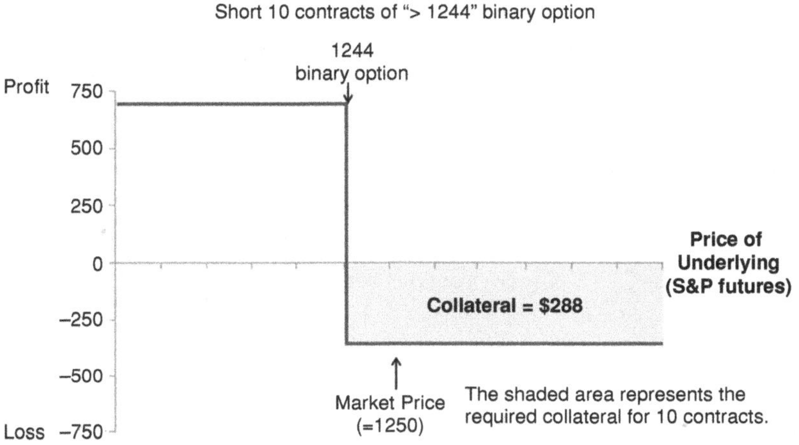

Short 10 contracts of "> 1244" binary option

EXHIBIT 4.14   P&L Graph of a Short Out-of-the-Money Binary Option Trade

In-the-Money Short Collateral Example

Rationale   Let's assume that you see a strong technical resistance level on the S&P futures at 1255. You are not sure where the futures will go, but you are fairly confident that they will not go above 1255. You may decide to sell the 1256 contract.

Entry Breakdown   Let's assume that you decide to sell one "> 1256" contract. The premium (bid price) of the 1256 contract is $26 per contract.

EXHIBIT 4.15   Data Points for Short Out-of-the-Money Binary Option Trade

Trade	Figure	Calculation
Underlying asset	S&P futures	
Market price	1250	
Expiration	1 day	
Strike price	1244	
Long/Short	Short (sell)	
Size	10 contracts	
Entry price	Bid price of $71.2/contract	
Max loss	$288	($100 − bid price) × number of contracts = max loss ($100 − $71.2) × 10 = $28.8 × 10 = $288
Collateral	$288	Collateral = max loss

If you hold the contract until expiration and the S&P futures close above 1256, the value of each contract will be $100. Therefore, your maximum loss per contract is $100 minus the option premium of $26. This equates to $74 dollars.

Because your maximum loss is always your collateral, you will have to put up $74 per contract in collateral when you sell the "> 1256" option.

Exhibit 4.16 depicts the required collateral for going short one contract of the 1256 US 500 binary option. The x-axis represents the price of the underlying, and the y-axis represents the traders profit/loss. In this example the collateral is represented as the shaded area and would be the maximum loss for this trade.

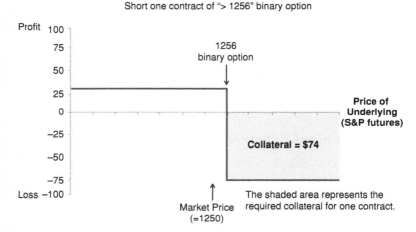

EXHIBIT 4.16   P&L Graph for a Short In-the-Money Binary Option Trade

Summary   Exhibit 4.17 contains all of the data points for this trade.

EXHIBIT 4.17   Data Points for Short In-the-Money Binary Option Trade

Trade	Figure	Calculation
Underlying asset	S&P futures	
Market price	1250	
Expiration	1 day	
Strike price	1256	
Long/Short	Short (sell)	
Size	1 contract	
Entry price	Bid price of $26/contract	
Max loss	$74	($100 − bid price) × number of contracts = collateral ($100 − $26) × 1 = $74 × 1 = $74
Collateral	$74	Collateral = max loss

At-the-Money Short Collateral Example

Rationale   If you would like to speculate that the S&P futures will simply go down and end up below their current price of 1250 at expiration, you can sell the "> 1250" contract. The premium of the "> 1250" contract is $48.1.

Entry Breakdown   You sell five contracts of US 500 binary options with a strike price of 1250 and a bid price of $48.1 per contract.

If the futures close above 1250, the contract value will go up to $100 and you will lose the difference between $100 and $48.1. This number is $51.9 per contract. Therefore, $51.9 is your maximum loss and collateral per contract.

If you trade five contracts, your total collateral will be 259.5. This is calculated by multiplying your collateral per contract ($51.9) by the number of contracts traded ($51.9 × 5).

Exhibit 4.18 depicts the required collateral for going short five contracts of the 1250 US 500 binary option. The x-axis represents the price of the underlying, and the y-axis represents profit and loss. In this example the collateral is represented as the shaded area and would be the maximum loss for this trade.

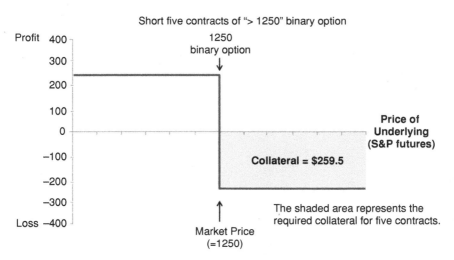

EXHIBIT 4.18   P&L Graph of an At-the-Money Binary Option Trade

Summary   Exhibit 4.19 contains all of the data points for this trade.

EXHIBIT 4.19   Data points for At-the-Money Binary Option Trade

Trade	Figure	Calculation
Underlying asset	S&P futures	
Market price	1250	
Expiration	1 day	
Strike price	1250	
Long/Short	Short (sell)	
Size	5 contracts	
Entry price	Bid price of $48.1/contract	
Max loss	$259.5	($100 − bid price) × number of contracts = max loss ($100 − $48.1) × 5 = $51.9 × 5 = $259.5
Collateral	$259.5	Collateral = max loss

CHAPTER 5

Settlement

Now that we covered collateral and looked at what your maximum losses are, let's look at what happens when you win on your binary options trades. Unlike stock options, binary options are never exercised. Due to the binary nature of the options, they are simply settled at either $0 or $100 at expiration.

Regardless of whether you buy or sell a binary option, if you are correct at expiration, your account will be credited $100 (settlement) per contract. If you are incorrect, you will get nothing.

When your trade settles at $100, your account gets credited very shortly after expiration and you will receive an e-mail notifying you that your trade was settled. Now let's look at the logistics of how a long and short binary options trade will settle.

SETTLEMENT ON BINARY OPTION LONG TRADES

If the condition for the option that you purchased is true at expiration, you will receive revenue of $100 per contract at settlement. Conversely, if this condition is false, you will receive nothing. For example, let's assume that the Standard & Poor's (S&P) futures were trading at 1280 when you entered your trade and you purchased a $1300 option for $30. If the price of the S&P futures is above 1300 at expiration, the option will settle at $100 and you will earn $70 on your $30 investment per contract or 233%. If, however, the S&P futures remain below 1300, the trade will settle at $0 per contract and you will get nothing and simply lose your $30 investment per contract.

Let's use the same examples from our section on collateral to learn how binary options positions are settled. Because we are using the same examples, we will also use the same option chain to examine how settlement works and assume that the S&P futures is the underlying and is trading at 1250 at the time the transaction is entered into.

Exhibit 5.1 is an image of an option chain of the US 500 binary options strike prices with 12 hours until expiration.

Contract	Bid	Offer
Daily US 500 (Mar) > 1268	2.1	5
Daily US 500 (Mar) > 1265	4.9	7.8
Daily US 500 (Mar) > 1262	9.7	12.7
Daily US 500 (Mar) > 1259	17	20
Daily US 500 (Mar) > 1256	26	29
Daily US 500 (Mar) > 1253	36.1	40.1
Daily US 500 (Mar) > 1250	48.1	51.6
Daily US 500 (Mar) > 1247	60.1	63.1
Daily US 500 (Mar) > 1244	71.2	73.9
Daily US 500 (Mar) > 1241	79.9	83.4
Daily US 500 (Mar) > 1238	87.4	90.4
Daily US 500 (Mar) > 1235	92.3	95.3
Daily US 500 (Mar) > 1232	95.4	98.4

12 hours to expiration, futures trading at 1250

EXHIBIT 5.1   Binary Option Chain

In-the-Money Long Settlement Example

Rationale   The S&P futures are currently trading at 1250. If you believe that the S&P futures will not drop below 1244, you would buy the 1244 contract.

Entry Breakdown   The ask price for this contract is $73.9. This is what you will have to put up for every contract that you want to trade. Therefore, on 10 contracts you are putting up $739.

Exit Breakdown   If the S&P futures close above 1244 at expiration and you don't exit your trade prior to expiration, the contract value will be $100. You will receive revenue of $1000 on your 10 contracts. Since you initially put up $739, your profit on the trade will be $261, or $26.1 per contract traded.

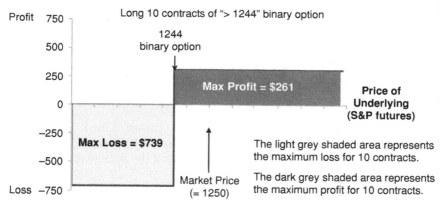

EXHIBIT 5.2   P&L Graph of a Long In-the-Money Binary Option Trade

Exhibit 5.2 depicts the profit and loss (P&L) of going long 10 contracts of the 1244 US 500 binary option. The x-axis represents the price of the underlying, and the y-axis represents P&L.

Summary   Exhibit 5.3 contains all of the data points for this trade.

EXHIBIT 5.3   Data Points for Long In-the-Money Binary Option Trade

Trade	Figure	Calculation
Underlying asset	S&P futures	
Market price	1250	
Expiration	1 day	
Strike price	1244	
Long/Short	Long (buy)	
Size	10 contracts	
Entry price	Ask price of $73.9/contract	
Max loss	$739	Ask price × number of contracts = max loss $73.9 × 10 = $739
Collateral	$739	Collateral = max loss
Max Profit	$261	($100 − ask price) × number of contracts = max profit ($100 − $73.9) × 10 = $26.1 × 10 = $261
Risk vs. reward	.35:1	Max profit/max loss = risk vs. reward $261 / $739 = .35:1

Out-of-the-Money Long Settlement Example

Rationale   The S&P futures are currently trading at 1250. If you believe that the S&P futures will go up in price, you would purchase a 1259 out-of-the-money option, hoping that the S&P futures will close above 1259 at expiration.

Entry Breakdown   You decide to buy one contract of the US 500 binary option with a strike price of 1259 and an ask price of $20 per contract. The required collateral to place this trade is $20, and the maximum you stand to lose is also $20.

Exit Breakdown   If you are correct and the S&P futures reach 1259 by expiration, then you will receive $100 per contract settlement at expiration. In this case your total profit will be $80 since total profit is equal to the difference between the collateral you put up and your settlement value of $100.

If you are wrong and the S&P futures do not settle above 1259 at expiration, your maximum loss will be $20 per contract, which is your entire collateral.

Exhibit 5.4 depicts the P&L of going long one contract of the 1259 US 500 binary option. The x-axis represents the price of the underlying, and the y-axis represents P&L.

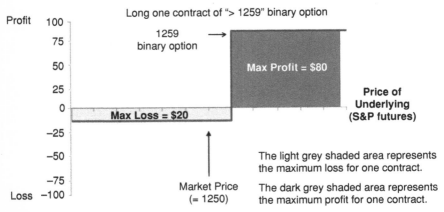

EXHIBIT 5.4   P&L Graph of a Long Out-of-the-Money Binary Option Trade

Summary   Exhibit 5.5 contains all of the data points for this trade.

EXHIBIT 5.5 Data Points for Long Out-of-the-Money Binary Option Trade

Trade	Figure	Calculation
Underlying asset	S&P futures	
Market price	1250	
Expiration	1 day	
Strike price	1259	
Long/Short	Long (buy)	
Size	1 contract	
Entry price	Ask price of $20/contract	
Max loss	$20	Ask price × number of contracts = max loss $20 × 1 = $20
Collateral	$20	Collateral = max loss
Max profit	$80	($100 − ask price) × number of contracts = max profit ($100 − $20) × 1 = $80 × 1 = $80
Risk vs. reward	4:1	Max profit / max loss = risk vs. reward $80 / $20 = 4:1

At-the-Money Long Trade Settlement Example

Rationale The S&P futures are currently trading at 1250. If you believe that the S&P futures will go up in price, but are unsure by how much, you would simply purchase a 1250 at-the-money option.

Entry Breakdown You buy five contracts of US 500 binary options with a strike price of 1250 and an ask price of $51.6 per contract. The required collateral to place this trade is $258, and the maximum you stand to lose is also $258.

Exit Breakdown If you are correct and the S&P futures are above 1250 by expiration, then you will receive $100 per contract on the trade. In this case your profit per contract will be $48.4 since it's the difference between the collateral you put up (options purchase price) and your settlement value of $100. Your total profit on this trade will be $48.4 × 5 contracts or $242.

If you are wrong and the S&P futures do not settle above 1250, your maximum loss will be $51.6 per contract. In this case you are trading five contracts, so your maximum loss is $258.

Exhibit 5.6 depicts the profit and loss of going long five contracts of the 1250 US 500 binary option. The x-axis represents the price of the underlying, and the y-axis represents P&L.

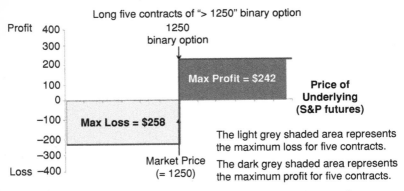

EXHIBIT 5.6 P&L Graph of a Long At-the-Money Binary Option Trade

Summary   Exhibit 5.7 contains all of the data points for this trade.

EXHIBIT 5.7   Data Point for a Long At-the-Money Binary Option Trade

Trade	Figure	Calculation
Underlying asset	S&P futures	
Market price	1250	
Expiration	1 day	
Strike price	1250	
Long/Short	Long (buy)	
Size	5 contracts	
Price	Ask price of $51.6/contract	
Max Loss	$258	Ask price × number of contracts = max loss $51.6 × 5 = $258
Collateral	$258	collateral = max loss
Max profit	$242	($100 − ask price) × number of contracts = max profit ($100 − $51.6) × 5 = $48.4 × 5 = $242
Risk vs. reward	.93:1	Max profit / max loss = risk vs. reward $242 / $258 = .93:1

SETTLEMENT ON BINARY OPTIONS SHORT TRADES

Settlement of short binary options trades is a bit trickier than settlement of long trades. But if you keep the basic principle of $100 per contract if you are correct and $0 per contract if you are wrong, you should be able to pick up the concept pretty quickly.

In order to have an understanding of how short binary option trades are settled, you must have a clear understanding of how short binary option trades work and how they are collateralized. If you need further clarification on these concepts, please refer to the section on collateral.

As you will recall from the section on collateral, when you sell a binary options contract, you put up the full collateral. Full collateral means that you are putting up your maximum potential loss to enter your trade.

The formula for maximum loss is:

$$\$100 - \text{Option Premium} = \text{Maximum Loss on Short Trade}$$

In a short trade your maximum potential loss per contract is $100 minus the option's premium.

Remember, the value of a contract goes to $100 at expiration if the underlying is trading above the strike price. For example, let's assume that you are selling a binary option for $40. The most you can lose when that option expires is $60.

Exhibit 5.8 is a graphical representation of the profit and loss on a short position. In this example the required collateral and maximum loss (dark grey shaded area) is $60, which is calculated by subtracting 100 from the option premium ($40). The maximum potential profit (light grey shaded area) is simply the option's premium, in this case $40.

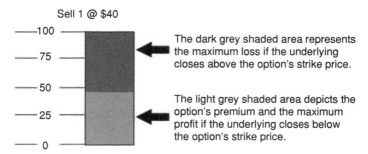

Sell 1 @ $40

———100

——— 75

The dark grey shaded area represents the maximum loss if the underlying closes above the option's strike price.

——— 50

——— 25

The light grey shaded area depicts the option's premium and the maximum profit if the underlying closes below the option's strike price.

——— 0

EXHIBIT 5.8 Image Depicting the Maximum Loss and Maximum Profit for Short Trades

If you are correct on your binary options short trade and the underlying does close below your strike price, then at trade settlement you will receive $100 per contract revenue. If you subtract the collateral that you put up from the $100, it will equate to the options premium.

Here is a simple formula to demonstrate this:

$$Profit = \$100 - Collateral$$

$$Collateral = \$100 - Premium$$

$$Profit = \$100 - (\$100 - Premium)$$

Therefore:

$$Profit = Premium$$

The key rules to remember are:

- In all binary options trades (long and short), at settlement you get $100 if you are correct and $0 if you are wrong.
- In all binary options trades, you put up your maximum loss as collateral. For short trades, collateral is equal to $100 minus the premium.
- Your profit in all binary options winning trades is $100 minus the collateral. On short trades, this is equivalent to the premium.

For example, if the S&P futures are trading at 1280, you may be able to sell a "> 1290" contract for $30. You will have to put up $70 per contract in collateral for this. If you decide to stay in your trade until expiration and the S&P futures close above 1290, you will lose your $70/contract collateral and end up with nothing.

However, if the S&P futures close below 1290 at expiration and you stay in your trade until expiration, your trade will settle at $100/contract to you. Your account will be credited $100/contract shortly after expiration and you will receive a notification e-mail. Your total profit per contract on the trade will be the $100 settlement minus the original $70 collateral that you put up. This equates to the $30 option premium of the "> 1290" contract.

Exhibit 5.9 depicts the P&L of going short one contract of the 1290 US 500 binary option. The x-axis represents the price of the underlying, and the y-axis represents profit and loss.

Summary   Exhibit 5.10 contains all of the data points for this trade.

Now let's look at some short settlement examples to solidify the concept. Once again, let's use the same option chain and assume that the S&P futures are trading at 1250 when you are entering your trades. Just as with long trades, you can trade in and out of your short binary options positions

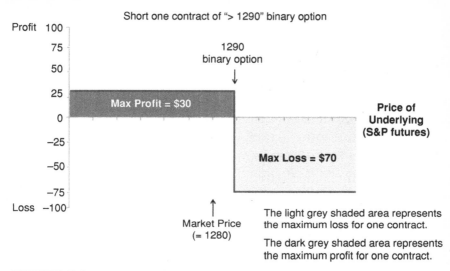

EXHIBIT 5.9 P&L Graph of a Short Binary Option Trade

EXHIBIT 5.10 Data Points for Short Binary Option Trade

Trade	Figure	Calculation
Underlying asset	S&P futures	
Market price	1280	
Expiration	1 day	
Strike price	1290	
Long/Short	Short (sell)	
Size	1 contract	
Price	Bid price of $30/contract	
Max loss	$70	($100 – bid price) × number of contracts = max loss ($100 – $30) × 1 = $70 × 1 = $70
Collateral	$70	Collateral = max loss
Max profit	$30	Bid price × number of contracts = max profit $30 × 1 =$30
Risk vs. reward	.42:1	Max profit / max loss = risk vs. reward $30 / $70 = .42:1

at any time before expiration. You will learn how this works in the subsequent sections of this text.

Exhibit 5.11 is an image of an option chain of the US 500 binary options strike prices with 12 hours until expiration.

Contract	Bid	Offer
Daily US 500 (Mar) > 1268	2.1	5
Daily US 500 (Mar) > 1265	4.9	7.8
Daily US 500 (Mar) > 1262	9.7	12.7
Daily US 500 (Mar) > 1259	17	20
Daily US 500 (Mar) > 1256	26	29
Daily US 500 (Mar) > 1253	36.1	40.1
Daily US 500 (Mar) > 1250	48.1	51.6
Daily US 500 (Mar) > 1247	60.1	63.1
Daily US 500 (Mar) > 1244	71.2	73.9
Daily US 500 (Mar) > 1241	79.9	83.4
Daily US 500 (Mar) > 1238	87.4	90.4
Daily US 500 (Mar) > 1235	92.3	95.3
Daily US 500 (Mar) > 1232	95.4	98.4

12 hours to expiration, futures trading at 1250

EXHIBIT 5.11   Option Chain

Out-of-the-Money Short Settlement Example

Rationale   The S&P futures are currently trading at 1250. You assume that the S&P futures will go down in price, ending up below 1244 at expiration.

Entry Breakdown   You sell 10 contracts of the US 500 binary option with a strike price of 1244 and a bid price of $71.2 per contract. The required collateral to place this trade is $288, and the maximum you stand to lose is also $288.

Exit Breakdown   If you hold until expiration and the S&P futures close below 1244, you will get a $100 settlement. This will provide you with a profit of $71.2 per contract, which is the option's premium.

If the futures close above 1244, you will get $0 per contract at expiration, and will lose your collateral of $28.8 per contract.

Exhibit 5.12 is a graph of the P&L of going short 10 contracts of the 1244 US 500 binary option. The x-axis represents the price of the underlying, and the y-axis represents P&L.

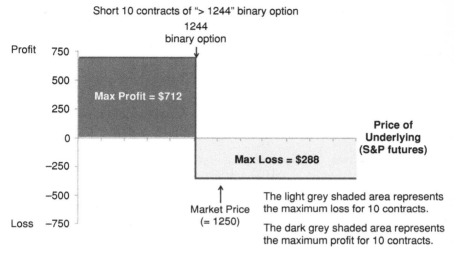

Short 10 contracts of "> 1244" binary option

EXHIBIT 5.12 P&L Graph of a Short Out-of-the-Money Binary Option Trade

Summary Exhibit 5.13 contains all of the data points for this trade.

EXHIBIT 5.13 Data Points for Short Out-of-the-Money Binary Option Trade

Trade	Figure	Calculation
Underlying asset	S&P futures	
Market price	1250	
Expiration	1 day	
Strike price	1244	
Long/Short	Short (sell)	
Size	10 contracts	
Price	Bid price of $71.2/contract	
Max loss	$288	($100 − bid price) × number of contracts = max loss ($100 − $71.2) × 10 = $28.8 × 10 = $288
Collateral	$288	Collateral = max loss
Max profit	$712	Bid price × number of contracts = max profit $71.2 × 10 =$712
Risk vs. reward	2.47:1	Max profit / max loss = risk vs. reward $712 / $288 = 2.47:1

In-the-Money Short Settlement Example

Rationale   If you would like to speculate that the S&P futures will stay below 1256 at expiration, you can sell the "> 1256" contract.

Entry Breakdown   You sell one contract of the US 500 binary option with a strike price of 1256 and a bid price of $26 per contract. The required collateral to place this trade is $74, and the maximum you stand to lose is also $74.

Exit Breakdown   If you hold until expiration and the S&P futures close below 1256, you will get a $100 settlement. This will provide you with a profit of $26 per contract ($100 settlement – $74 collateral). The $26 is the option's premium.

If the futures close above 1256, you will get $0 per contract at expiration, and will lose your collateral of $74 per contract.

Exhibit 5.14 depicts the P&L of going short one contract of the 1256 US 500 binary option. The x-axis represents the price of the underlying, and the y-axis represents P&L.

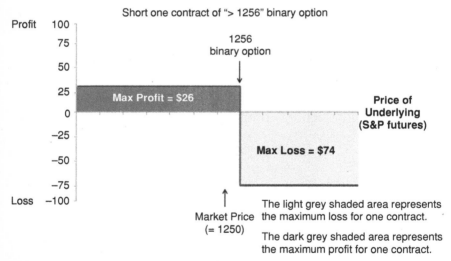

EXHIBIT 5.14   P&L Graph of a Short In-the-Money Binary Option Trade

Summary   Exhibit 5.15 contains all of the data points for this trade.

EXHIBIT 5.15 Data Points for Short In-the-Money Binary Option Trade

Trade	Figure	Calculation
Underlying asset	S&P futures	
Market price	1250	
Expiration	1 day	
Strike price	1256	
Long/Short	Short (sell)	
Size	1 contract	
Price	Bid price of $26/contract	
Max loss	$74	($100 − bid price) × number of contracts = max loss ($100 − $26) × 1 = $74 × 1 = $74
Collateral	$74	Collateral = max loss
Max profit	$26	Bid price × number of contracts = max profit $26 × 1 = $26
Risk vs. reward	.35:1	Max profit / max risk = risk vs. reward 26 / 74 = .35:1

At-the-Money Short Settlement Example

Rationale   If you would like to speculate that the S&P futures will simply go down and close below 1250 at expiration, you can sell the "> 1250" contract.

Entry Breakdown   You sell five contracts of the US 500 binary option with a strike price of 1250 and a bid price of $48.1 per contract. The required collateral to place this trade is $259.5 ($100 − $48.1) × 5 contracts, which, of course, is the maximum you stand to lose.

Exit Breakdown   If you hold until expiration and the S&P futures close below 1250, you will get a $100 settlement. This will provide you with a profit of $48.1 per contract ($100 settlement − $51.9/contract collateral). The $48.1 is also the option's premium. On five contracts this is $240.5.

If the S&P futures close above 1250, you will get $0 per contract at expiration and will lose your collateral of $51.9 per contract.

Exhibit 5.16 depicts the P&L of going short five contracts of the 1250 US 500 binary option. The x-axis represents the price of the underlying, and the y-axis represents P&L.

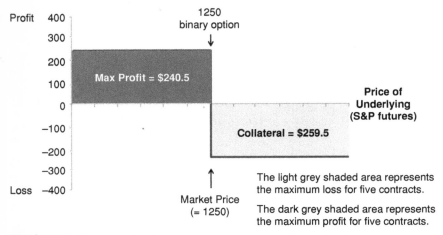

Short five contracts of "> 1250" binary option

1250 binary option ↓

Max Profit = $240.5

Collateral = $259.5

Price of Underlying (S&P futures)

↑ Market Price (= 1250)

The light grey shaded area represents the maximum loss for five contracts.

The dark grey shaded area represents the maximum profit for five contracts.

EXHIBIT 5.16 P&L of a Short At-the-Money Binary Option Trade

Summary Exhibit 5.17 contains all of the data points for this trade.

EXHIBIT 5.17 Data Points for Short At-the-Money Binary Option Trade

Trade	Figure	Calculation
Underlying asset	S&P futures	
Market price	1250	
Expiration	1 day	
Strike price	1250	
Long/Short	Short (sell)	
Size	5 contracts	
Price	Bid price of $48.1/contract	
Max Loss	$259.5	($100 − bid price) × number of contracts = max loss ($100 − $48.1) × 5 = $51.9 × 5 = $259.5
Collateral	$259.5	Collateral = max loss
Max profit	$240.5	Bid price × number of contracts = max profit $48.1 × 5 = $240.5
Risk vs. reward	.93:1	Max profit / max loss = risk vs. reward $240.5 / $259.5 = .93:1

Collateral and Max Profit Summary Table

Exhibit 5.18 should help you easily remember how to determine the collateral and maximum profit for both long and short binary option trades.

Exhibit 5.18 depicts how the collateral and the maximum profit are calculated for long and short binary option trades. As you can see, the calculation for max profit and collateral is inverse for the two trade types.

EXHIBIT 5.18 Collateral and Max Profit Summary Table

Trade	Collateral/Max Loss at Expiration	Max Profit at Expiration
Long trade	Premium	$100 – Premium
Short trade	$100 – premium	Premium

COMMISSIONS AND FEES

When trading binary options contracts, typically you are charged a commission for each contract. With some brokers you will also be charged a settlement fee if the option goes until expiration. You pay the settlement fee only if you win on the trade. To be precise, if you purchase an option and hold it until expiration and it settles above a strike price, then you will pay a settlement fee. If you sell an option and hold it until expiration, then you will pay a settlement fee if it closes below the strike price. If you choose to exit your trade prior to expiration, you will typically pay the same commissions regardless of whether you win or lose.

An example of a commission fee could be $1 per side per contract. So if you enter five contracts, you will pay $5 to enter your trade and $5 to exit.

Exhibit 5.19 shows the commission and settlement variables for binary options.

EXHIBIT 5.19 Breakdown of Commissions and Fees

Trade Type	Win	Loss
Entry	Commission	N/A
Exit prior to settlement	Commission	Commission
Settlement	Settlement fee	Nothing

CHAPTER 6

Entering and Exiting Binary Option Trades

READING QUOTES

When reading a binary option quote, there are several fundamental components that you should understand and identify. These fundamental components are: the underlying asset, the strike price, the expiration time and date, and the bid/offer.

- *Underlying asset or market.* This component of the quote identifies the underlying asset on which the binary option contract is traded. As you learned in Part Two, binary options can be traded on multiple instruments, including index futures, commodity futures, spot forex, and economic data releases.

US 500 (Mar)

In the image above, the underlying asset is the March Standard & Poor's (S&P) 500 futures.

- *Strike price.* The strike price represents the true or false condition relative to the underlying market. More simply put, the strike price is your price target to be achieved or not achieved based on your position (long or short).

US 500 (Mar >1223.0 4:15PM)

In the image above, the strike price for this US 500 (S&P 500) binary is 1223.0.

- *Expiration time and date.* As you have learned, binary options are available with multiple expiration times and dates. The possibilities are weekly options, daily options, and hourly options. This component is critical, based on your trading strategy.

US 500 (Mar) >1223.0 (4:15PM)

In the image above, the expiration time for this binary option is 4:15 P.M. EST.

- *Bid and offer.* When viewing a price quote, you will see two different prices; these are known as the *bid* and *offer.* The bid is the price at which you sell the binary option. The offer is the price at which you sell the binary option. These two prices will fluctuate until expiration. Both the bid and the offer prices of binary options must remain in a range from $0 to $100. Also, please keep in mind that each point on a binary option is equivalent to $1.

  Bid—the price to sell the binary option.

60.50   64.00

Above, you see an example of the bid for this US 500 binary. As you can see, if you were to sell the US 500 option discussed above, you would do so at the $60.50 price.

  Ask—the price to buy the binary option.

60.50   64.50

Above, you see an example of the offer for this US 500 binary option. In this example the current price to buy this binary option is $64.50. The price quote above shows a spread of $3.50.

READING AN ORDER TICKET

Now that you are able to identify the underlying asset, strike price, and bid/offer prices, let's take a look at an order ticket. As you can see, the order ticket in Exhibit 6.1 has the same parameters you just learned about. The underlying asset is the US 500 (S&P 500 futures), with a strike price of 1248.5 and a bid/offer of 41.00/45.50.

  Anatomy of an order ticket:

  Contract information. Underlying asset, strike price, and expiration time and date.

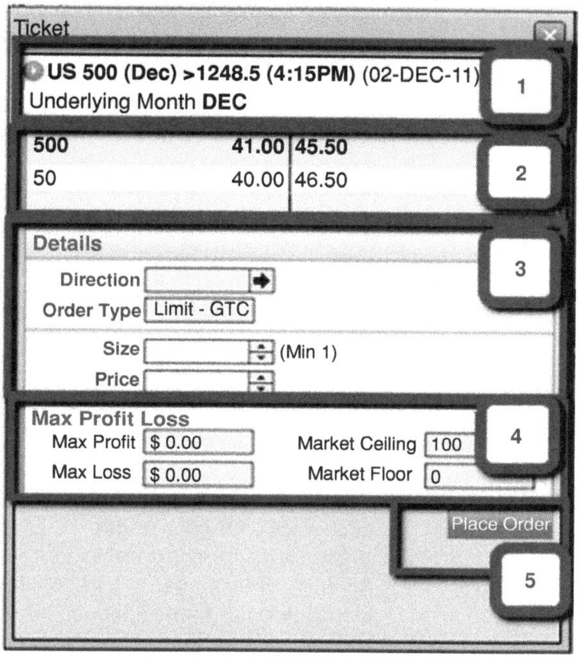

EXHIBIT 6.1 Order Ticket

Bid and offer prices.

Order details. This is where the direction (buy or sell), number of con-
    tracts (size), and price are displayed. If you believe that the US 500
    will go up and close above 1248.5 at expiration, then you would
    buy. If you believe that it will go down or stay at its current price
    and close below 1248.5, then you would sell.

Also, in this section you can enter the order type that you want to place.
If you want to simply take what the market is giving you, you can place a
market order to buy now at the ask price or sell now at the bid price.

If you want to get a better price than the current asking price, you can
place a limit order. When buying, you will attempt to get in below the ask
price, and when selling, you will attempt to get in above the bid price. You
can also go in between the spread with a limit order. For example, in this
particular case you can place your limit order at 43 to get a better fill than
is currently being offered. Of course, when you use a limit order to enter
your trade, it may take longer to get filled, or you may not get filled at all
and miss your opportunity.

You can also place a stop order to buy or sell. If you believe that the underlying needs to break out of a price range and want to enter only if it does, then you can place your stop order above the offer price. If you believe that the underlying will break below a price range and want to enter only if it does, then you can place your entry order below the bid.

Exhibit 6.2 details the various types of entry and exit orders.

Max profit, max loss, market ceiling, and *market floor* are defined for you. It simply shows what is the most you can make and the most you can lose on the trade if you hold until expiration.

EXHIBIT 6.2   Order Types

Type of Order	Entry/Exit	Result
Market order	Entry/Exit	Places an order at the current price
Limit entry order	Entry	An order type that the trader would use to get into a trade at a better price than offered
		Lower price for long trades
		Higher price for short trades
Stop	Entry	An entry order to get in a trade when the instrument has made a move
		Higher price for long trades
		Lower price for short trades
Stop loss (stop)	Exit	An exit order to cut losses in case of an adverse move
		Lower than market price for long trades
		Higher than market price for short trades
Take profit (limit)	Exit	An order used to lock in profit on trades
		Higher than market price for long trades
		Lower than market price for short trades

EXITING TRADES

When trading binary options, you can exit your trade in two different ways: (1) You can wait until expiration and have your trade settled at $0 or $100 per contract, or (2) you can exit your trade before expiration for the fair market price.

Commissions for Trade Exit and Settlement

Unlike with regular put and call options, binary options brokers typically will require you to pay commissions any time that your trade is settled in-the-money. You will always have to pay commissions to enter the trade.

EXHIBIT 6.3 Commission Requirements before and after Expiration

Type of Exit	Win	Loss
Exit before expiration	Commissions	Commissions
Expiration and settlement	Commissions	No Commissions

You will also always have to pay commissions to exit the trade prior to expiration whether it is profitable or not. If you wait until expiration, typically you will have to pay commissions only if the trade is settled in profit. If your trade loses and is settled at $0, then you will not have to pay commissions.

Look at Exhibit 6.3 to determine the cases in which you typically will or will not be required to pay commission. This table details the commissions resulting from exiting a trade before expiration or after expiration.

Exit at Trade Expiration

If you followed the prior examples in this text, you should have a pretty basic understanding of what happens with binary options when they expire or are settled. Each contract will have a predefined expiration time and date (if necessary).

- Daily contracts will expire every day at 4:15 P.M. New York time.
- Hourly contracts expire at specific times: 11 A.M., 12 P.M., 2 P.M., and 4:15 P.M. New York time.
- Weekly contracts will expire on Fridays at varying times depending on the underlying asset.

Losing at Expiration

If you wait until expiration and your trade expires for a loss, then you will simply lose your collateral and not get anything at expiration. This holds true whether you bought or sold an options contract.

For example, if the underlying is trading at 1250 and you purchase a 1230 contract for $70 and the underlying falls below 1230, then you will lose the $70 that you purchased the contract for at expiration.

Now let's looks at a sell example. Let's assume that the underlying is also trading at 1250 when you make your trade, and you sell a 1280 option for $30. You will have to put up $70 collateral ($100 – $30 options premium). If the underlying is trading at or above 1280 at expiration, then you will lose on your trade. In this case you will again simply lose the $70 collateral that you put up to enter the trade.

Since both of the previous scenarios ended up in a loss, you will not be required to pay commissions to exit your trade.

Winning at Expiration

If your trade ends up in-the-money at expiration, you will collect $100 regardless of whether you entered a short or a long position.

Exhibit 6.4 details the payout of a trade expiring in the money.

Let's look at a basic example where the underlying is the S&P 500 futures and it is trading at 1250:

EXHIBIT 6.4 Payout of Long and Short In-the-Money Binary Options

Long or Short In-the-Money	Payout
Long at expiration	$100
Short at expiration	$100

If you purchase a 1270 call for $30 and the S&P 500 futures go up and close above 1270 at expiration, you will collect $100 revenue per contract.

Exhibit 6.5 depicts a long 1270 binary option at expiration with a payout of $100. The x-axis represents the price of the underlying, and the y-axis depicts profit. The shaded area represents the payout that will be credited to your account if the S&P futures are above the 1270 strike price at expiration.

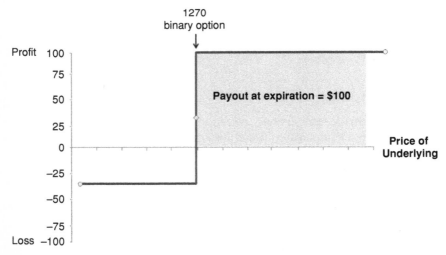

EXHIBIT 6.5 P&L Graph of a Long Binary Option Trade Depicting a Payout of $100 at Expiration

If you sell a 1270 call for $30 per contract, you will have to put up the $70 collateral. As long as the US 500 stays below 1270, you will be able to collect $100 revenue per contract at settlement.

Exhibit 6.6 depicts a short 1270 binary option at expiration with a payout of $100. The x-axis represents the price of the underlying, and the y-axis depicts profit. The shaded area represents the payout that will be credited to your account if the S&P futures are below the 1270 strike price at expiration.

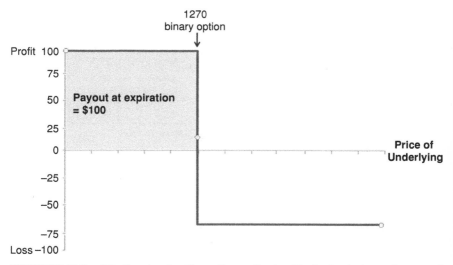

EXHIBIT 6.6   P&L Graph of a Short Binary Option Trade Depicting a Payout of $100 at Expiration

When you receive the $100/contract trade settlement on your winning trades, you typically will be charged a commission on your exit. This commission may be referred to as a settlement fee. Once the broker settles, your account balance will go up by $100 per winning contract and you will typically receive an e-mail confirming that you won on the trade and received a settlement fee.

EXITING YOUR TRADE BEFORE EXPIRATION

With binary options you do not have to wait for the contract to expire to exit your trade. You may want to exit your trade prior to expiration for one of two reasons: (1) to lock in your profit or (2) to minimize your losses.

Contract	Bid	Offer
Daily US 500 (Mar) > 1268	2.1	5
Daily US 500 (Mar) > 1265	4.9	7.8
Daily US 500 (Mar) > 1262	9.7	12.7
Daily US 500 (Mar) > 1259	17	20
Daily US 500 (Mar) > 1256	26	29
Daily US 500 (Mar) > 1253	36.1	40.1
Daily US 500 (Mar) > 1250	48.1	51.6
Daily US 500 (Mar) > 1247	60.1	63.1
Daily US 500 (Mar) > 1244	71.2	73.9
Daily US 500 (Mar) > 1241	79.9	83.4
Daily US 500 (Mar) > 1238	87.4	90.4
Daily US 500 (Mar) > 1235	92.3	95.3
Daily US 500 (Mar) > 1232	95.4	98.4

12 hours to expiration, futures trading at 1250

EXHIBIT 6.7   Option Chain

Exhibit 6.7 is an example of a US 500 binary option chain with 12 hours until expiration. Let's use the option chain in the exhibit to illustrate a few examples of exiting the trade prior to expiration.

Exit to Lock In Profit

If you wait until expiration and the underlying ends up even one cent below your strike price, you will get $0 instead of $100 per contract at settlement. Therefore, you may not want to take that chance and exit that trade prior to expiration if your trade is profitable. You simply may want to lock in the profit on your trade prior to settlement. Let's examine this principle with two basic examples.

Example 1 (Long Position)   Let's use a long binary option trading position to demonstrate why you would want to lock in your profit prior to expiration.

Entry Breakdown   Let's assume that the S&P futures are trading at 1250 when you place your trade. You purchase a "> 1244" option in the morning with the assumption that the underlying will be above 1244 at the end of the day. You decide to buy one contract for $73.90.

In Exhibit 6.8, the y-axis represents available strike prices. The dark grey dashed line represents the market price of S&P futures and the light

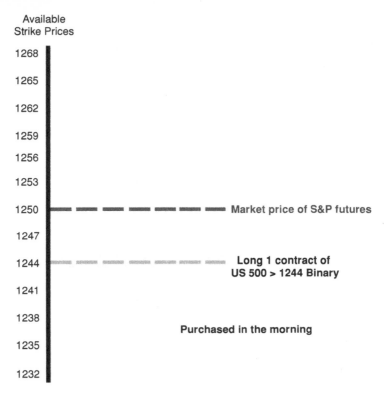

EXHIBIT 6.8 Binary Option Condition Purchased in the Morning

grey dashed line represents the binary option contract. With one day until expiration, the 1244 binary option is purchased with the assumption that the S&P futures will close above 1244 at expiration.

Exit Breakdown Halfway through the day, you see that the S&P 500 futures broke through 1260 and then started to fall. At this point, the price of your option is up to $85. However, due to the downward move, you are concerned that the S&P 500 futures may drop below 1244. If this occurs, you will not make a profit.

Exhibit 6.9 depicts a price chart of the S&P futures. The x-axis represents the time, and the y-axis represents price. Halfway through the day the S&P futures have risen above 1260 but are now starting to move down.

In Exhibit 6.10, the y-axis represents available strike prices. The dark grey dashed line represents the market price of S&P futures, and the light grey dashed line represents the binary option contract. Halfway through the day, the S&P futures have risen 10 points to 1260 and are now starting to fall.

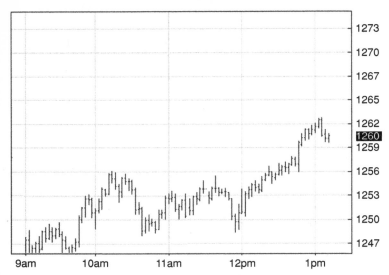

EXHIBIT 6.9   Price Chart of S&P Futures Halfway through the Trading Day

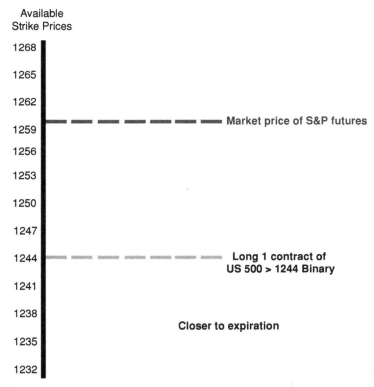

EXHIBIT 6.10   Binary Option Condition Closer to Expiration

You exit the position early when the bid price is $85, giving you a total profit of $11.10. Your profit is calculated by simply subtracting $73.9 (your purchase collateral) from $85 (the bid price of the option when you decide to exit your trade). To do this, you simply sell the "> 1244" option and lock in your profit.

Summary   Exhibit 6.11 contains all of the data points for this trade.

EXHIBIT 6.11   Data Points for Long Binary Option Trade Demonstrating Early Exit to Lock in Profits

Trade	Figure	Calculation
Underlying asset	S&P futures	
Market price	1250	
Expiration	1 day	
Strike price	1244	
Long/Short	Long (buy)	
Size	1 contract	
Entry price	Ask price of $73.9/contract	
Max loss	$73.9	Ask price × number of contracts = max loss $73.9 × 1 = $73.9
Collateral	$73.9	Collateral = max loss
Max profit	$26.1	($100 – ask price) × number of contracts = max profit ($100 – $73.9) × 1 = $26.1 × 1 = $26.1
Exit price	Bid price of $85	
Profit or loss	Profit of $11.10	Bid price when position closed – ask price when position opened = profit $85 – $73.9 = $11.10

Example 2 (Short Position)

Now let's use a short binary option trading position to demonstrate why you would want to lock in your profit prior to expiration.

Entry Breakdown   Based on the same option chain we discussed, let's assume again that the S&P futures were trading at 1250 when you entered your trade. But this time you sold the "> 1241" option in the morning with the anticipation that the underlying will go down by the end of the day. The option's bid price is $79.9; therefore, you put up $20.1 collateral per contract.

In Exhibit 6.12, the y-axis represents available strike prices. The dark grey dashed line represents the market price of S&P futures, and the light

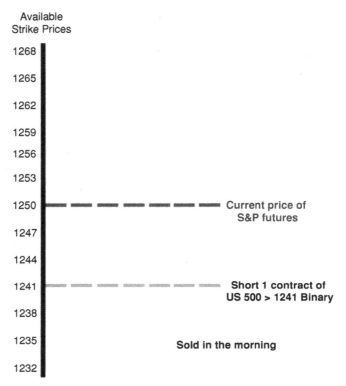

EXHIBIT 6.12   Binary Option Condition Sold in the Morning

grey dashed line represents the binary option contract. With one day until expiration, the 1241 binary option is sold with the assumption that the S&P futures will close below 1241 at expiration.

Exit Breakdown   As expiration approaches, the S&P futures drop and are priced at 1244. The price of the "> 1241" option goes down to $65.

You become concerned that the S&P futures will rebound and decide to exit your trade early. In order to do this, you will now need to buy back the "> 1241" option.

Since initially you sold the option for $79.9 and now you are buying it back at $65, your account will be credited the difference between the two strike prices. This figure is $14.9. Additionally, you will receive your trade collateral back since you exited your trade. So for a max risk of $20.1 per contract, you will receive a reward of $14.9 per contract.

In Exhibit 6.13, the y-axis represents available strike prices. The dark grey dashed line represents the market price of S&P futures, and the light grey dashed line represents the binary option contract. As expiration approaches, the S&P futures have fallen six points and are currently trading at 1244.

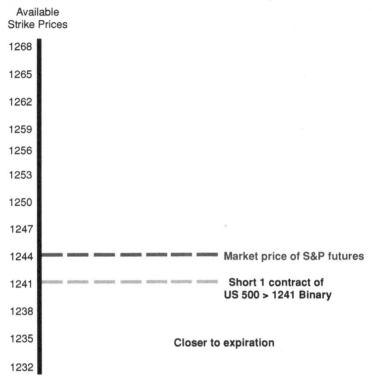

EXHIBIT 6.13 Binary Option Condition Closer to Expiration

Summary Exhibit 6.14 contains all of the data points for this trade.

Of course, in all cases you are paying commission on your way in and out of the trades.

EXHIBIT 6.14 Data Points for Short Binary Option Trade Demonstrating Early Exit to Lock in Profits

Trade	Figure	Calculation
Underlying asset	S&P futures	
Market price	1250	
Expiration	1 day	
Strike price	1241	
Long/Short	Short (sell)	
Size	1 contract	
Entry price	Bid price of $79.9/contract	
Max loss	$20.1	($100 − bid price) × number of contracts = max loss ($100 − $79.9) × 1 = $20.1 × 1 = $20.1

(Continued)

EXHIBIT 6.14 (Continued)

Trade	Figure	Calculation
Collateral	$20.1	Collateral = max loss
Max profit	$79.9	Bid price × number of contracts = max profit $79.9 × 1 = $79.9
Exit price	Ask price of $65/contract	
Profit or loss	Profit of $14.9	Bid price when position opened – ask price when position closed = profit $79.9 – $65 = 14.9

Exit to Minimize Losses

Let's assume that you enter into a binary options contract and it's simply not working out in your favor. The way things are going, it clearly looks like you are going to lose on the trade and the underlying is going to end up in a situation where your contract will be worth $0 at expiration.

One great feature of binary options is that you do not have to wait until expiration and lose your entire collateral. You can simply cut your losses short by exiting the trade before expiration and preserve at least a portion of your investment on the trade.

Let's look at a few examples of where this can be done using the option chain in Exhibit 6.15.

Contract	Bid	Offer
Daily US 500 (Mar) > 1268	2.1	5
Daily US 500 (Mar) > 1265	4.9	7.8
Daily US 500 (Mar) > 1262	9.7	12.7
Daily US 500 (Mar) > 1259	17	20
Daily US 500 (Mar) > 1256	26	29
Daily US 500 (Mar) > 1253	36.1	40.1
Daily US 500 (Mar) > 1250	48.1	51.6
Daily US 500 (Mar) > 1247	60.1	63.1
Daily US 500 (Mar) > 1244	71.2	73.9
Daily US 500 (Mar) > 1241	79.9	83.4
Daily US 500 (Mar) > 1238	87.4	90.4
Daily US 500 (Mar) > 1235	92.3	95.3
Daily US 500 (Mar) > 1232	95.4	98.4

12 hours to expiration, futures trading at 1250

EXHIBIT 6.15 Binary Option Chain

Exhibit 6.15 is an example of a US 500 binary option chain with 12 hours until expiration. Let's assume that the market price of the underlying is 1250 when you enter your trade for both examples.

Example 1 (Long Position)   Let's use a long binary option trading position to demonstrate why you would want to exit your trade prior to expiration to cut losses.

Entry Breakdown   Let's assume that you purchase a "> 1256" option with 12 hours until expiration. You put up the asking price, $29, as collateral for the trade.

In Exhibit 6.16, the y-axis represents available strike prices. The dark grey dashed line represents the market price of the S&P futures, and the light grey dashed line represents the binary option contract. With one day until expiration, the S&P futures are trading at 1250 and you buy the 1256 binary option with the assumption that the S&P futures will be above 1256 at expiration.

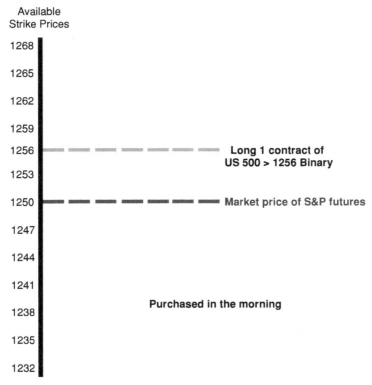

EXHIBIT 6.16   Binary Option Condition Purchased in the Morning

Exit Breakdown Unfortunately, the market moves down as expiration approaches. Now you have two factors working against you: time value and price.

Let's assume the S&P futures dropped to 1247 and the price of the "> 1256" option is now $10. You may decide to at least preserve some of your investment by exiting the trade. In order to do this, you would simply sell the option.

To summarize, you purchased the option at $29 and now you can exit at $10 for a loss of $19. This way, instead of waiting until expiration and watching your $29 per contract investment turn to $0, you at least salvage roughly 30 percent of your investment.

In Exhibit 6.17, the y-axis represents available strike prices. The dark grey dashed line represents the market price of the S&P futures, and the light grey dashed line represents the binary option contract. As expiration approaches, the S&P futures fall three points and are trading at 1247.

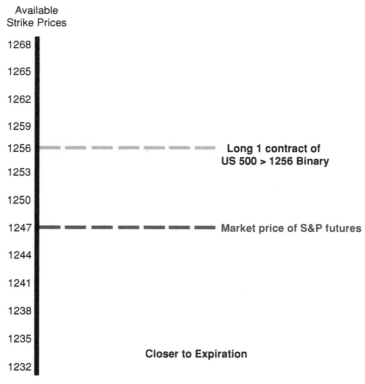

EXHIBIT 6.17 Binary Option Condition Closer to Expiration

Summary Exhibit 6.18 contains all of the data points for this trade.

EXHIBIT 6.18	Data Points for Long Binary Option Trade Demonstrating Early Exit to Cut Losses	
Trade	**Figure**	**Calculation**
Underlying asset	S&P futures	
Market price	1250	
Expiration	1 day	
Strike price	1256	
Long/Short	Long (buy)	
Size	1 contract	
Price	Ask price of $29/contract	
Max loss	$29	Ask price × number of contracts = max loss $29 × 1 = $29
Collateral	$29	Collateral = max loss
Max profit	$71	($100 − ask price) × number of contracts = max profit ($100 − $29) × 1 = $71 × 1 = $71
Exit price	Bid price of $10/contract	
Profit or loss	Loss of $19	Bid price when position closed − ask price when position opened = loss $10 − $29 = −$19

Example 2 (Short Position) Now let's use a short binary option trading position to demonstrate why you would want to exit your trade prior to expiration to cut losses.

Entry Breakdown You sell one contract of US 500 binary options with a strike price of 1256 and a bid price of $26 per contract in the morning. You assume that the underlying asset will be above 1256 at the end of the day. The required collateral to place this trade is $74, which is the maximum you stand to lose on the trade.

As a seller, you are hoping that the S&P 500 futures will close below 1256 at expiration so that you can collect a $100 settlement on your $74 collateral, for a profit of $26 per contract. Of course, $26 is the option's premium.

In Exhibit 6.19, the y-axis represents available strike prices. The dark grey dashed line represents the market price of the S&P futures, and the light grey dashed line represents the binary option contract. With one day until expiration, the S&P futures are trading at 1250. You sell the 1256 binary option with the assumption that the S&P futures will be below 1256 at expiration.

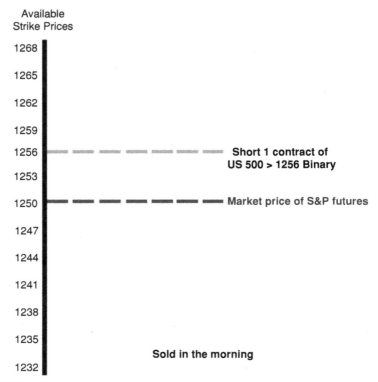

EXHIBIT 6.19 Binary Option Condition Sold in the Morning

Exit Breakdown Let's assume that after you enter the trade, the S&P futures break out of a range and trade seven points higher to 1257. You notice that the option is now trading at a $55 ask, which is higher than what you originally sold it for.

You don't want to wait until expiration to see the option jump to $100 and lose your entire collateral. In order to get out and minimize your losses, you will need to buy back the option. You can buy the option back at $55 per contract. Since you sold the option for $26 and bought it back at $55, you will incur a $29 loss and your account will be debited accordingly. However, you will receive your $74 collateral back.

By exiting your trade early instead of waiting for expiration, you are able to turn a $74 loss into a $29 loss.

Of course, there was also the possibility that the underlying would go back below 1256 and you would earn the $26 premium. That is the drawback of exiting early. But these are the risks and rewards that you have to weigh.

In Exhibit 6.20, the y-axis represents available strike prices. The dark grey dashed line represents the market price of the S&P futures, and the light grey dashed line represents the binary option contract. As expiration approaches, the S&P futures have risen seven points and are currently trading at 1257.

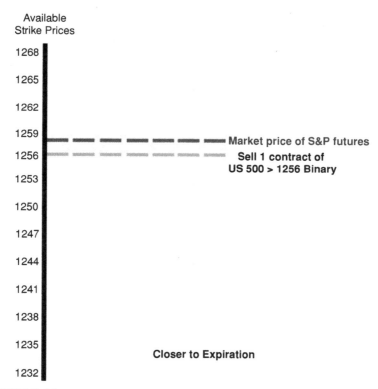

EXHIBIT 6.20 Binary Option Condition Closer to Expiration

Summary Exhibit 6.21 contains all of the data points for this trade.

To drill this concept down even further, you can see more trade examples on www.traderschoiceoptions.net. Deciding on when to get out early and when to hold until expiration is something that you have to determine based on your desired profitability and risk tolerance. It will be further discussed in our strategy guides and courses.

Of course, when exiting long and/or short trades early, you will still have to pay commission when you exit the trade.

EXHIBIT 6.21 Data Points for Short Binary Option Trade Demonstrating Early Exit to Cut Losses

Trade	Figure	Calculation
Underlying asset	S&P futures	
Market price	1250	
Expiration	1 day	
Strike price	1256	
Long/Short	Short (sell)	
Size	1 contract	
Price	Bid price of $26/contract	
Max loss	$74	($100 – bid price) × number of contracts = collateral ($100 – $26) × 1 = $74 × 1 = $74
Collateral	$74	Collateral = max loss
Max profit	$26	Bid price × number of contracts = max profit $26 × 1 = $26.
Exit price	Ask price of $55/contract	
Profit or loss	Loss of $29	Bid price when position opened – ask price when position closed = profit $26 – $55 = –$29

CHAPTER 7

Keys to Trading Binary Options and More Examples

L et's review some key facts to remember when trading binary options:

- **Fact 1:** If the market price is above the strike price at expiration, the contract value goes to $100. If the market price is below the strike price at expiration, the contract value goes to $0.
- **Fact 2:** You can always trade in and out of a binary option contract any time before expiration and settlement.
- **Fact 3:** The collateral you put up for a binary option trade is always equivalent to your maximum loss on the trade.
- **Fact 4:** Binary options have no calls or puts. They simply have conditions (also known as strike prices) that you can speculate on to be true or not. If you believe a condition to be true by expiration, you buy the binary option; if you would like to speculate for it to be false, you sell the binary option on that condition.
- **Fact 5:** You can never lose more than you put into a binary options trade. You put up your maximum loss as the collateral and can never lose more than you put up on your trade.
- **Fact 6:** The most collateral any contract will require you to put up on a trade is $100; typically, the collateral you put up will be less than $100 on any binary option contract.
- **Fact 7:** When trading a binary option, if you are correct on your trade at expiration, your account will always be credited $100 per contract. If you are incorrect at expiration, your account will always receive nothing.

Taking these facts into consideration, let's look at some simple trade examples to solidify the concepts.

GOLD BINARY EXAMPLES

Based on the option chain in Exhibit 7.1, let's look at some possible trade examples based on gold binary options.

Exhibit 7.1 is an image of an option chain of gold binary options strike prices with 12 hours until expiration.

Gold (Feb) > 1730.5	15.00	20.00
Gold (Feb) > 1720.5	27.00	32.50
Gold (Feb) > 1710.5	41.50	47.50
Gold (Feb) > 1700.5	56.00	62.50
Gold (Feb) > 1690.5	71.00	76.50
Gold (Feb) > 1680.5	83.00	88.00
Gold (Feb) > 1670.5	91.00	95.50
Gold (Feb) > 1660.5	95.50	-
Gold (Feb) > 1650.5	96.00	-
Gold (Feb) > 1640.5	96.00	-
Gold (Feb) > 1630.5	96.00	-
Gold (Feb) > 1620.5	96.00	-
Gold (Feb) > 1610.5	96.00	-

EXHIBIT 7.1   Gold Binary Option Chain

Buy: At-the-Money Example

Let's review the following at-the-money trade example:

Rationale   Gold futures are currently trading at 1700.5. You assume that gold futures will be above 1700.5 at expiration.

Entry Breakdown   You buy one contract of gold binary options with a strike price of 1700.5 and an ask price of $62.5 per contract. The required collateral to place this trade is $62.5, which is your maximum potential loss on the trade.

Exit Breakdown   If the market closes above 1700.5 at expiration, the contract will be worth $100 and you will make a profit of $37.5 per contract or 60 percent on your trade.

However, if the market closes below 1700.5, the option will expire worthless and you will lose $62.5 per contract.

Exhibit 7.2 depicts the profit and loss (P&L) of going long the 1700.5 gold binary option. The x-axis represents the price of the underlying, and the y-axis represents P&L.

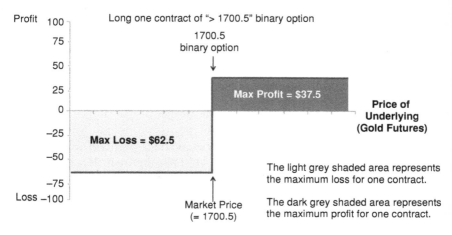

Profit

Long one contract of "> 1700.5" binary option

1700.5 binary option

Max Profit = $37.5

Price of Underlying (Gold Futures)

Max Loss = $62.5

Loss

Market Price (= 1700.5)

The light grey shaded area represents the maximum loss for one contract.

The dark grey shaded area represents the maximum profit for one contract.

EXHIBIT 7.2 P&L Graph of a Long At-the-Money Binary Option Trade

Summary Exhibit 7.3 contains all of the data points for this trade.

EXHIBIT 7.3 Data Points for Long At-the-Money Binary Option Trade

Trade	Figure	Calculation
Underlying asset price	Gold futures	
Market price	1700.5	
Expiration	1 day	
Strike price	1700.5	
Long/Short	Long (buy)	
Size	1 contract	
Price	Ask price of $62.5/contract	
Max loss	$62.5	Ask price × number of contracts = max loss $62.5 × 1 = $62.5
Collateral	$62.5	collateral = max loss
Max profit	$37.5	($100 − ask price) × number of contracts = max profit ($100 − $62.5) × 1 = $37.5 × 1 = $37.5
Risk vs Reward	.6:1	Max profit / max loss = risk vs. reward $37.5 / $62.5 = .6:1

Sell: Out-of-the-Money Example

Let's review the following out-of-the-money trade example:

Rationale   Gold futures are currently trading at 1690. You assume that gold futures will go down and close below 1680 at expiration.

Entry Breakdown   You sell three contracts of gold binary options with a strike price of 1680.5 and a bid price of $83 per contract. In order to get into the position, you will need to put up $17 in collateral per contract (this is the difference between the option premium and $100), for a total of $51.

Exit Breakdown   If gold futures go below 1680, you will win on your trade and your account will be credited $100 per contract. If you subtract the $17 per contract collateral from this revenue, your profit will be the option's premium, $83 per contract, for a total of $249. However, if the market stays above $1680, you will lose the $17 per contract collateral for a total loss of $51.

   Exhibit 7.4 depicts the P&L of going short the 1680 gold binary option. The x-axis represents the price of the underlying, and the y-axis represents profit and loss.

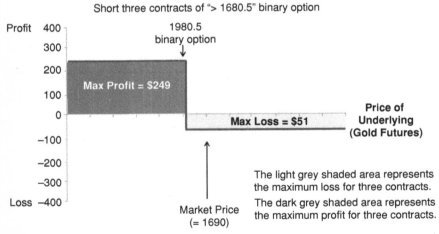

EXHIBIT 7.4   P&L Graph of a Short Out-of-the-Money Binary Option Trade

Summary   Exhibit 7.5 contains all of the data points for this trade.

EXHIBIT 7.5 Data Points for Short Out-of-the-Money Binary Option Trade

Trade	Figure	Calculation
Underlying asset	Gold futures	
Market price	1690	
Expiration	1 day	
Strike price	1680.5	
Long/Short	Short (sell)	
Size	3 contracts	
Price	Bid price of $83/ contract	
Max loss	$51	($100 – bid price) × number of contracts = max loss ($100 – $83) × 3 = $17 × 3 = $51
Collateral	$51	Collateral = max loss
Max profit	$249	Bid price × number of contracts = max profit $83 × 3 = $249
Risk vs. reward	4.88:1	Max profit / max loss = risk vs. reward $249 / $51 = 4.88

COPPER BINARY EXAMPLES

Exhibit 7.6 is an image of an option chain of copper binary options strike prices with 12 hours until expiration. Based on this option chain, let's look at some possible trade examples based on copper binary options.

Copper (Mar) > 404.5	-	10.00
Copper (Mar) > 399.5	-	10.00
Copper (Mar) > 394.5	5.50	16.00
Copper (Mar) > 389.5	21.00	31.50
Copper (Mar) > 384.5	44.00	54.50
Copper (Mar) > 379.5	67.50	78.00
Copper (Mar) > 374.5	84.00	94.50
Copper (Mar) > 369.5	90.00	-
Copper (Mar) > 364.5	90.00	-
Copper (Mar) > 359.5	90.00	-
Copper (Mar) > 354.5	90.00	-
Copper (Mar) > 349.5	90.00	-
Copper (Mar) > 344.5	90.00	-

EXHIBIT 7.6 Copper Binary Option Chain

Buy: In-the-Money Example

Let's review the following in-the-money trade example:

Rationale   Copper futures are currently trading at 384.5. You forecast that copper futures will stay above 379.5 at expiration.

Entry Breakdown   You buy five contracts of copper binary options with a strike price of 379.5 and an ask price of $78 per contract. The required collateral to place this trade is the premium of $390 ($78 × 5), which is also your maximum loss.

Exit Breakdown   If copper futures close above 379.5 at expiration, each contract will be worth $100 and you will make a profit of $22 per contract or 28 percent on your trade. On a five-contract position, you will make a profit of $110 on this trade.

    However, if copper futures close below 379.5, the option will expire worthless. The collateral you put up here is $78 per contract, which is the price of the option. On a five-contract position your loss is $390, the collateral.

    Exhibit 7.7 depicts the P&L of going long the 379.5 copper binary option. The x-axis represents the price of the underlying, and the y-axis represents P&L.

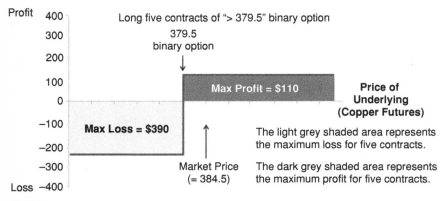

EXHIBIT 7.7   P&L Graph of a Long In-the-Money Binary Option Trade

Summary Exhibit 7.8 contains all of the data points for this trade.

EXHIBIT 7.8 Data Points for Long In-the-Money Binary Option Trade

Trade	Figure	Calculation
Underlying asset	Copper futures	
Market price	384.5	
Expiration	1 day	
Strike price	379.5	
Long/Short	Long (buy)	
Size	5 contracts	
Price	Ask price of $78/contract	
Max loss	$390	Ask price × number of contracts = max loss $78 × 5 = $390
Collateral	$390	Collateral = max loss
Max profit	$110	($100 − ask price) × number of contracts = max profit ($100 − $78) × 5 = $22 × 5 = $110
Risk vs. reward	.28:1	Max profit / max loss = risk vs. reward $110 / $390 = .28:1

Sell: At-the-Money Example

Rationale Copper futures are currently trading at 384.5. You assume that copper futures will drop below 384.5 at expiration.

Entry Breakdown You sell one contract of copper binary options with a strike price of 384.5 and a bid price of $44 per contract. In order to get into the position, you will need to put up $56 in collateral.

Exit Breakdown If the copper futures go below 384.5, you will win on your trade and your account will be credited revenue of $100 per contract. After subtracting the collateral, your profit per contract will be $44. However, if the market stays above $384.5, you will lose your collateral of $56 per contract.

Exhibit 7.9 depicts the P&L of going short the 384.5 copper binary option. The x-axis represents the price of the underlying, and the y-axis represents P&L.

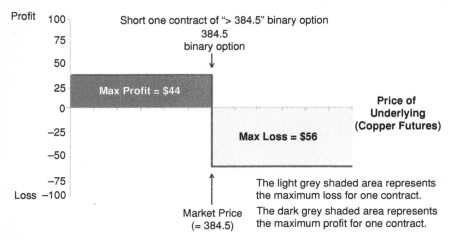

EXHIBIT 7.9　P&L Graph of a Short At-the-Money Binary Option Trade

Summary　Exhibit 7.10 contains all of the data points for this trade.

To see even more trade examples based on the theories you just learned, simply visit our companion site, www.traderschoiceoptions .net.

EXHIBIT 7.10　Data Points for Short At-the-Money Binary Option Trade

Trade	Figure	Calculation
Underlying asset	Copper futures	
Market price	384.5	
Expiration	1 day	
Strike price	384.5	
Long/Short	Short (sell)	
Size	1 contract	
Price	Bid price of $44/ contract	
Max loss	$56	($100 – bid price) × number of contracts = max loss ($100 – $44) × 1 = $56 × 1 = $56
Collateral	$56	Collateral = max loss
Max profit	$44	Bid price × number of contracts = max profit $44 × 1 = $44
Risk vs. reward	.78:1	Max profit / max loss = risk vs. reward $44 / $56 = .78:1

KEY POINTS: PART 3

To take a quiz on this section, simply visit our companion education site, www.traderschoiceoptions.net.

- Binary options are fully collateralized. This means that regardless of whether you are buying or selling an option, you cannot lose more than you put up per contract on the trade.
- The collateral on a long binary option contract is always the premium.
- The collateral on a short binary option contract is always $100 minus the premium.
- Regardless of whether you buy or sell a binary option, if you are correct at expiration, your account will be credited $100 (settlement) per contract. If you are incorrect, you will get nothing.
- If you hold a binary option until expiration and lose, your loss will always be your collateral.
- If you hold a binary option trade until expiration and win, your profit is always going to be equal to $100 minus your collateral.
- The profit on a successful short binary option trade is always the premium.
- The profit on a successful long binary option trade is always $100 minus the premium.
- When trading binary options contracts, typically you are charged a commission on each contract. With some brokers you will also be charged a settlement fee if the option goes until expiration. You pay the settlement fee only if you win on the trade.
- When reading a binary option quote, there are several fundamental components that you should understand and identify:
  - The underlying asset
  - Strike price
  - Expiration time and date
  - Bid/Offer
- When reading a binary option order ticket, there are several fundamental components that you should understand and identify:
  - Contract information
  - Bid and offer prices
  - Order details
  - Max profit, max loss, market ceiling, market floor

- When trading binary options, you can exit your trade in two different ways: (1) You can wait until expiration and have your trade settled at $0 or $100 per contract, or (2) you can exit your trade before expiration for the fair market price.

- If you wait until expiration and your trade expires at a loss, then you will simply lose your collateral and not get anything at expiration. This holds true whether you bought or sold an options contract.

- If your trade ends up in-the-money at expiration, you will collect $100 regardless of whether you entered a short or a long position.

- You can trade in and out of binary options at any time up until expiration to either lock in your profits or mitigate your losses.

PART IV

Binary Options Trading Strategies

This section will teach you some basic trading strategies that you can implement with binary options.

What You Will Learn:

- How do you use binary options to forecast where the underlying asset will *not* go?
- What is volatility trading with binary options?
- What is the difference between directional and volatility trading?
- How do you use binary options to forecast a market range of an underlying asset?
- How do you use binary options to forecast the magnitude of a move rather than direction?
- How do you use binary options with technical analysis?
- How do you use binary options with news trading and fundamental analysis?

When you complete this section, you should understand various binary options trading strategies.

CHAPTER 8

Volatility Trading Explained

With binary options you are not limited to directional trading only. Volatility trading presents a unique opportunity to trade based on the magnitude of market moves rather than market direction. Volatility trading means that you are not trying to predict a direction in the market, but rather you are simply speculating whether the market will stay in a certain range or come out of the range in either direction. In other words, you no longer need to predict where the underlying will go. Instead, you are trying to speculate how much it is going to move.

You can also use binary options to speculate on where the market will not go. Let's assume that you see a strong support area and are confident that the underlying asset will not reach this area. Yet you are unsure if it is going to go up or down in the short term. You can use binary options to simply speculate on the assumption that the underlying will not breach the support area without having to worry about forecasting the directional move.

Before we go into the mechanics of volatility trading with binary options, here are a few terms you need to be familiar with:

- *Option spread.* An option strategy that involves buying and selling two or more different option strike prices.
- *Leg.* An options term that refers to one side of a spread transaction. For instance, a trader might buy an option that has a particular strike price and expiration date and then sell another option that has a different strike price and the same expiration date. The two options are called legs of the spread.
- *Long strangle (buying volatility).* A binary option strategy that consists of buying a binary option with a strike price above an underlying

asset's market price and also selling a binary option with a strike price below the underlying asset's market price. A long strangle is used when a trader assumes that an underlying asset will move in one direction or another. This concept will be covered in greater detail in this section.

- *Short strangle (selling volatility).* A binary option strategy that consists of selling a binary option with a strike price above an underlying asset's market price and also buying a binary option with a strike price below the underlying asset's market price. A short strangle is used when a trader assumes that an underlying asset will remain within a range. This concept will be covered in greater detail in this section.

TAKING A VOLATILITY LONG POSITION (BUYING VOLATILITY)

Binary options can be used to build strategies that can profit in the event of unexpectedly high volatility, even if a trader is unsure as to whether this volatility will cause a large upward move in the market or a sudden and dramatic decline. This can happen in times of instability in the underlying asset, or after news releases such as the nonfarm payroll or gross domestic product (GDP) announcements.

Buying volatility means that you are making a speculation that the underlying asset will make a large move in one direction or another. This type of trade may be referred to as a long spread, also known as a long strangle.

Exhibit 8.1 is the profit-and-loss (P&L) graph for a long volatility trade. The x-axis represents the price of the underlying, and the y-axis represents P&L.

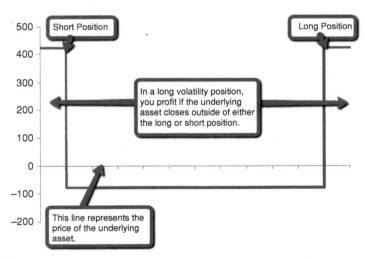

EXHIBIT 8.1   P&L Graph of a Long Volatility Binary Option Trade

Long Volatility Example

So now let's walk through a complete "long volatility" trading example:

If the underlying is trading at 1250 and you expect it to make a large move either up or down, you can buy volatility. Here is a way to do it:

Buying volatility: Short 1 lot of "> 1235" @ 92.3, long 1 lot of "> 1265" @ 7.8.

Rationale   The S&P futures are currently trading at 1250. A trader expects a large move of 15 points or more but is unsure of the direction in which the move will occur.

Entry Breakdown   A trader sold one contract of the US 500 > 1235 binary option for $92.3, and also bought one contract of the US 500 > 1265 for $7.8. The collateral for this trade is $15.5, which is the collateral of the long position, $7.8, added to the collateral of the short position, $7.7 ($100 − $92.3).

Exit Breakdown   If this position is held until expiration and the S&P futures close above 1265 or below 1235, the trader will make a profit of $84.5, which is calculated by subtracting the combined collateral from $100 ($100 − $15.5 = $84.5).

The trader can potentially profit on only one of these contracts at the most. This is due to the fact that the futures cannot settle above 1265 *and* below 1235 at the same time.

If the S&P futures do not settle above 1265 or below 1235, the trader will lose the combined collateral of $15.5. $15.5 is calculated by adding the $7.8 collateral for the long position and the $7.7 collateral for the short position.

So now let's look at the two potential outcomes for this trade:

Winning Outcome: If the market does indeed move by 15 points in one direction or another, you would collect the $100 settlement payout. Your cash outlay was the $7.8 for the long "> 1265" contract and $7.7 for the short "> 1235"contract, for a total cash outlay of $15.5. This will give you a total profit of $84.5 ($100 − $15.5) for every contract that you trade. So your reward/risk ratio is equal to $84.5 divided by $15.5, or 5.45:1.

Losing Outcome: If the US 500 does not move by 15 points in one direction or another, you would lose both the long and the short collateral, totaling $15.5.

Exhibit 8.2 is the P&L graph for a long volatility trade. The x-axis represents the price of the underlying, and the y-axis represents P&L. In this example a trader sells one contract of the 1235 binary option and also buys one contract of the 1265 binary option. If at expiration the underlying has closed below 1235 or above 1265, the trader will profit.

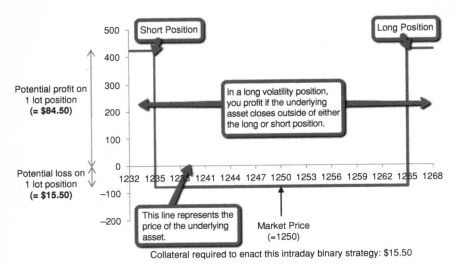

Collateral required to enact this intraday binary strategy: $15.50

EXHIBIT 8.2   P&L Graph of a Long Volatility Binary Option Trade

Summary   Exhibit 8.3 contains all of the data points for this trade.

EXHIBIT 8.3   Data Points for Long Volatility Binary Option Trade

Trade	Figure	Calculation
Underlying asset	S&P futures at 1250	
Market price	1250	
Expiration	1 day	
Strike price long	1265	
Strike price short	1235	
Size long	1 contract	
Size short	1 contract	
Price	Ask price of $7.8/ contract Bid price of $92.3/ contract	
Max loss	$15.50	(($100 – bid price) + ask price) × number of contracts = max loss (($100 – $92.3) + $7.8) X 1 = ($7.7 + $7.8) × 1 = $15.50 × 1 = $15.50
Total collateral	$15.50	Collateral = max loss
Max profit	$84.50	$100 – total collateral = profit $100 – $15.5 = $84.5
Risk vs. reward	5.45:1	Max profit / max loss = risk vs. reward $84.5 / $15.5 = 5.45

REGULATING SUCCESS PROBABILITY AND PAYOUT WITH STRIKE PRICES

When trading long volatility, the strike prices of the options that you choose will determine how large a move you need in order to make money. Naturally, the larger a move that you try to predict, the bigger your payout will be.

Exhibit 8.4 shows the relationship between an anticipated movement and the payout of a binary option. Typically, when a trader speculates that an underlying will have a larger move, the payout tends to be higher. This phenomenon is directly related to the probability of the move. A smaller move could be considered much more likely than a larger move.

EXHIBIT 8.4 How the Size of a Move Affects the Potential Payout

Size of Move Speculated	Payout
Larger	Higher
Example: 20 points	Example: $80 per contract
Smaller	Less
Example: 10 points	Example: $40 per contract

For example, let's assume that the underlying is trading at 1200 and you decide to speculate that it will move at least 10 points by expiration. To do this, you would purchase a 1210 strike price and sell an 1190 strike price. The 1210 strike price may cost $40, and the 1190 put may cost $60. Each of these options would give you a potential reward of $60 with a risk of $40.

If the market moves by at least 10 points in one direction or another, you would take in $100 total, which is the settlement for the winning trade. But you spent $80 (the combined collateral of the long and short position, $40 + $40 = $80), which is the collateral that you put up.

Another way to look at this trade is that if the S&P futures move in one direction by 10 points, you will make $60, but you will also lose $40 on the other trade. Your profit if you win is $20, which is the profit on the winning leg minus the loss on the losing leg position ($60 – $40 = $20).

Your reward/risk ratio on the trade is your maximum profit of $20 divided by the maximum loss of $80. The $80 is the total loss if the underlying stays within the range of the two strike prices. For this example the reward/risk ratio will be $20 divided by $80 or 1:4.

Exhibit 8.5 depicts the P&L of going long a binary option and short a binary option. The x-axis represents the price of the underlying, and the y-axis represents the P&L.

Short one contract of "> 1190" binary option and long one contract "> 1210" binary option

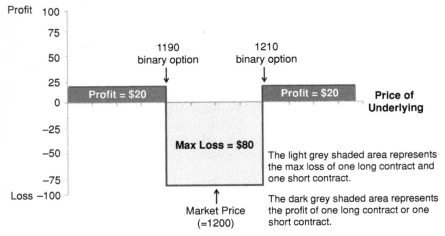

EXHIBIT 8.5   P&L Graph of a Long Volatility Binary Option Trade

However, if you are speculating that the S&P futures will move at least 20 points in one direction or another, you will obviously have a lower chance of winning yet a better potential reward/risk ratio. In other words, you will get better payout odds.

Using the same example, if the S&P 500 futures underlying is trading at 1200, a 1220 option may cost you $20 and you may be able to sell an

Short one contract of "> 1180" binary option and long one contract "> 1220" binary option

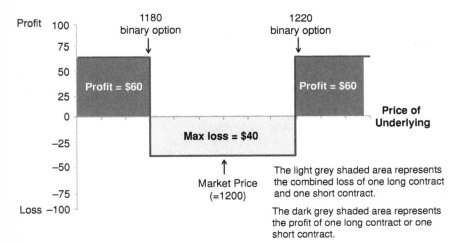

EXHIBIT 8.6   P&L Graph of a Long Volatility Binary Option Trade

1180 option for $80. This will give you the same $100 potential payout, but your risk in this case is only $40. This will give you a $60 profit if you win. So if the US 500 does move 20 points in one direction or another, you will have a reward/risk ratio of 3:2 (60/40) instead of the 1:4 reward/risk ratio discussed in the previous example.

Exhibit 8.6 depicts the profit and loss of going long a binary option and short a binary option. The x-axis represents the price of the underlying, and the y-axis represents the profit and loss.

TAKING A VOLATILITY SHORT POSITION (SELLING VOLATILITY)

You would sell volatility if you felt that the underlying asset would remain in a certain range by expiration. This strategy seeks to profit from volatility slowing down and price staying within a given range. This type of trade may be referred as a short volatility trade (also known as a short strangle). With a short strangle, a trader will sell a binary option at the top of the range and buy a binary option at the bottom of the range. Going short volatility is the exact opposite of going long volatility.

Exhibit 8.7 depicts the profit and loss of going long a binary option and short a binary option. The x-axis represents the price of the underlying, and the y-axis represents the profit and loss. If at expiration the underlying has closed below the short position and/or above the long position, the trader will profit.

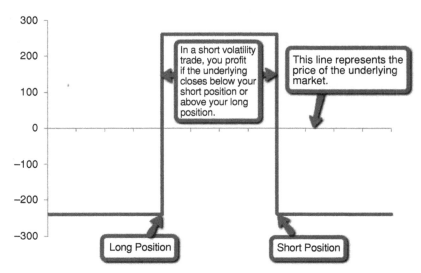

EXHIBIT 8.7 P&L Graph of a Short Volatility Binary Option Trade

Short Volatility Example

Let's look at a specific trade example to get a bit more clarity.

Rationale   In Exhibit 8.8 the market price of the US 500 is 1250. A trader speculates that the S&P futures will remain in a range, staying above 1244 and below 1256.

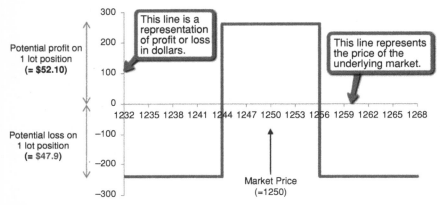

EXHIBIT 8.8   P&L Graph of a Short Volatility Binary Option Trade

Entry Breakdown   A trader sold one contract of the US 500 > 1256 binary option for $26, and also bought one contract of the US 500 > 1244 binary option for $73.9. The collateral for this trade is $147.9, which is the collateral of the long position, $73.9, added to the collateral of the short position, $74 ($100 – $26).

Long-Trade Logic   Since you are assuming that the S&P 500 futures will stay within your desired range, you would put up 73.9 for the "> 1244" option and hope that the price would indeed close greater than 1244, which would give you a $100 total payout on the 1244 option for a potential profit of $26.1 per contract ($100 – $73.9).

Short-Trade Logic   With the short position, you are assuming that the underlying will stay in the desired range and therefore it will not cross above 1256. So you sell short (sell) the "> 1256" option. You would put up $74 in collateral (this is the difference between $100 and the $26 premium of the option you sell). As long as the market does not go above 1256, you will receive the settlement of $100, for a profit of $26 ($100 – $74).

Total Collateral Your total collateral on the spread is $147.9. This is $73.9 option premium for the long trade plus $74 collateral for the short trade ($100 – $26).

Exit Breakdown

Maximum Risk If, however, the S&P futures move outside of either strike price, the trader will lose $47.9. The calculations for these numbers are explained below.

When going short volatility you cannot lose on both legs of your position at the same time if you hold until expiration. The futures cannot be both below 1244 and above 1256 at the same time. Therefore, you have to win on at least one of your positions if you hold until expiration.

Upper Strike Price Breach Your maximum risk if the S&P 500 futures close above 1256 at expiration is equal to the $26.1 gain from the "> 1244" option that you bought minus the $74 loss on the "> 1256" option that you sold; $26.1 minus $74 equals a total loss of $47.9.

Lower Strike Price Breach Your maximum risk if the S&P 500 futures close below 1244 at expiration is equal to the $26 profit that you take in on the "> 1256" option minus the $73.9 loss that you will incur with the "> 1244" option. This also equals a total loss of $47.9.

Now let's look at what happens if the underlying stays between 1244 and 1256 by expiration.

Maximum Reward If the US 500 stays between 1244 and 1256 at expiration, your cash inflow would be $100 on both the long and the short options. So you would collect a total of $200 at expiration. To find out your profit, simply subtract the collateral that you put up from your cash inflow at expiration.

As you recall, your total collateral is $147.9. Subtract that number from the $200 revenue at expiration and you arrive at a maximum profit of $52.1.

Reward/Risk Ratio Your reward/risk ratio on this trade is simply equal to 52.1 (max profit at expiration) divided by 47.9 (max risk at expiration) or 1.09:1.

Exhibit 8.8 depicts the profit and loss of going long the 1244 binary option and short the 1256 binary option when the underlying instrument is trading at 1250. The x-axis represents the price of the underlying and the y-axis represents the P&L. If at expiration the underlying has closed below 1256 and above 1244, the trader will profit.

Summary Exhibit 8.9 contains all of the data points for this trade.

116

BINARY OPTIONS

EXHIBIT 8.9 Data Points for Short Volatility Binary Option Trade

Trade	Figure	Calculation
Underlying asset	S&P futures	
Market price	1250	
Expiration	1 day	
Strike price long	1244	
Strike price short	1256	
Size long	1 contract	
Size short	1 contract	
Price	Ask price of > 1244 contract: $73.9 Bid price of > 1256 contract: $26	
Total collateral	$147.9	(Ask price + ($100 − bid price)) × number of contracts = total collateral ($73.9 + ($100 − $26)) × 1 = ($73.9 + $74) × 1= $147.9 × 1 = $147.9
Max loss	$47.9	Higher of: (collateral of short position − profit of long position) × number of contracts = max loss (($100 − $26) − ($100 − $73.9)) × 1 = ($74 − $26.1) × 1 = $47.9 × 1 Or (collateral of long position − profit of short position) × number of contracts = max loss ($73.9 − $26) × 1 = $47.9 × 1 = $47.9
Max profit	$52.1	Revenue − total collateral = max profit $200 − $147 = $52.1
Risk vs. reward	1.09:1	Max profit / max loss = risk vs. reward $52.1 / $47.9 = 1.09:1

Exhibit 8.10 depicts the maximum loss and maximum gain for each leg of the short volatility trade above. The light grey shaded area represents the maximum profit for each position, and the dark grey shaded area represents the maximum loss for each position.

REGULATING RANGE AND PAYOUT WITH STRIKE PRICES

Just like with going long volatility, you determine your desired range to speculate on and payout odds by the strike prices that you choose. The farther away the strike prices that you choose, the more likely you are to

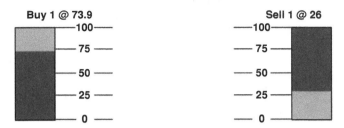

EXHIBIT 8.10 Graphical Representation of the P&L on Both the Long and Short Position

win on your trade. At the same time, the farther the strike prices that you choose, the lower your payout odds will be.

If you speculate that the underlying will stay in a tighter range, you would choose to trade closer strike prices. Since it is less likely that your underlying would stay in a tighter range than a wider one, your payout odds (return on collateral) will be higher than with a wider range.

Exhibit 8.11 is an option chain of US 500 binary options with 12 hours until expiration. As you can see, the options farther away from the underlying's market price require more collateral (pay less premium) to go short volatility. And the options closer to the market price of the underlying require less collateral (pay more premium) to go short volatility. This is simply due to the fact that the underlying is more likely to end up in a wider range than a narrower range at expiration.

Contract	Bid	Offer
Daily US 500 (Mar) > 1268	2.1	5
Daily US 500 (Mar) > 1265	4.9	7.8
Daily US 500 (Mar) > 1262	9.7	12.7
Daily US 500 (Mar) > 1259	17	20
Daily US 500 (Mar) > 1256	26	29
Daily US 500 (Mar) > 1253	36.1	40.1
Daily US 500 (Mar) > 1250	48.1	51.6
Daily US 500 (Mar) > 1247	60.1	63.1
Daily US 500 (Mar) > 1244	71.2	73.9
Daily US 500 (Mar) > 1241	79.9	83.4
Daily US 500 (Mar) > 1238	87.4	90.4
Daily US 500 (Mar) > 1235	92.3	95.3
Daily US 500 (Mar) > 1232	95.4	98.4

12 hours to expiration, futures trading at 1250

EXHIBIT 8.11 Binary Option Chain

Exhibit 8.12 is an image of a normal distribution curve. Due to the principle of normal distribution, the price of a tradable instrument has a higher probability of eventually ending up where it started. To get a realistic picture of how much the S&P moves in a given day or week, you can check out our distribution tool at www.traderschoiceoptions.net.

For example, the US 500 is more likely to end up in a price range between 1265 and 1235 than in a range between 1256 and 1244.

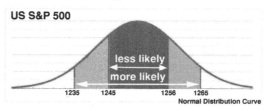

EXHIBIT 8.12   A Normal Distribution Curve

Let's look further at this example to drive the concept home. The short volatility example demonstrated that to speculate that the S&P 500 futures would end up in a price range between 1244 and 1256, you would need to purchase the "> 1244" option for $73.9 collateral per contract, and you would need to sell the "> 1256" option for $74 collateral per contract. Your total collateral is 147.9, and your potential inflow if the S&P 500 futures stay within your desired range is $200. Therefore, your maximum profit is $200 – $147.9 or $52.1. Your maximum risk is $47.9 ($73.9 – (100 – 74)), so your reward/risk ratio is 52.1/47.9 or 1.09:1.

Exhibit 8.13 depicts the P&L of going long the 1244 binary option and short the 1256 binary option. The x-axis represents the price of the underlying, and the y-axis represents the P&L.

If you want to speculate that the S&P 500 futures will stay in a wider range, say between 1235 and 1265, you would do the following: You would purchase the "> 1235" option for $95.3 collateral per contract and sell the "> 1265" option for $4.9 (collateral per contract would be $100 minus the $4.9 option premium or $95.1). Your total collateral will be $190.4 ($95.3 + $95.1). Your total potential inflow will be $200 as long as the market stays within your desired range. Therefore, your total potential profit will be $9.6 per contract, which is $200 minus $190.4.

If you hold this trade until expiration and the S&P 500 futures go below 1235 at expiration, you would lose $95.3 per contract on that leg. However, you would still get to keep $4.9 per contract that you would collect from the 1265 leg. This will give you a net loss of 90.4 ($4.9 – $95.3).

If the US 500 goes above 1265 at expiration, then you would lose $95.1 on the short "> 1265" contract; however, you would still make $4.7 on the long "> 1235" contract. This would give you a net loss of $90.4 ($4.7 – $95.1).

Short one contract of "> 1256" binary option and long one contract of "> 1244" binary option

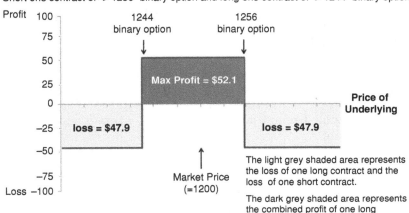

EXHIBIT 8.13 P&L Graph of a Short Volatility Binary Option Trade

Therefore, on this particular trade, your max loss is $90.4 and your max profit is $9.6. This gives you a reward/risk ratio of .106:1. Simply divide 9.6 by 90.4 to come up with this number.

Exhibit 8.14 depicts the P&L of going long the 1235 binary option and short the 1265 binary option. The x-axis represents the price of the underlying, and the y-axis represents the P&L.

Short one contract of "> 1265" binary option and long one contract "> 1235" binary option

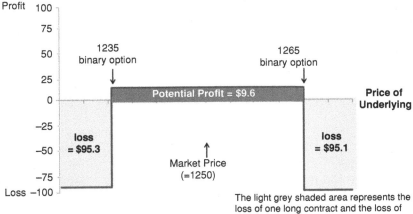

EXHIBIT 8.14 P&L Graph of a Short Volatility Binary Option Trade

As you can see by this example, the larger a price range that you bet the underlying will end up in at expiration, the lower your payout ratio will be. Think of it this way: Let's assume that a machine is going to randomly spit out a number between 1 and 10 and pay you if you guess correctly. Also, let's assume that each guess costs you money. Naturally, the more guesses you have, the more likely you are to guess correctly. However, because each guess costs you, your payout ratio is going to drop with every guess you make. Picking a wider range when going short volatility is simply like making more guesses of where the price will end up at expiration.

Based on this example, you should now see that by trading volatility with binary options, you control your probability to win and your payout ratio by modifying the strike prices that you trade.

MAX LOSS, COLLATERAL, AND MAX PROFIT SUMMARY TABLE

Exhibit 8.15 will help you remember how to calculate the max loss, max profit, and collateral for long, short, volatility long, and volatility short binary option trades.

EXHIBIT 8.15   Max Loss, Max Profit, and Collateral Table for Binary Option Trades and Spreads at Expiration

Type of trade	Max Loss	Max Profit	Collateral
Long	Premium	$100 – premium	Premium
Short	$100 – premium	Premium	$100 – Premium
Volatility long	Premium long leg + ($100 – premium short leg)	$100 – (Collateral long leg + collateral short)	Long leg: Premium short leg ($100 – premium) Total: Premium long + ($100 – premium short)
Volatility short	Higher of Lower breach: Premium long leg – premium short leg Or Upper breach: ($100 – Premium short leg) – ($100 – premium long leg)	Premium short leg + ($100 – premium long leg)	Premium long leg + ($100 – premium short leg)

As you can see from the table, the collateral is equal to the max loss for all types of trades except for volatility short. Also, you can see that the max profit is simply $100 minus collateral for all examples except for volatility short. For volatility short, max profit can be calculated by subtracting total collateral from $200 or by adding the premium for the short leg to ($100 – premium for the long leg). Please keep in mind that all these examples are based on your holding the position until expiration.

CHAPTER 9

Binary Option Behavior as Expiration Approaches

With regular put/call options, as expiration approaches, the time value goes down. This is known as *time decay*. With binary options, as expiration approaches, you will start to notice a very interesting phenomenon. This phenomenon occurs due to the binary nature of these options. It also presents some interesting opportunities and should be addressed, as it is a key attribute of binary options.

UNDERSTANDING DELTA

In order to illustrate this phenomenon, you must understand the concept of delta. Delta is simply the amount that the price of the option changes for every dollar that the price of the underlying changes. For example, with a deep-in-the-money option, the delta will be 1 to 1 since for every dollar that the underlying grows, the option will also grow by $1.

If you have a deeply out-of-the-money option, the option will have a lower delta. This is due to the fact that as the underlying grows by $1, the option does not become significantly more likely to be in-the-money. Therefore, the $1 growth in the underlying will have only a minimal impact on the price of the option.

As you will shortly see, the delta will behave significantly differently with vanilla put/call options than with binary options.

To learn more about delta and other option parameters, you can visit our companion site, www.traderschoiceu.com.

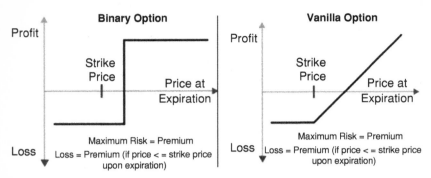

EXHIBIT 9.1   P&L Graph of a Long Binary Option Next to a Vanilla Call Option

In Exhibit 9.1 a profit-and-loss (P&L) graph of a long binary option is juxtaposed with a P&L graph of a vanilla call option. A vanilla option has a smoother graph than a binary option.

To demonstrate this concept further, let's once again use the same option chain that we have been using in the majority of the examples provided in this text.

12 Hours to Expiration Example

Exhibit 9.2 is an example of a US 500 binary option chain with 12 hours until expiration.

Contract	Bid	Offer
Daily US 500 (Mar) > 1268	2.1	5
Daily US 500 (Mar) > 1265	4.9	7.8
Daily US 500 (Mar) > 1262	9.7	12.7
Daily US 500 (Mar) > 1259	17	20
Daily US 500 (Mar) > 1256	26	29
Daily US 500 (Mar) > 1253	36.1	40.1
Daily US 500 (Mar) > 1250	48.1	51.6
Daily US 500 (Mar) > 1247	60.1	63.1
Daily US 500 (Mar) > 1244	71.2	73.9
Daily US 500 (Mar) > 1241	79.9	83.4
Daily US 500 (Mar) > 1238	87.4	90.4
Daily US 500 (Mar) > 1235	92.3	95.3
Daily US 500 (Mar) > 1232	95.4	98.4

12 hours to expiration, futures trading at 1250

EXHIBIT 9.2   A Binary Option Chain

With traditional put/call options, the principle is simple: The closer you get to being "in-the-money," the higher the delta. Also, the closer you get to expiration, the lower the delta becomes for each strike price.

Now let's look at what happens with binary options around expiration time:

Let's assume that you purchased a "> 1250" at-the-money option when the underlying was trading at 1250. Based on the option chain above, you would have purchased that call for $51.6 per contract.

As expiration approaches, if the S&P 500 futures close above 1250, your collateral investment of $51.6 will turn into $100. However, if the S&P 500 futures close at 1249.99 or below, your initial investment of $51.6 will turn to $0.

Exhibit 9.3 demonstrates the price behavior of a binary option at expiration. If at expiration the underlying is above the 1250 strike price, the initial investment of $51.6 is in-the-money and worth $100. If at expiration the underlying is below the 1250 strike price, the initial investment of $51.6 is out-of-the-money and worth $0.

As you can see, this is a huge difference. A one-cent move in the price of the underlying right before expiration represents a difference of $100 in the price of the option at expiration.

If there is still a lot of time before expiration, then a $1 move around the "at-the-money" price point of the underlying is fairly insignificant since there is still plenty of time for it to make a move in one direction or another and still roughly a 50 percent chance that it will end up above or below the at-the-money price.

However, as expiration approaches, the underlying has less time to move in one direction or another. For this very reason, the premiums of the options with strike prices around market price will have huge deltas, as every dollar move can potentially make the difference between a $0 value at expiration and a $100 value at expiration.

So now let's look at the option chain again and make some assumptions about where the options premiums are likely to end up as expiration approaches, based on these principles.

EXHIBIT 9.3 Depiction of Binary Option at Expiration

Binary Option	Price	S&P futures above 1250	S&P futures below 1249.99
Long > 1250	$51.6	Initial investment grows to $100	Initial investment turns to $0

20 Minutes to Expiration Example

Exhibit 9.4 is an example of a US 500 binary option chain with 20 minutes until expiration.

Assuming that the S&P futures remain at 1250 at expiration, here is what the strike prices in the options chain are likely to do and why, as you get within 10 to 20 minutes of expiration:

Strike prices of 1256 and up will all decrease at a very quick rate. This is due to the fact that it is very unlikely for the S&P 500 futures to jump six points in 10 to 20 minutes. No one wants to buy these options anymore. And the traders holding these options are all trying to get rid of them to at least salvage some of their investment. Therefore, because of the basic rules of supply and demand, the price of these options will drop quickly.

Strike prices of 1244 and down will all head toward $100 at a very fast rate. Once again, this is due to the fact that it is highly unlikely that the S&P 500 futures will drop by six points in 10 to 20 minutes. All traders will want these options since they are all highly likely to expire at $100. Traders holding them may as well wait until expiration to get the full $100 return on their invested collateral. Further, anyone that was short will be trying to buy the options back to at least salvage some of their investment. So what's happening is that no one is selling here and traders want to buy, so the price naturally starts to move toward $100 very rapidly for these options.

Contract	Bid	Offer
Daily US 500 (Mar) > 1268	-	3.0
Daily US 500 (Mar) > 1265	-	3.0
Daily US 500 (Mar) > 1262	-	7.0
Daily US 500 (Mar) > 1259	-	7.0
Daily US 500 (Mar) > 1256	-	7.0
Daily US 500 (Mar) > 1253	54.00	55.00
Daily US 500 (Mar) > 1250	56.00	57.00
Daily US 500 (Mar) > 1247	70.00	71.00
Daily US 500 (Mar) > 1244	97.00	-
Daily US 500 (Mar) > 1241	97.00	-
Daily US 500 (Mar) > 1238	97.00	-
Daily US 500 (Mar) > 1235	97.00	-
Daily US 500 (Mar) > 1232	97.00	-

20 Minutes to expiration, futures trading at 1250

EXHIBIT 9.4   A Binary Option Chain

Now, as you look at strike prices close to the market price of the underlying (like 1253 and 1247), things get a bit interesting. The delta becomes huge, as every dollar move represents the potential difference between a $100 payout and a $0 payout for the trader at expiration.

For example, if the S&P futures are sitting right at 1250, as the market approaches expiration, the 1253 strike price will start to head toward $0. However, every single one-point move up will have a significant positive effect on the premium of the > 1253 option. For example, the premium may be $20 when the S&P futures are at 1250, and it may jump to $30 if the futures move to 1251, since with every one-point move in the direction of the strike price, the likelihood of the underlying's breaching it by expiration grows substantially.

If the S&P futures are sitting at 1250 and drop to 1248 with a short amount of time until expiration, the "> 1247" option may also drop in price significantly, since now there is a higher chance of the S&P futures dropping below 1247, which would cause that option to settle at $0.

DELTA AND PRICE

To summarize, as expiration approaches, the delta (sensitivity to the movement of the underlying) increases significantly with option strike prices that are around the market price of the underlying.

Exhibit 9.5 depicts the reaction of price and delta for an option as expiration approaches. Notice that the options farther away from market price will be heading toward the expiration value points of $0 or $100 and will not be very susceptible to the price movement of the underlying. However, the options closer to the market price of the underlying will be much more susceptible to the price movement of the underlying because there is a good chance that they will be affected by the value of the underlying at expiration.

EXHIBIT 9.5 Relationship of Delta to Option Price

Strike Prices	Above/Below Market Price	Delta as Expiration Approaches	Option Price Direction
Strike prices close to market price	Above	Grows	Toward $0
Strike prices further from market price	Above	Shrinks	Toward $0
Strike prices close to market price	Below	Grows	Toward $100
Strike prices further from market price	Below	Shrinks	Toward $100

CHAPTER 10

Technical Trading Strategies with Binary Options

T echnical analysis is the art of forecasting the future price of a trading instrument based on historic price. Typically, technical traders use price charts to conduct their analysis with the x-axis being time and the y-axis being price. See Exhibit 10.1.

When trading an underlying instrument, you are typically trying to forecast direction. One of the great aspects of option trading is that you don't necessarily have to forecast where an instrument will go, but you can simply forecast where it will *not* go.

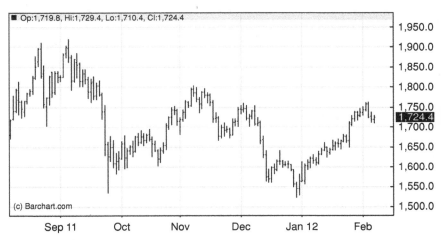

EXHIBIT 10.1 Gold Daily OHLC Chart

There are certain technical principles that focus on areas where an instrument will not go. Once again, with the use of options you can speculate on such future conditions.

One of the great advantages of binary options is that you can speculate on volatility without having to fear that you will lose more than you put into the trade.

SUPPORT AND RESISTANCE

One of the most popular and simplistic technical trading methods is using the theory of support and resistance. Support is a level that an underlying asset has previously had difficulty penetrating to the downside. The theory behind support areas on charts is that, typically, when price hits support, it stops and then reverses direction, moving higher.

Resistance is the exact opposite. Resistance is a price level that an underlying asset has had difficulty penetrating to the upside. The theory behind resistance is that typically when price hits resistance, it stops and then reverses direction, moving lower. Exhibit 10.2 is a diagram demonstrating support and resistance.

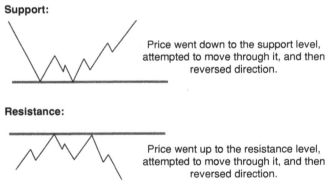

Support:

Price went down to the support level, attempted to move through it, and then reversed direction.

Resistance:

Price went up to the resistance level, attempted to move through it, and then reversed direction.

EXHIBIT 10.2   Depiction of Support and Resistance

Support is a price level that an underlying asset has difficulty moving below. The more times price bounces off a support level, the more significant that level becomes. Resistance is the exact opposite. Resistance is a price level that an underlying asset has difficulty moving above. The more times price bounces off a resistance level, the more significant that level becomes.

If you see a support/resistance area on a chart and believe that it will not be breached, you may be able to use binary options to speculate on this.

Let's look at a basic example.

Long Trade Forecasting Where Gold *Will Not* Trade Based on Support

Let's review the following trade example:

Rationale   Gold futures are trading at 1610 and you notice a support area at 1600 and decide to speculate that the price will not breach 1600 to the downside.

Exhibit 10.3 depicts a price chart of gold futures. The x-axis represents time, and the y-axis represents the price of the gold futures. The straight line represents a strong support level at 1600. Support is a price level that an underlying asset has difficulty moving below. In this example, price reached 1600 multiple times but failed to go below 1600.

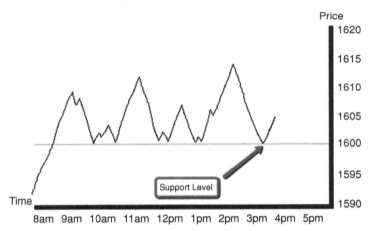

EXHIBIT 10.3   Gold Futures Price Chart Showing Support

Trade Entry   You buy one contract of the 1599 option for $90. You put up $90 as collateral for the trade.

Trade Outcome   If you are correct and gold futures stay above the 1600 level, you will receive revenue of $100 at expiration for a $10 profit on your $90 investment ($100 − $90).

If you hold until expiration and the price of the underlying closes below 1599 at expiration, you will lose your entire collateral of $90.

You can, of course, get out of this trade earlier to cut your losses or lock in a smaller profit.

Exhibit 10.4 depicts the profit and loss (P&L) of going long the 1599 binary option. The x-axis represents the price of the underlying, and the y-axis represents the P&L.

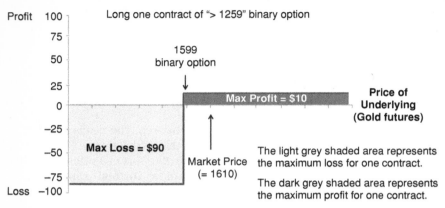

EXHIBIT 10.4 P&L Graph of a Long Binary Option Trade

Summary Exhibit 10.5 contains all of the data points for this trade.

When an underlying asset becomes trapped between a heavy area of support and a heavy area of resistance, it becomes range bound. Range bound is also known as a consolidation, and in the simplest of terms it means that the underlying asset has not moved more than a certain amount in one direction or the other over a certain period of time.

EXHIBIT 10.5 Data Points for Long Binary Option Trade

Trade	Figure	Calculation
Underlying asset	Gold futures	
Market price	1610	
Expiration	1 day	
Strike price	1599	
Long/Short	Long (buy)	
Size	1 contract	
Price	Ask price of $90/contract	
Max loss	$90	Ask price × number of contracts = max loss $90 × 1 = $90
Collateral	$90	Collateral = max loss
Max Profit	$10	($100 − ask price) × number of contracts = max profit ($100 − $90) × 1 = $10 × 1 = $10
Risk vs. reward	.11:1	Max profit / max loss = risk vs. reward $10 / $90 = .11:1

Resistance

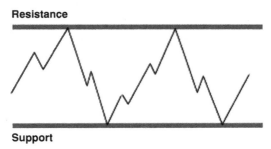

Support

EXHIBIT 10.6   Depiction of a Consolidation or a Range

When an underlying asset is range bound, we can use a short volatility binary option strategy to capitalize on the theory that price will continue to stay within the range of support and resistance. Exhibit 10.6 is a diagram of a range-bound asset.

When an underlying asset has difficulty moving above a resistance level and below a support level, it becomes caught in a range. When this happens, you may want to speculate that the underlying asset will remain within this range in the future.

Range Trade Example

Let's review the following trade example:

Rationale   Let's assume that gold futures are trading at 1600 and you see a top-side resistance of 1610 and a bottom support at 1590. You believe that gold futures will stay within this range.

Trade Entry   You sell one contract of the 1610 option for $10, and you purchase one contract of the 1590 option for $90. Your collateral is $90 for the long leg of your trade (the option premium) and also $90 for the short leg ($100 – option premium), for a total collateral of $180.

Trade Exit   If at expiration the price of gold futures is between 1590 and 1610, then you will get a $100 settlement on both the short and long legs of your trade. You will take in revenue of $200—$100 for each leg. Your profit will be $20 ($200 revenue – $180 collateral).

If you are incorrect and one of the levels is breached prior to expiration, then you will lose the collateral on that leg. So you will lose $90 on one of the legs and make $10 on the other, for a net loss of $80.

Exhibit 10.7 depicts the P&L of going long the 1590 binary option and short the 1610 binary option. The x-axis represents the price of the underlying, and the y-axis represents the P&L.

Short one contract of "> 1610" binary option and long one contract of "> 1590" binary option

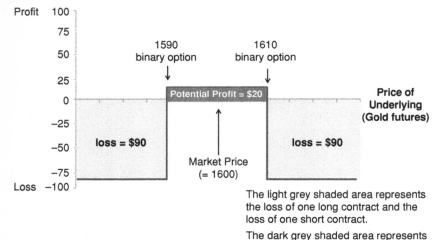

EXHIBIT 10.7   P&L Graph of a Short Volatility Binary Option Trade

Summary   Exhibit 10.8 contains all of the data points for this trade.

EXHIBIT 10.8   Data Points for Short Volatility Binary Option Trade

Trade	Figure	Calculation
Underlying asset	Gold	
Market price	1600	
Expiration	1 day	
Strike price long	1590	
Strike price short	1610	
Size long	1 contract	
Size short	1 contract	
Price	Long leg: Ask price of $90/contract	
	Short Leg: Bid price of $10/contract	
Total collateral	$180	(Ask price + ($100 − bid price)) × number of contracts = total collateral ($90 + ($100 − $10)) × 1 = ($90 + $90) × 1 = $180 × 1 = $180

(continued)

EXHIBIT 10.8 *(Continued)*

Trade	Figure	Calculation
Max loss	$80	Higher of: (collateral of short position – profit of long position) × number of contracts = max loss (($100 – $10) – ($100 – $90)) × 1 = ($90 – $10) × 1 = $80 × 1 = $80 OR (collateral of long position – profit of short position) × number of contracts = max loss ($90 – $10) × 1 = $80
Max profit	$20	Revenue – total collateral = max profit $200 – $180 = $20
Risk vs. reward	.25:1	Max profit / max loss = risk vs. reward $20 / $80 = .25:1

BREAKOUT TRADING

If a particular trading instrument has been trapped in a consolidation pattern for a while, a technical trader may want to make an assumption that it will break out either to the upside or the downside. One of the biggest difficulties of breakout trading is that it is extremely hard to forecast the direction of the breakout. In other words, you never know whether the instrument will break out and go up or break out and go down.

Exhibit 10.9 illustrates a technical breakout to the upside. In this diagram, the price of an underlying was caught in a tight range between support and resistance. Eventually, enough momentum occurred, causing the price to push through the resistance level and climb higher.

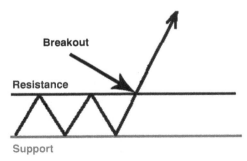

EXHIBIT 10.9 Technical Breakout to the Upside

Exhibit 10.10 illustrates a technical breakout to the downside. In this diagram, the price of an underlying was caught in a tight range between support and resistance. Eventually, enough momentum occurred, causing the price to push through the support level and move lower.

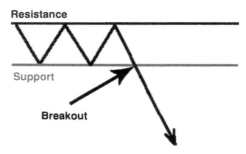

EXHIBIT 10.10   Technical Breakout to the Downside

Fortunately, binary options offer you a way to take advantage of a breakout without having to be concerned about the direction of the trade. You can simply buy an option that speculates on the underlying's going up and sell an option that speculates on the underlying's going down at the same time.

As long as you buy the options relatively equidistant from the market price of the underlying, if one of the options is correct, your profit on one leg of the trade will be enough to overcome for the loss on the other leg and yield a net profit. This type of trade is called a *strangle*.

Breakout Strangle Trade Example

Let's review the following trade example:

Rationale   Let's assume that the Standard & Poor's (S&P) futures are trading at 1250 and they have been stuck in a range between 1240 and 1260. You may decide that they are about to break out of this range but are not sure about the direction.

Trade Entry   You buy one contract of the "> 1260" option, and you sell one contract of the "> 1240" option. Let's assume that the price of the 1260 contract is $20 and the price of the 1240 contract is $80. In both cases, your collateral is $20. So your total collateral is $40.

Trade Exit   If the S&P futures stay within the range of 1240 to 1260, you will lose your entire collateral of $40.

Short one contract of "> 1240" binary option and long one contract of "> 1260" binary option

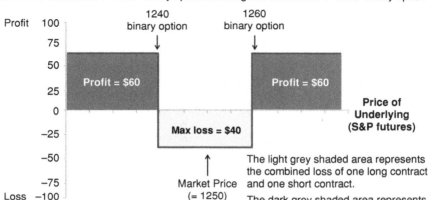

EXHIBIT 10.11 P&L Graph of a Long Volatility Binary Option Trade

If the S&P futures do indeed break out of the range and you hold until expiration, the winning leg will give you revenue of $100, and the losing leg will expire worthless. This will give you a profit of $100 minus your total collateral of $40. This equals a $60 profit per contract.

Exhibit 10.11 depicts the P&L of going long the 1260 binary option and short the 1240 binary option. The x-axis represents the price of the underlying, and the y-axis represents the P&L.

Summary   Exhibit 10.12 contains all of the data points for this trade.

EXHIBIT 10.12   Data Points for Long Volatility Binary Option Trade

Trade	Figure	Calculation
Underlying asset	S&P futures	
Market price	1250	
Expiration	1 day	
Strike price long	1260	
Strike price short	1240	
Size long	1 contract	
Size short	1 contract	
Price	Long leg: Ask price of $20/contract	
	Short leg: Bid price $80/contract	

(continued)

EXHIBIT 10.12 *(continued)*

Trade	Figure	Calculation
Max loss	$40	(($100 – bid price) + ask price) × number of contracts = max loss (($100 – $80) + $20) × 1 = ($20 + $20) × 1 = $40 × 1 = $40
Total collateral	$40	Collateral = max loss
Max profit	$60	$100 – total collateral = profit $100 – $40 = $60
Risk vs. reward	1.5:1	Max profit / max loss = risk vs. reward $60 / $40 = 1.5:1

CHAPTER 11

Fundamental Trading Strategies with Binary Options

A s you may know, the central banks of various countries are always releasing key economic data reports. These reports include unemployment data, gross domestic product (GDP), interest rates, and more.

NEWS RELEASES

Exhibit 11.1 depicts some relevant news releases and the effect they have on the appropriate underlying asset.

EXHIBIT 11.1 Relevant News Releases and Their Effect on the Underlying Asset

Data	Released	Definition	Underlying and Effect
Consumer credit Released by the U.S. Federal Reserve	Monthly; typically 37 days after the month ends	Change in the total value of outstanding consumer credit that requires installment payments	AUD/USD: Better than expected = bearish EUR/USD: Better than expected = bearish GBP/USD: Better than expected = bearish USD/CAD: Better than expected = bullish USD/CHF: Better than expected = bullish USD/JPY: Better than expected = bullish US 500: Better than expected = bullish

(continued)

EXHIBIT 11.1 *(Continued)*

Data	Released	Definition	Underlying and Effect
Unemployment claims Released by the U.S. Department of Labor	Weekly; typically 5 days after the week ends	The number of individuals who filed for unemployment insurance for the first time during the past week	AUD/USD: Better than expected = bearish EUR/USD: Better than expected = bearish GBP/USD: Better than expected = bearish USD/CAD: Better than expected = bullish USD/CHF: Better than expected = bullish USD/JPY: Better than expected = bullish US 500: Better than expected = bullish
Federal budget balance Released by the U.S. Department of Treasury	Monthly; typically on the 8th business day after the month ends	Difference in value between the federal government's income and spending during the previous month	AUD/USD: Better than expected = bearish EUR/USD: Better than expected = bearish GBP/USD: Better than expected = bearish USD/CAD: Better than expected = bullish USD/CHF: Better than expected = bullish USD/JPY: Better than expected = bullish US 500: Better than expected = bullish
Nonfarm payroll Released by the U.S. Bureau of Labor and Statistics	First Friday of each month	Change in the number of employed people during the previous month, excluding the farming industry and government jobs	AUD/USD: Better than expected = bearish EUR/USD: Better than expected = bearish GBP/USD: Better than expected = bearish USD/CAD: Better than expected = bullish USD/CHF: Better than expected = bullish USD/JPY: Better than expected = bullish US 500: Better than expected = bullish
Retail sales Released by the U.S. Census Bureau	Monthly; typically 14 days after the month ends	Change in the total value of sales in the retail sector	AUD/USD: Better than expected = bearish EUR/USD: Better than expected = bearish GBP/USD: Better than expected = bearish USD/CAD: Better than expected = bullish USD/CHF: Better than expected = bullish USD/JPY: Better than expected = bullish US 500: Better than expected = bullish
Existing home sales Released by the U.S. National Association of Realtors	Monthly; typically 20 days after the month ends	Annualized number of residential buildings that were sold during the previous month, excluding new construction	AUD/USD: Better than expected = bearish EUR/USD: Better than expected = bearish GBP/USD: Better than expected = bearish USD/CAD: Better than expected = bullish USD/CHF: Better than expected = bullish USD/JPY: Better than expected = bullish US 500: Better than expected = bullish

Data compiled from www.forexfactory.com.

This table depicts several important data releases that impact various underlying assets. These news releases have forecasts that economists make prior to the data release.

Exhibit 11.2 is an example of an economic calendar.

If the actual data release is in line with the forecast, the markets will remain fairly stable. However, if the actual news release deviates from the forecast, the markets may move rather quickly and drastically.

For example, if the forecast for U.S. jobless claims is 350,000 and the actual number comes up at 360,000, then you can expect that the U.S. dollar will lose value relative to other currencies. This is due to the fact that the jobless claims came out higher than expected, which is a negative sign for the U.S. economy and thus the U.S. dollar.

Certain economic releases have more impact on the markets than others. This is typically noted in an economic calendar. Economic releases typically have a significant effect on the value of a country's currency relative to other currencies.

If you believe that an economic event will have a significant impact on a currency pair but are not sure of the direction, you may decide to enter a long strangle (long volatility) trade. You can do this by buying a binary option with a strike price higher than market price and selling a binary option with a strike price lower than the market price.

Strangle at News Example

Let's review the following trade example:

Rationale   The EUR/USD pair is trading at 1.3000 and the jobless claims report is coming out. The forecast for the report is 350,000. You believe that once the actual report comes out, it will have an impact on the EUR/USD cross.

Trade Entry   Let's assume that you can purchase a 1.3100 option for $20 and you can sell 1.2900 option for $80. Your total collateral for this trade will be $40; $20 premium for the long trade and $100 minus the $80 premium for the short trade ($20).

Trade Exit   If you are wrong and the EUR/USD pair stays within the range at expiration, then you will lose your collateral on both legs of the trade, for a loss of $40.

If you are correct and the EUR/USD pair closes above 1.3100 or below 1.2900 at expiration, then you will receive a $100 revenue settlement for the winning leg, and your cash outflow is the total collateral of $40, for a total profit of $60.

Especially for this trade, you may want to exit early if the price spikes during the release and places one of your trades in-the-money. By doing so, you may be able to lock in a profit due to a spike prior to expiration.

EXHIBIT 11.2 Example of an Economic Calendar

Date		Currency	Impact		Detail	Actual	Forecast	Previous	Chart
Tue Feb 7	12:00	JP		Leading Indicators		94.3%	93.9%	93.7	
	2:45am	EU		French Trade Balance		-5.0B	-5.2B	-4.1B	
	3:00am	CHF		Foreign Currency Reserves		227.2B		254.3B	
	6:00am	EUR		German Industrial Production m/m		-2.9%	-0.1%	0.0%	
	6:15am	CHF		Gov Board Member Jordan Speaks					
	8:05am	CAD		Gov Council Member Macklem Speaks					
	8:30am	CAD		Building Permits m/m		11.1%	0.2%	-2.6%	
	10:00am	USD		Fed Chairman Bernanke Testifies					
	10:00am	USD		IBD/TIPP Economic Optimism		49.4	48.1	47.5	
	3:00pm	USD		Consumer Credit m/m			7.7B	20.4B	
	6:50pm	JPY		Bank Lending y/y				0.4%	
	6:50pm	JPY		Current Account			0.63T	0.48T	
	7:01pm	GBP		BRC Shop Price Index y/y				1.7%	

Economic Calendar provided by www.forexfactory.com.

1. This column shows the time a particular news release will be issued.
2. This column shows which underlying asset will be affected.
3. This column details the severity of the impact a news event will have on the underlying. Red means the data release may have a large impact, orange means the data release may have a moderate impact, and yellow means the data release may have less of an impact (color not shown in print book).
4. This column provides the name of the data release.
5. This column provides the actual numbers of the release, the forecasted numbers, and the previous report's numbers.

142

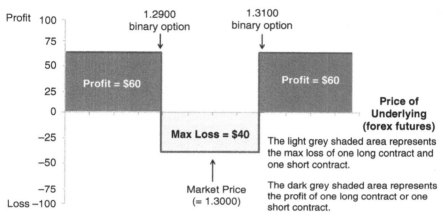

Short one contract of "> 1.2900" binary option and long one contract of "> 1.3100" binary option

EXHIBIT 11.3   P&L Graph of a Long Volatility Binary Option Trade

For example, if the release is higher than expected, the EUR/USD pair may shoot up. This will cause the "> 1.3100" to jump in price to $80. In this case, you can simply get out and lock in your profit of $40 for the entire long strangle.

One thing that you may want to consider is entering a take-profit order as soon as you get in on the trade. This way, as soon as a certain profit target of an option is hit, the entire long strangle will close and lock in a profit for you. Of course, you can also exit this trade early to mitigate losses.

Exhibit 11.3 depicts the profit and loss (P&L) of going long the 1.3100 binary option and short the 1.2900 binary option. The x-axis represents the price of the underlying, and the y-axis represents the profit and loss.

Summary   Exhibit 11.4 contains all of the data points for this trade.

EXHIBIT 11.4   Data Points for Long Volatility Binary Option Trade

Trade	Figure	Calculation
Underlying asset	EUR/USD	
Market price	1.3000	
Expiration	1 day	
Strike price long	1.3100	
Strike price short	1.2900	
Size long	1 contract	
Size short	1 contract	

(continued)

EXHIBIT 11.4 *(Continued)*

Trade	Figure	Calculation
Price	Long leg: Ask price of $20/contract Short leg: Bid price of $80/contract	
Max loss	$40	(($100 − bid price) + ask price) × number of contracts = max loss (($100 − $80) + $20) × 1 = ($20 + $20) × 1 = $40 × 1 = $40
Total collateral	$40	Collateral = max loss
Max profit	$60	$100 − total collateral = profit $100 − $40 = $60
Risk vs. reward	1.5:1	Max profit / max loss = risk vs. reward $60 / $40 = 1.5:1

POLITICAL EVENTS

The markets are also always reacting to news that is related to political and economic stability or instability. If you see that there is instability in certain parts of the world, presidential elections, or new policy that may affect the economy, you can implement binary options to take advantage of it.

For example, when a new president is elected, the market moves. If you are not sure who will be elected and how the market will react, you may decide to enter a long volatility strangle trade. This way, you don't have to forecast the direction of the market, just simply the fact that the market will move. If you believe that a certain political event will not cause a drastic move in the markets, you can take a short volatility strangle trade.

Volatility Short Trade during Instability

Let's review the following trade example:

Rationale   Let's assume that there is a key economic data release coming out and you believe that it will not affect the Standard & Poor's (S&P) 500 futures significantly. Because of the release, the option premiums are up significantly.

The S&P futures are trading at 1250, and you are able to sell the 1310 option for $20 and buy the 1190 option for $80.

Trade Entry   You decide to sell the short strangle with one contract. You sell the 1310 option and buy the 1190 option. Your collateral for the 1310 option will simply be $100 minus the premium of $20, and your collateral for the 1190 option will be the premium of $80, for a total collateral of $160.

Trade Exit   If the underlying closes within the range of 1310 and 1190 regardless of the outcome of the data release, then you will receive $100 for each leg of the option, giving you a total profit of $40 (total settlement $200 minus total collateral $160).

If the S&P futures do in fact end up moving significantly as a result of the data release and close either above 1310 or below 1190, then you will lose the collateral for one leg of your short strangle, but still keep the profit on the other leg, since the S&P futures cannot be above 1310 and below 1190 at the same time at expiration.

Therefore, your revenue will now be only $100 for the winning leg, and your outflow will be the total collateral of $160. This will give you a $60 net loss on the trade if one of the strike prices is breached.

Exhibit 11.5 depicts the P&L of going long the 1190 binary option and short the 1310 binary option. The x-axis represents the price of the underlying, and the y-axis represents the P&L.

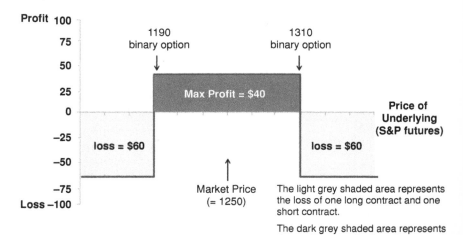

Short one contract of "> 1310" binary option and long one contract of "> 1190" binary option

EXHIBIT 11.5   P&L Graph of a Short Volatility Binary Option Trade

Summary Exhibit 11.6 contains all of the data points for this trade.

EXHIBIT 11.6 Data Points for Short Volatility Binary Option Trade

Trade	Figure	Calculation
Underlying asset	S&P futures	
Market price	1250	
Expiration	1 day	
Strike price long	1190	
Strike price short	1310	
Size long	1 contract	
Size short	1 contract	
Price	Long leg: Ask price of $80/contract Short leg: Bid price of $20/contract	
Total collateral	$160	(Ask price of long leg + ($100 − bid price of short leg)) × number of contracts = total collateral ($80 + ($100 − $20)) × 1 = ($80 + $80) × 1= $160 × 1 = $160
Max loss	$60	Higher of: (collateral of short position − profit of long position) × number of contracts = max loss (($100− $20) − ($100 − $80)) × 1 = ($80 − $20) × 1 = $60 × 1 = $60 Or (collateral of long position − profit of short position) × number of contracts = max loss ($80 − $20) × 1 = $60
Max profit	$40	Revenue − total collateral = max profit $200 − $160 = $40
Risk vs. reward	.67:1	Max profit / max loss = risk vs. reward $40 / $60 = .67:1

SPECULATING ON ACTUAL NEWS RELEAS

In addition to speculating how various underlying ir
an economic data release, you can actually speculat
economic data release itself.

You can find upcoming economic data releaಎ ....
www.traderschoiceoptions.net.

Let's take a look at a binary options trade on an economic event.

Binary Option Trade on an Economic Event

Let's review the following trade example:

Rationale   Let's say that you are interested in taking a position on the jobless claims report that will be coming out on Thursday. You think that fewer people have filed for unemployment benefits and that the job market as a whole has been improving.

Last week 352,000 new unemployment claims were filed, and you believe that this week the number will be less.

Trade Entry   You sell one jobless claims binary option with a strike price of 352,000. You sell this contract for $50. With this binary option, the assumption is made that on Thursday the jobless claims number will be less than 352,000. Your collateral for this trade is $50.

Trade Exit   If the jobless claims come out lower than 352,000, you will earn a premium of 50. If they come out higher, then you will lose your collateral of $50.

Exhibit 11.7 depicts the P&L of going short the 352,000 jobless claims binary option. The x-axis represents the price of the underlying, and the y-axis represents the P&L.

Summary   Exhibit 11.8 contains all of the data points for this trade.

At this point, you are able to trade binary options only on certain types of economic data releases. More releases are likely to be tradable in the future. In some cases, you may be able to speculate based on presidential elections.

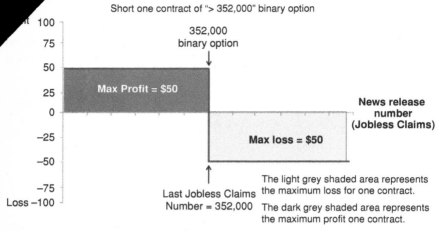

Short one contract of "> 352,000" binary option

EXHIBIT 11.7 P&L Graph of a Short Binary Option Trade

EXHIBIT 11.8 Data Points for Short Binary Option Trade

Trade	Figure	Calculation
Underlying asset	Jobless claims	
Last jobless claims number	352,000	
Expiration	1 day	
Strike price short	1310	
Size short	1 contract	
Price	Bid price of $50/ contract	
Max loss	$50	($100 – bid price) × number of contracts = max loss ($100 – $50) × 1= $50
Collateral	$50	Collateral = max loss
Max profit	$50	Bid price × number of contracts= max profit $50 × 1 = $50
Risk vs. reward	1:1	Max profit / max loss = risk vs. reward $50 / $50 = 1:1

ECONOMIC DATA RELEASES THAT YOU CAN SPECULATE ON

Exhibit 11.9 depicts the economic events that one can speculate on with binary options. You can find upcoming data releases, their consensus, and results at www.traderschoiceoptions.net.

> *Federal funds rate.* U.S. banks are obligated to maintain certain levels of reserve funds at all times. These reserves are either held with the Federal Reserve Bank (the central bank for the United States) or in cash located in their vaults. Sometimes when a bank issues a loan, it depletes part of this required reserve. When this occurs, the bank must borrow funds from another bank with a surplus. The federal funds rate is the interest rate at which these banks lend funds to each other. The federal funds target rate is determined by a meeting of the members of the Federal Open Market Committee, the committee in charge of the U.S. government's money supply and interest rates. The federal funds rate is released once a month.
>
> *Jobless claims.* This is a report issued by the U.S. Department of Labor on Thursday of each week. The jobless claims report tracks how many individuals have filed for new unemployment benefits during the past week. Jobless claims are an important way to gauge the U.S. job market. More people filing for unemployment indicates that there are fewer jobs. Fewer people filing for unemployment indicates that there are more jobs.
>
> *Nonfarm payrolls.* This is a report issued by the U.S. Bureau of Labor Statistics on the first Friday of each month. This report was created to describe the total number of U.S. employees, excluding government employees, nonprofit employees, and farm employees. This report also estimates the average weekly earnings of all employees, excluding those outlined above. This report essentially looks at whether businesses are hiring people or not.

EXHIBIT 11.9 Relevant News Releases and Their Effect on the Underlying Asset

Release Name	Released	Definition	Effected Underlying	Significance
Federal Funds Rate Released by the U.S. Department of Treasury	Released 8 times per year	Interest rate at which banks lend balances held at the Federal Reserve to other banks overnight	AUD/USD EUR/USD GBP/USD USD/CAD USD/CHF USD/JPY US 500	Extremely significant

(continued)

EXHIBIT 11.9 *(Continued)*

Release Name	Released	Definition	Effected Underlying	Significance
Jobless Claims Released by the U.S. Department of Labor	Weekly; typically 5 days after the week ends	The number of individuals who filed for unemployment insurance for the first time during the past week	AUD/USD EUR/USD GBP/USD USD/CAD USD/CHF USD/JPY US 500	Extremely significant
Nonfarm Payroll Released by the U.S. Bureau of Labor and Statistics	First Friday of each month	Change in the number of employed people during the previous month, excluding the farming industry and government jobs	AUD/USD EUR/USD GBP/USD USD/CAD USD/CHF USD/JPY US 500	Extremely significant

 KEY POINTS: PART 4

To take a quiz on this section, simply visit our companion site, www.traderschoiceoptions.net.

- Volatility trading means that you are not trying to predict a direction in the market. You are simply speculating whether the underlying will stay in a certain range or come out of the range in either direction.
- Buying volatility means that you are making a speculation that the underlying asset will make a large move in one direction or another.
- Selling volatility means that you are making a speculation that the underlying asset will remain in a certain range by expiration.
- As binary options approach expiration, premiums of options with strike prices around market price will have large deltas, as every dollar move can potentially make the difference between a $0 value at expiration and a $100 value at expiration.
- You can use binary options to speculate on where an underlying asset will not go.
- If you think that an underlying asset will not go below a certain price, you simply buy that in-the-money binary option.

- If you think that an underlying asset will not go above a certain price, you simply sell the option with a higher strike price than the market price of the underlying.

- The wider a range that you speculate an underlying asset will trade in, the lower your payout odds on the trade.

- The tighter the range that you speculate an underlying asset will stay in, the higher your payout odds are on the trade.

- The larger a move that you speculate an underlying asset will make, regardless of direction, the better your payout odds are on the trade.

- When going long volatility, the smaller a move you try to speculate on using binary options, the lower your payout odds will be on the trade.

- You can use binary options to speculate during economic data and news releases by trading volatility.

PART V

Creating Your Binary Options Strategy

T his section will teach you how to test an edge in the market and use proper risk management in order to create your very own binary options trading strategy.

What You Will Learn:

- Why can binary options mitigate the two emotions that are detrimental to your trading: greed and fear?
- What is the inverse relationship between your chances of winning on binary option trades and your potential payout?
- What are the basics of strategy development using any instrument?
- How many binary option contracts should you trade based on your account size and system?
- What types of strategies can you create with binary options?

When you complete this section, you should be well on your way to developing a binary options trading strategy that is suited to your needs.

CHAPTER 12

Systems with Binary Options

Some people do not understand what binary options are. Due to the two possible fixed payouts at expiration, people automatically assume that trading binary options is almost like gambling.

This could not be further from the truth. As this text has already covered, binary options are a tradable instrument. You can trade in and out of your positions anytime up until expiration. There are multiple strike prices and expirations, and you can trade binaries on a plethora of underlying instruments.

The fact that there are two possible outcomes at expiration actually provides binary options with a unique attribute that is not available with most other trading products.

The "binary nature" of binary options makes them act in a certain way as expiration approaches. This attribute can actually provide intermediate and advanced traders with unique trading opportunities. However, for beginner traders it serves another purpose. It actually allows the traders to enter into the market with a controlled instrument that can mitigate the two biggest enemies of any trader, fear and greed.

FINDING YOUR EDGE

Just as with all instruments, when trading binary options, you need to find an edge in the market and create a system around it. However, unlike many instruments, binary options allow for many different types of trades. As you know, you can use binary options to speculate on ranges, breakouts, economic events, and all other kinds of trades.

⌐ an edge is certainly not easy to do. The idea is to take some ⌐oncepts covered in this text and on our companion website, www ⌐aderschoiceoptions.net, and practice trading them in a free demo account that you can pick up on the website until you find something that works for you.

To make things even more interesting, finding an edge is not the Holy Grail; another key component is risk management and trading psychology. These components are so intertwined that neither one can be mentioned without the other. And both of these components can be your worst enemy if they are not properly used. Having said that, if properly used, they can also be your best friend.

It has been hypothesized that, with proper risk management, a simple system like flipping a coin to buy or sell could be successful. However, having even the slightest edge should enhance your chances a great deal. An edge is something that will make you more money than you lose over a big enough sample size of trades.

You can take advantage of your edge by trading it manually, or you can create an algorithmic system to trade your edge. What's most important is that you make money in the long run.

A perfect example of this is the game of blackjack. The house has a very slight edge, less than 2 percent. But by repetitive play, they consistently end up profitable. This is because they have a set approach, an edge, and they don't get emotional when a player goes on a winning streak. Good traders put themselves in the position of a casino.

To begin, one needs to calculate a system's expectancy, develop trading and risk management rules, and follow those rules religiously to generate profits. Because most systems have life cycles, it is very important with any system to create a reevaluation point. This is a point where the trader starts to question the system's effectiveness and begins to look for other systems that he expects to be profitable. The reevaluation point should be decided upon before trading begins. It should be based on the back-tested data, and take into account concepts that will be discussed such as a drawdown, consecutive losing sessions, and reward/risk ratio. The next sections will cover these concepts in greater detail. The key is to develop and utilize a system that fits your trading style and personality.

PROPER TRADING SYSTEM DEVELOPMENT

We will go into the calculations and common misconceptions about expectancy later. But, for now, it is just important to understand that an edge should ideally make the system profitable in the long run and make

you more likely to make money than lose money over a larg
sample size of trades.

Indicator Colinearity

When selecting an edge, it is very important not to overoptimize or fit the data. One common mistake that people make when developing a system is relying too heavily on technical analysis and using two confirming indicators and optimizing them. This causes the system to look great historically; however, the system will not do as well in the future.

This is not a book on technical analysis, but it is important to point out that when using multiple technical indicators in your system, it is critical to make sure that you are using uncorrelated indicators. Using two or more indicators that confirm each other and then assuming that they are giving you a trade signal is a big mistake.

Indicators are broken down into five types, listed in Exhibit 12.1. And if you are using two or more indicators, make sure that at least two of them are from a different group.

EXHIBIT 12.1 Examples of Indicators

Indicator Type	Example	Example
Trend	Moving averages	ADX
Volume	On-balance volume	Accumulation/ Distribution
Volatility	Bollinger bands	Keltner bands
Momentum	Stochastics	Rate of change
Overbought/Oversold	CCI	RSI

- Trend
- Volume
- Overbought/Oversold
- Momentum
- Volatility

System Robustness

It is important that the edge is robust. A system is robust when it remains profitable during up, down, and sideways markets. Many trend-following systems perform well when the instrument trends, but don't do as well when the instrument is in a sideways, whipsaw period. It is crucial that the period is taken into account during back-testing. A system that works well in only one kind of market needs an "on/off" indicator if it is to be used, so that the system can be shut down when market conditions are not favorable. Or it may be possible to use two systems in conjunction with each other that work well in opposite market conditions and together give a more positive return than alone.

Amount to Back-Test

Before even demo trading a system, you will want to conduct some kind of a back-test. With instruments such as futures, forex, and stocks, this can be done with a simple software program or trading platform that you can get online. You can also back-test manually by simply following the chart of the instrument.

BACK-TESTING BINARY OPTIONS STRATEGIES

Because binary options are derivatives of stocks, futures, contracts for differences (CFDs), and forex, back-testing will not be as easy, as there is no readily available data on each option historically.

While some people may look at this as a problem, it can also be used as an opportunity, since your competition in a zero-sum game will not have certain tools readily available to them. You should check our companion site, www.traderschoiceoptions.net, for various tools and reports that will historically analyze the underlying instruments on which binary options are available.

Also, there are some creative ways to back-test for binary option trades even without knowing the data of each option. Here are some examples:

If you are going to be speculating on weekly ranges, you can take historical data for an underlying instrument and see what percentage of the time the price of the underlying moved outside of this range.

Let's clarify this concept with a simple example. Let's assume that you will make weekly trades with binary options, speculating that the Standard & Poor's (S&P) futures will not move up by more than 3 percent and will not move down by more than 3 percent.

Taking this into consideration, you can get weekly data for the S&P futures from the Chicago Mercantile Exchange (CME) website and determine how many times over the past five years the S&P futures moved up or down by more than 3 percent. Based on this information, you will know the percentage of the time that this range was breached.

Another way to approach back-testing option strategies is
back-test the underlying instrument itself. For example, let's say
have a short-term system that you want to use to forecast the pr.
You can back-test the price of oil very easily using a back-testing program
such as Metastock, Wealthlab, or Metatrader. Once you back-test your system, you can use options to trade your edge. For example, instead of trading oil futures, you can use binary options on oil futures.

There are quite a few benefits with this. First, if you use out-of-the-
money options, you can have a higher return on investment (ROI) on your
trades. Also, the option itself can act as a natural stop-loss. You will no
longer have to worry about setting your stop or the market's moving too
fast and moving past your stop. You can simply use the option premium as
your stop. If the market moves in your favor, you cash out at settlement;
if it moves against you, you get nothing at settlement. Essentially, you are
using the option premium as your stop-loss with this approach.

Of course, this will work only with directional strategies. It is harder
to implement with volatility strategies. There are, however, some ways that
you can back-test volatility strategies.

One technical strategy that traders often use is a breakout strategy.
With a breakout strategy a technical trader observes an instrument trading in a tight range with increasing volume for an extended period of time.
Typically, after this happens, the instrument makes a big move in one direction or another as it breaks out of a range. Exhibit 12.2 depicts a breakout
above resistance.

One big issue with a breakout strategy is that it's hard to forecast
which direction the breakout will be in. Is the price going to break above

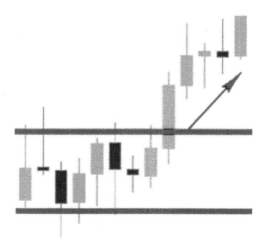

EXHIBIT 12.2   Chart of a Breakout

the upper level of the range? Or is it going to break down below the lower level? By using binary options you can solve this problem. You can simply get into a long volatility spread. This way, the direction of the breakout does not matter to you. By using the long volatility spread, you make money as long as the breakout happens—it does not matter if it is to the downside or to the upside.

The way that you would test a system like this is by simply manually going back on a chart and looking for where you forecast a breakout to take place. If a breakout did in fact happen, you can assume that you would win on your option trade; if there were no breakout, you can assume that you would lose on the trade. Of course, this is a discretionary manual strategy, so you would want to trade it on a demo account and then on a small live account, both of which can be set up at www.traderschoiceoptions.net, before applying any serious money to it.

In the same manner, you can use binary options with a support resistance system. Support resistance areas are areas on the chart that price has difficulty breaching. Exhibit 12.3 depicts support and resistance.

It is likely that there is a big buyer or seller in the market of the underlying that is either buying or selling at a certain level. For example, let's assume that the EUR/USD pair is trading at 1.3550. A big bank may be

Support:

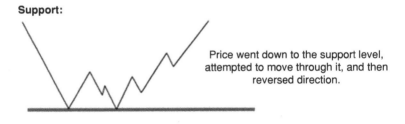

Price went down to the support level, attempted to move through it, and then reversed direction.

Resistance:

Price went up to the resistance level, attempted to move through it, and then reversed direction.

EXHIBIT 12.3   Support and Resistance

accumulating the euro, and it has an order to buy everything up at 1.3540 or lower.

Exhibit 12.4 depicts a large buy order at the 1.354 level. In this scenario, the large buy order will cause price to bounce up from the 1.354 level. As soon as the price drops to 1.3540, the bank will step in and buy the euro. This causes the price to stay above 1.3540.

On the chart, this area will look like a support. Let's say that you are not sure what the EUR/USD cross is going to do, but you see this clear area of support. You may decide to purchase an in-the-money binary option with a 1.3540 strike price. This way, as long as the EUR/USD stays above 1.3540, you will win on your trade.

To test this strategy you can pull up a charting application, mark all areas of support, and see if price breaks below it on upcoming trades. For example, you can find an area of support from 2011 and see what price does around this level in 2012. You can simply test whether the price drops below the support line or not. If it bounces off support, you can assume that you would win on the trade. If it crosses below the support line, then you can assume that you would have lost on the trade. This is a way that you can manually back-test such a strategy.

Once again, this is not 100 percent quantifiable. Therefore, you will need to play with this strategy on a demo account to make sure that it works for you and then trade it with a very small real account to get comfortable before applying any serious money to it.

To sum things up, if used incorrectly, back-testing can be very dangerous, as traders often don't test during correct ranges and overoptimize with confirming indicators. This practice is typically called *curve fitting.* In other words, people adjust nonrobust parameters in a way to make their system look good on historical data. The key is to use unconfirming indicators to test your edge on a robust period of time.

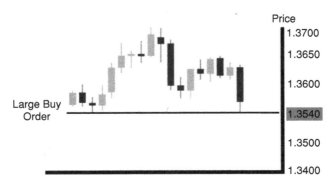

EXHIBIT 12.4 Support

THREE BACK-TESTING RULES

There are three practical rules that you want to apply when back-testing.

Rule 1: Back-Test over a Sufficient and a Robust Sample Size of Data

Many traders will make the extremely dangerous mistake of not back-testing over a sufficient data range. For example, they may take a long biased trend-following system and back-test it on a short uptrend. The results will be spectacular! You will probably see extremely high accuracy and huge profits on your trades.

Exhibit 12.5 depicts an upward trend. An upward trend occurs when price continuously climbs higher. Pretty much any long trade will win here, so testing on strictly an uptrend will not provide you with sufficient information.

The problem is: What happens during a downtrend? And what happens during a choppy period or a sideways market? There is a good chance that this system will fail miserably. For this reason, you must back-test on a sufficient number of data points, and you must back-test on a robust period.

A good rule of thumb is to back-test on at least 1,000 data points. So if you are back-testing a system on a daily chart, you will want to back test at least four years of data. In addition to just making sure that you are getting four years, make sure that the range has an uptrend, a downtrend, and a sideways choppy area. This will show you if the system can really stand up over time.

If you are back-testing a weekly system, you don't really need to go too much farther back than 10 years. Ten years on a weekly system would be about 520 data points. For an intraday system, you will want to test more like 2,000 data points since there are more data available. The logic

EXHIBIT 12.5   Uptrend

behind this is that the overall market direction and behavior do not change as quickly on intraday time frames, so you want to get more data to really prove the system to yourself.

Additionally, back-testing on a robust data range will tell you what market conditions are most conducive to your system and where to proceed with caution, for example, if you have a reversion to the mean system. Basically, this is a system that does well in a ranging market; if you see a clear trend, you may decide to cut down on your position size.

Rule 2: Do Not Curve Fit

This was already covered in this section, but the idea is to not use confirming indicators and not overoptimize data. Try to use at least two indicators that are uncorrelated. For example, moving average convergence/divergence (MACD) and moving averages will not work since they are essentially both trend indicators. But MACD and volume may work since one is a trend indicator and the other one is a volume indicator.

Rule 3: Progress to Your Live Account

Although you will be eager and excited to get money out of the market, you must prove to yourself that your system can work with real money. So after you back-test, always demo trade for a bit. Then start with a very small amount of money to make sure that the system works. Once you do this, and if you are happy with the performance of the system, you can start to scale it up until you reach your desired trading amount.

As you can see, especially with options, back-testing is much more of an art than a science. Past performance is never an indication of future performance, and there is no guarantee whatsoever that you will achieve the results of what you back-tested in the real market. Additionally, there are no data to back-test with options. So the key is to demo trade the strategy until you reach your desired performance and then to trade the strategy with a small account. Take notes on everything that you see about your system/strategy, and only then apply real live money to it on a big scale.

CHAPTER 13

Negative Emotions

M any traders discount the detriment of negative emotions on their trading. They greatly overestimate their emotional intelligence and thus assume that they will be able to follow any trading system without negative intervention due to negative emotions.

The real fact of the matter is that traders unnecessarily intervene even with fully automated trading robots, causing them to lose almost all the time. If people intervene even with automated trading robots due to negative emotions, you can only imagine just how much negative effect these emotions have when trading manually. In fact, there are extremely successful market-making operations set up simply to take advantage of people's negative emotions.

Almost any market maker will tell you that if you give any trader enough time, two catastrophic emotions will kick in and the statistics will catch up. These two catastrophic emotions are *fear* and *greed*.

It is very likely that if you've read at least one trading book in your life, you have heard about these two emotions. However, it is equally as likely that you are unaware of their practical relation to your trading. In order to have a true understanding of how these two emotions can negatively affect your trading, it is necessary to look into how each of them practically relates to your trading.

GREED AND FEAR

When you are trading any instrument, you have to ask yourself the following basic questions.

- When do I enter the trade?
- How much money do I put up?
- How long should I stay in my trade?
- When do I exit if the trade goes my way?
- When do I exit if the trade goes against me?

Most traders find a reason to get in based on some kind of fundamental or technical analysis. They typically put up more money than they should to enter the trade, as they are not familiar with proper risk management. They do not decide ahead of time how long they plan to stay in the trade. Because they don't have a time limit on their trade, they typically are too greedy to realize a loss when they need to. To make things worse, when they do have a profit, they immediately start to fear losing it and end up getting out too early.

These are the two biggest problems with greed and fear. People stay in their losing trades for too long because they are too greedy to close out a trade for a loss. People also cut their losses short because they are too fearful to give up their profits. These two negative emotions pretty much control all of the actions of most traders.

If you think that you can control these two emotions, or if you think that you are not one of the traders who is controlled by these two emotions, think again. There is another mental process that is detrimental to the success of most trades, and that process is *justification*—making an emotional decision and then trying to rationalize and justify it after the fact.

This is basically how the majority of traders function. There is a lot of emotion tied to money. Therefore, most traders make decisions purely based on emotion. The issue is that they don't realize this until it is too late. And the reason for that is justification. If they don't want to get out of a trade, they will find 10 reasons to stay in. If they want to cut their losses short, they will find 10 reasons to get out of the trade prematurely. They will also usually find reasons to interfere with just about every trading system and break it due to their emotions.

HOW TO HANDLE NEGATIVE EMOTIONS

Most books, tutorials, and classes on trading discuss the concepts of fear and greed and how they can be extremely detrimental to your trading, but few discuss specific ways that you can mitigate the emotions. The problem is that you are conditioned to act and think in a certain way from the moment you are born. And emotions like fear and/ or greed can actually be good emotions to have in certain areas of your life, just not in trading.

The fact is that you cannot control your emotions. So simply telling yourself to stop being greedy or stop being fearful will do nothing. Also, telling yourself to be disciplined and simply follow your system will most likely do nothing. Most traders will once again make an emotional decision based on these negative emotions and end up trying to rationalize it after the fact.

The key is that you need to create practical parameters for yourself that will mitigate the magnitude of negative emotions. Let's look at a basic example to illustrate the concept.

Let's assume that you have a trading system and you make a trade that goes against you, and the rules of your system are telling you to cut your losses. If you close out your trade, you will lose $5. Most likely, you are not going to have a problem exiting your trade for a loss. This is due to the fact that the emotion of greed will not kick in as much when it comes to a $5 loss. Basically, most people are not very emotionally attached to $5.

Now let's imagine the same scenario, but now you have to realize an $80,000 loss, which also happens to be half of your life savings. Now, there is a very good chance that most traders are going to have a pretty big problem pulling the trigger and exiting the trade for a loss.

It is highly likely that the trader who is experiencing the $5 loss wagered less money on his trade than the trader who is experiencing the $80,000 loss.

This is obviously a fairly drastic example, but it is meant to emphasize the point that you can set specific conditions on your trading strategy that will be able to mitigate negative emotions.

There is a famous saying by Sun Tzu in his book *The Art of War:* "Every battle is won before it is ever fought." The same concept applies to trading systems. Unless properly set up from the onset, trading systems may be doomed before you ever even make your first trade. This is regardless of how great your indicator, trading robot, market research, or signal service is.

Conversely, if you set up proper parameters for your trading system, particularly risk and money management, from the start, you will have a much higher likelihood of avoiding the detrimental effects of negative emotions such as fear and greed. This is not to say that your system will necessarily win or be profitable. Setting up proper parameters means that you will have better control of your trading and will be less likely to lose an amount that will have a drastic impact on your financial well-being.

If you want your system to perform well for an extended period of time, it is absolutely a must that you take practical steps to diminish the negative effects of greed, fear, and justification on your trading system.

FIND THE RIGHT SYSTEM FOR YOU

The first step that you need to take in order to avoid the doom of negative emotions when trading is to select a system that is compatible with your trading personality. If you select a system that is wrong for you, no matter how great it is, your emotions will take over and cause you to break the system.

You almost have to look at it in the way you would look at a spouse. If your spouse has completely different interests and goals than you, things simply will not work out, no matter how great that person is.

Without going too deep into it and asking you to take personality profile tests, you simply have to ask yourself one crucial question: What is going to make me react in a worse way—a lot of small consecutive losses, or sporadic large losses?

To clarify, think of it this way: One type of a winning system will have more losses than gains, but the gains will be bigger than the losses. Another type of a winning system will have a lot of small gains, with a few occasional losses that are big and will wipe out quite a few gains.

This is, of course, a gray scale, and there will be different size gains and losses; however, almost no system is going to be right in the middle. It is always going to be skewed to one side or another.

So the key *practical* question is: Which extreme makes you cringe more—lots of wins but huge losses, or lots of losses but bigger wins? Most of the other components of a trader profile simply do not apply to practical situations.

The reason that this is a critical component is a principle known as *system trade expectancy*. Many traders think that having a high reward/risk ratio is important for successful trading. This is not true at all. In order for a system to be successful, it needs to have positive expectancy. Essentially, expectancy measures how much you should expect from every trade that you make with a trading system.

If you have historical data of trades on a system, you can calculate expectancy as follows. Take the average historical loss and multiply it by your losing percentage. Then take that number and subtract it from your average historical win multiplied by your winning percentage.

The expectancy formula is:

$$\text{Expectancy} = \text{Average Gain (\% winning trades)} - \text{Average Loss}$$
$$\text{(\% losing trades)}$$

The main purpose of the expectancy formula is that it should tell you how much you can expect to make on a trade over a large enough sample size of trades. Obviously, you want this number to be positive and large enough to make you want to trade the system.

You can relate this formula to trading binary options in a practical way. Let's look at two examples: One would be most compatible with a trader who prefers many consecutive wins and a few large losses, and the other is more compatible with a trader who would prefer more small losses and compensating for them a few large wins. Let's look at each of these examples.

More Small Wins and Fewer Big Losses

Let's say that you are buying deep-in-the-money options. As you know, with these options you are paying a fairly high premium. If you are correct, you will receive $100 per contract at settlement. This means that you will earn only a small percent return on your collateral. However, you have a higher chance of winning on the trade because you win as long as the underlying does not drop below the strike price of the option. If you hold until expiration and lose, you will lose much more than you make on your winning trades with this approach.

Therefore, this approach has a low reward/risk ratio but a high accuracy. And this is one type of trade that you can get into if you prefer to win more frequently than you lose but are okay with having a few larger losses (Exhibit 13.1). Let's look at a trade example with this strategy.

EXHIBIT 13.1 Support at the 1244 Level

Rationale The Standard & Poor's (S&P) futures are currently trading at 1250. If you believe that the S&P futures will not drop below 1244, you would buy the 1244 contract.

169

n The ask price for this contract is $73.9. This is what
up for every contract that you want to trade. Therefore,
are putting up $739.

....own As long as the S&P futures don't drop below 1244
.. expiration, you will win. You will receive revenue of $1,000 on your 10
contracts. Because you initially put up $739, your profit on the trade will be
$261, or $26.1 per contract traded.

Exhibit 13.2 depicts the profit and loss (P&L) of going long 10 contracts of the 1244 US 500 binary option. The x-axis represents the price of
the underlying, and the y-axis represents P&L.

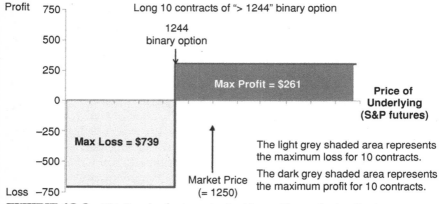

EXHIBIT 13.2 P&L Graph of a Long In-the-Money Binary Option Trade

Summary Exhibit 13.3 contains all of the data points for this trade.

As you can see, with this trade you are more likely to be correct than
incorrect. If the S&P futures go up, you win; if the S&P futures go down,
you also win; and if the S&P futures stay where they are, you also win.
Keeping in mind that due to normal distribution the price at expiration is
most likely to end up where it was at the time you entered the trade, you
have a greater than 50 percent chance of winning on this trade. In fact, if
the price of a binary option can be used as a market consensus here, you
have a 73.9 percent chance of winning on this trade.

However, your payout will be less than 50 percent on this trade; also,
in fact, you will receive a 35 percent return on collateral. The reward/risk
ratio on this trade is only .35:1. If you take on these types of trades over and
over, you have to assume that you will have losses, and each loss may wipe
out two to three wins.

So now the question that you have to ask yourself is: How okay will I
be taking on such big losses that will wipe out a large number of my wins?

EXHIBIT 13.3 Data Points for a Long In-the-Money Binary Option Trade

Trade	Figure	Calculation
Underlying asset	S&P futures	
Market price	1250	
Expiration	1 day	
Strike price	1244	
Long/Short	Long (buy)	
Size	10 contracts	
Entry price	Ask price of $73.9/ contract	
Max loss	$739	Ask price × number of contracts = max loss $73.9 × 10 = $739
Collateral	$739	Collateral = max loss
Max Profit	$261	($100 – ask price) × number of contracts = max profit ($100 – $73.9) × 10 = $26.1 × 10 = $261
Risk vs. reward	.35:1	Max profit/max loss = risk vs. reward $261 / $739 = .35:1

More Small Losses and a Few Big Wins

The next scenario that you will have to look at is taking on a lot more small losses but occasionally having big wins that can potentially compensate for the smaller losses.

With this strategy, you may be wrong week after week after week and have to wait out losing streaks in order to catch a big win. Once again, you have to ask yourself the question: How do I feel about waiting out losing streaks?

When plugged into an expectancy formula, these trades will have a low winning percentage and a high average win. At the same time, they will have a higher losing percentage and a lower average loss.

From a practical standpoint, you can look at an out-of-the-money long binary option trade. Here, you have a less than 50 percent chance of winning. Now if the underlying stays where it started when you entered the trade, you lose; if the underlying goes down, you also lose; and even if the underlying goes up but fails to reach your strike price, you will also lose. Your only chance of winning with these trades is if the underlying ends up above your strike price.

If you make this trade day after day or week after week, you will have more losing trades than winning trades. However, to enter this type of trade you will not need to put up a lot of collateral, and your return on collateral will be higher.

Let's look at a trade example to illustrate this concept.

Rationale   Let's assume that the S&P futures are trading at 1250. You decide that the S&P futures will go up in price substantially and buy a 1259 out-of-the-money option, hoping that the S&P futures will close above 1259 at expiration.

Entry Breakdown   You decide to buy one contract of the US 500 binary option with a strike price of 1259 and an ask price of $20 per contract. The required collateral to place this trade is $20, and the maximum you stand to lose is also $20.

Exit Breakdown   If you are correct and the S&P futures reach 1259 by expiration, then you will receive $100 per contract settlement at expiration. In this case, your total profit will be $80 because total profit is equal to the difference between the collateral you put up and your settlement value of $100.

If you are wrong and the S&P futures do not settle above 1259 at expiration, your maximum loss will be $20 per contract, which is your entire collateral.

Exhibit 13.4 depicts the P&L of going long one contract of the 1259 US 500 binary option. The x-axis represents the price of the underlying, and the y-axis represents P&L.

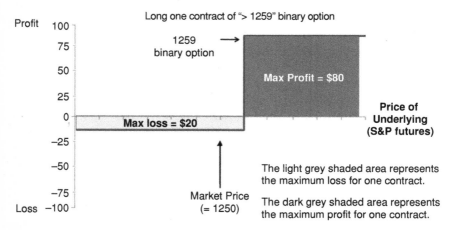

EXHIBIT 13.4   P&L Graph of a Long Out-of-the-Money Binary Option Trade

Summary   Exhibit 13.5 contains all of the data points for this trade.

EXHIBIT 13.5   Data Points for a Long Out-of-the-Money Binary Option Trade

Trade	Figure	Calculation
Underlying asset	S&P futures	
Market price	1250	
Expiration	1 day	
Strike price	1259	
Long/Short	Long (buy)	
Size	1 contract	
Entry price	Ask price of $20/ contract	
Max loss	$20	Ask price × number of contracts = max loss $20 × 1 = $20
Collateral	$20	Collateral = max loss
Max profit	$80	($100 − ask price) × number of contracts = max profit ($100 − $20) × 1 = $80 × 1 = $80
Risk vs. reward	4:1	Max profit / max loss = risk vs. reward $80 / $20 = 4:1

Notice now that you are taking on a much smaller risk, $20, to get a po-
tentially higher reward, $80. Your reward/risk ratio is 4:1, and your return
on collateral is 400 percent. However, with this trade, you have a much
lower chance of winning than you would with the in-the-money trade.

Once again, the key is that you have to take on the lesser evil here.
It is not possible to take on only a few small losses. You have to assume
that you will be faced with a lot of small losses or a few big losses and find
which one sits better with you.

This principle also works with spreads. For example, some people will
enter into volatility long spreads and simply buy out-of-the-money options
both above and below the market price. With this strategy, you are not really putting up a lot of collateral, but the underlying has to make a large move
in one direction or another in order for you to win on the trade. Based on
the normal distribution principle, the probability of that is fairly low.

Exhibit 13.6 is the P&L graph for a long volatility trade. The x-axis represents the price of the underlying, and the y-axis represents P&L.

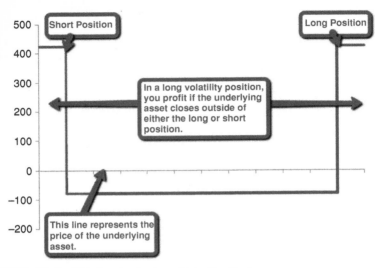

EXHIBIT 13.6   P&L Graph of a Long Volatility Trade

Exhibit 13.7 shows a normal distribution curve. Due to the principle of normal distribution, the price of a tradable instrument has a higher probability of eventually ending up where it started. To get a realistic picture of how much the S&P moves in a given day or week, you can check out our distribution tool on www.traderschoiceoptions.net.

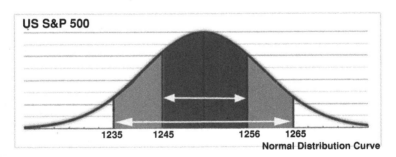

EXHIBIT 13.7   Normal Distribution Curve

However, certain traders are known as premium collectors in the traditional option world. They are simply betting for the underlying to remain in a certain wide range by expiration. They may be earning only 5 to 10 percent return on collateral on the trade, and they are perfectly content with that. These traders know well in advance that they will have a lot of winning days and week. And they also know far in advance that they will have losing trades that will wipe out a ton of their wins, but they are prepared and comfortable with that in the same way that the volatility long trader is comfortable sitting through losing streaks.

If you are not sure which group you fall into, you may want to look into a couple of other strategy types. One would be a binary options strategy where the winning-to-losing trade ratio would be as close to 50-50 as possible. This way, you will have similar losses to gains and should have similar average losses to average gains.

You also may want to consider a combo strategy where you go volatility long on certain instruments and volatility short on others. This way, you will be waiting for occasional big moves on certain spreads, while consistently accumulating small wins on other spreads. With this approach, you want to analyze the type of underlying instrument that you are trading.

As a rule of thumb, U.S. indexes such as the S&Ps and Nasdaq tend to revert to the mean, while commodities and commodity currencies tend to be more trending. You may consider trading volatility long strategies on the trending underlying assets and volatility short strategies on ranging underlying assets.

PRACTICAL STEPS TO MITIGATE THE NEGATIVE EMOTIONS

Now that you have selected a system that can work well with your trading personality, let's discuss the practical steps that you can take to mitigate negative emotions when trading your system.

One huge reason that many traders lose is that they don't have a specified predetermined trading system. They are simply entering trades based on their emotions, then rationalizing them and losing.

It is an absolute must that you create a trading system that has predetermined rules and addresses exactly what you are going to do no matter what happens. It is also preferable that you back-test this system and demo trade it before allocating real live money to it to make sure that it can perform. Risking your hard-earned money on a trading system before developing specific rules and testing them is pretty much guaranteed financial suicide.

A system does not just mean waiting for a moving average to cross, or trading based on the news that comes out. Each system must have specific components. These components are basically rules that you will need to have to deal with all the possible events that can happen when you are trading. These include at least the following.

Entering Trades

An entry strategy is the market condition that will have to be true in order for you to enter. This can be a 100 percent quantifiable condition, or it can be slightly subjective to the trader. The key is that you will need to have specific rules in place in order to enter the trade. This has to be specified and predetermined. Otherwise, you will be making decisions based on your emotions, which we just learned is not a good thing.

Traders typically implement a few different conditions for entering trades, for example:

- *Technical conditions.* These are the conditions in the historic price of a trading instrument. For example, you buy if the price drops for x number of days in a row. Also, technical indicators such as moving averages, Bollinger bands, and stochastics could trigger a buy condition.
- *Fundamental conditions.* Traders may want to enter trades based on certain economic data releases. They may also look at news and geopolitical events.

Exiting Trades

Just as you have to know when you have to enter a trade, you will have to predetermine when you will have to exit the trade. There are typically two reasons for you to exit your trade: (1) If you lose on the trade and you need to cut losses, and (2) if you win on your trade and you need to take profit.

Traders typically implement many different tactics for exiting trades. Let's cover some basic ones.

- *Take-profit.* With a take-profit, you simply exit your trade after it makes a certain dollar or percentage return to lock in your profit.
- *Stop-loss.* You can use a stop-loss to cut your losses. This means that if you enter the trade and it goes against you by a certain percentage, points, or dollars, you get out. Additionally, you can move your stop-loss up to protect your winnings. If a trade actually goes in your favor, you can move your stop-loss to lock in at least some profit on the trade. One thing that you should never do is move the stop-loss against you.
- *Time stop.* The time stop is a great exit strategy that is fairly straightforward and is a great way to discipline traders, but it is often overlooked. With this approach you simply predetermine the amount of time that you plan to stay in your trade after you enter it. For example, you can enter a trade and plan to be in the trade for one hour. Or you can plan to stay in the trade for a day or a week. This actually coincides with options quite well because options have expiration dates. With this approach, you are exiting your trade based on time regardless of whether the trade is winning or losing.

- *Conditional stop.* With a conditional stop, you will be exiting your trade based on certain technical or fundamental conditions in the market, for example, if an indicator can tell you to enter a trade and to exit a trade. Or you can get into your trade and hold it until a certain economic data release is scheduled to come out. The idea here is that you exit based on the condition regardless of the profitability of the trade that you are in.
- *Stop-loss based on underlying.* When trading options and binary options, you may want to implement a stop-loss rule that is based on the underlying instrument that you are trading. Here are some ways in which you can do this. You may decide to enter an in-the-money trade and cut your losses as soon as the option goes out-of-the-money. Or you may sell an out-of-the-money option and decide to cut your losses when the option goes in-the-money. Additionally, you may want to get out of your option trade if the underlying instrument moves against you by a certain number of points.

If you are looking to track the prices of the underlying instruments right from the Web, you can simply visit TradersChoiceOptions.com to look at quotes and charts for commodities, forex, futures, and CFDs.

For example, let's assume that the S&P futures are trading at 1250 and you decide to buy an option with a 1240 strike price. When you enter the trade, your option is in-the-money, and as long as the S&P futures do not move below 1240, you will win at expiration. This option may cost you $80 per contract. You will be okay on this trade until the underlying drops below 1240; once it does, you will be in jeopardy of losing your entire collateral if the S&P futures end up below 1240 at expiration. You may decide to cut the position when this happens (Exhibit 13.8).

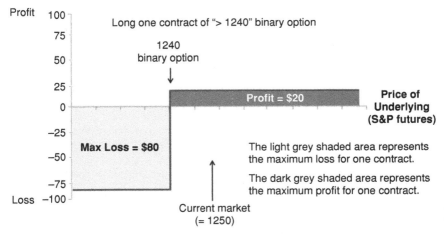

EXHIBIT 13.8 P&L Graph of a Long Out-of-the-Money Binary Option Trade

Therefore, your cutoff rule on this type of trade may be to exit your trade as soon as your position gets out-of-the-money and not wait to see what happens at expiration.

- *Stop based on option premium.* Another stop-loss approach is to exit your trades based on the premium of the option that you entered. With this approach, you are also not holding to expiration, but rather you are cutting your trade when the option's premium changes by a predetermined amount.

Out-of-the-Money Binary Option Trade

Here is an example.

Entry Breakdown   Let's assume that the S&P futures are trading at 1300 and you decide to sell an out-of-the-money binary options contract with a strike price of 1320 and a premium of $10. With this trade, as long as the S&P futures are below 1320 at expiration, you will make the $10 premium, but if the futures rise above 1320, you will lose $90 collateral per contract.

Exit Breakdown   You may decide that you don't want to risk the entire $90 collateral and thus implement a cutoff strategy. One way to do this is to say that when the option premium triples, you will exit your trade no matter what.

Exhibit 13.9 depicts the P&L of going long one contract of the 1240 US 500 binary option. The x-axis represents the price of the underlying, and the y-axis represents P&L.

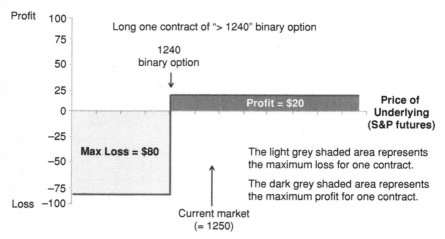

EXHIBIT 13.9   P&L Graph of a Short Binary Option Trade

Summary   Exhibit 13.10 contains all of the data points for this trade.

EXHIBIT 13.10   Data Points for Short Binary Option Trade

Trade	Figure	Calculation
Underlying asset	S&P futures	
Market price	1300	
Expiration	1 day	
Strike price	1320	
Long/Short	Short (Sell)	
Size	1 contract	
Entry price	Bid price of $10/contract	
Max loss	$20 Stop loss	Cut off if option triples and value goes to $30
Collateral	$90	Collateral = max loss
Max profit	$10	Bid price × number of contracts = max profit $10 × 1 = $10
Risk vs. reward	1:2	Max profit / max loss = risk vs. reward $10 / $20 = .5

With this approach, if the S&P futures go up and the trade moves against you, causing the options contract to go up in price to $30 or more, you will cut off your trade no matter what. This will cause you to have a $20 loss rather than the $90 loss that you would experience if you stayed in your trade until expiration.

Buying an In-the-Money Binary Option

You can also implement this strategy if you are buying an in-the-money binary option.

Entry Breakdown   Let's assume that gold futures are trading at 1600 and you believe they will not drop below 1580. You may find a binary option with this strike price. Let's assume that the premium of this option is $85.

Exit Breakdown   If gold futures drop below 1580 at expiration, you will lose your entire $85 premium per contract. Thus, you may decide to cut off the trade based on the premium of the option.

The most you stand to collect is $15 if you are correct. This is calculated by subtracting $85 from the $100 potential settlement. You may decide to implement a 1:2 reward/risk ratio and cut the trade if your max open loss exceeds $30.

If gold futures start to drop and head toward 1580, your option premium may drop below $55. If this happens, you can simply get out of your trade prior to expiration and incur the $30 per contract loss rather than waiting until expiration and taking on the entire $85 per contract loss.

Exhibit 13.11 depicts the P&L of going long one contract of the 1580 US 500 binary option. The x-axis represents the price of the underlying, and the y-axis represents P&L.

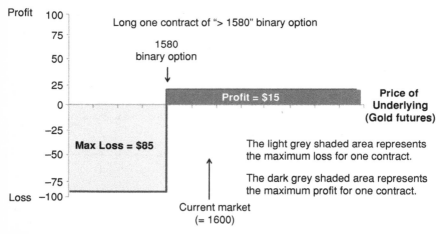

EXHIBIT 13.11   P&L Graph of a Long Binary Option Trade

Summary   Exhibit 13.12 contains all of the data points for this trade.

Please keep in mind that with these cutoff strategies, stop losses are never guaranteed and you may get out past your stop if the market moves quickly against you.

The idea with this type of a stop-loss strategy is that it is mathematically related to the options premium. Or it may be better even to look at your maximum potential profit or reward risk ratio with this approach.

So if you stand to collect x amount of dollars if you are correct on the trade, you may decide to cut your trade if your loss becomes x × y.

EXHIBIT 13.12   Data Points for Long Binary Option Trade

Trade	Figure	Calculation
Underlying asset	Gold futures	
Market price	1600	
Expiration	1 day	
Strike price	1580	
Long/Short	Long (buy)	
Size	1 contract	
Entry price	Ask price of $85/ contract	
Max loss	$30	Cut off if option drops to $55
Collateral	$85	Collateral = max loss
Max profit	$15	($100 − ask price) × number of contracts = max profit ($100 − $85) × 1 = $15 × 1 = $15
Risk vs. reward	1:2	Max profit / max loss = risk vs. reward $15 / $30 = .1:2

The main theme with all of these trade exit rules is that they absolutely *must* be predetermined in advance of your entering the trade. In fact, they must be created when you develop the rules for your trading system.

CHAPTER 14

Risk
Management

The next big component of a trading system is determining how much to risk on each trade. This is probably the most important aspect of a trading system. The point is that you are always going to be right on some trades and wrong on others. The idea is to make the numbers work out in a way so that you will make more money on your winners than you will lose on your losers.

This, of course, is not an easy task. The first component is to determine trade size so that you don't have a single trade that will wipe out your entire account or, even worse, your life savings.

The first question that you have to ask yourself is: How much am I willing to risk on any one single trade? There is a risk management principle referred to as the *2 percent rule*. And this is basically a rule of thumb stating that you should not exceed a loss of over 2 percent of your account balance on any one single trade.

For example, if you have a $10,000 account, you should not lose more than 2 percent of that account ($200) on any one single trade.

The 2 percent rule is a great rule of thumb to use; however, the numbers should vary a bit. They should be anywhere from 1 to 5 percent, depending on how many consecutive losing trades your entry and exit condition produced historically.

THE PROCESS

Here is how the process works:

The first thing you need to do is to check how many consecutive losing trades your system can have in a row and how much dollar/point profit you are going for on each trade. If your system historically has had a fairly large number of losing trades in a row, then you want to make sure that the most that you risk on the trade is 2 percent or less. If the system historically has not had a large number of losing trades in a row, then you may want to risk slightly more than 2 percent.

Consecutive losses are what will get you here. They will create what is known as a *drawdown*. A drawdown is a dip in the equity curve of your trading account from the net new equity high. For example, let's assume that your account starts out at $10,000 and then grows to $25,000 until you hit a series of losing trades. Let's say you have a bunch of losing trades in a row and your account value falls to $15,000. Your account will be in the drawdown until it breaks the previous equity high of $25,000.

Your strategy will always cause your account to go into drawdowns simply because some trades will go against you. It is important to know how to handle these drawdowns, and this will be covered more in the account/money management section. The idea is that you want your losses small enough so that the drawdowns stay relatively small. As a rule of thumb, most good trading systems have drawdowns of under 20 percent.

Keeping this in mind, you can now look at your consecutive losing trades and plug in account percentage levels to each trade to see what the total drawdown will be based on how much you risk. For example, if you risk 2 percent of your account on each trade and you have a total of five consecutive losing trades, your total drawdown would be slightly less than 10 percent. Here is how it would be calculated:

Let's assume that you are trading a $10,000 account. The balance is really arbitrary; it is simply used here to illustrate an example.

Exhibit 14.1 shows the numerical and percentage-based breakdown of what a 10 percent drawdown on a $10,000 account would look like on five 2 percent losses.

EXHIBIT 14.1   Drawdown Analysis on $10,000 Account, 2 Percent Losses

Loss	Preloss Balance	$ Loss	% Loss	Postloss Balance	Total $ DD	Total % DD
1	$10,000	$200	2%	$9,800	($200)	−2.00%
2	$9,800	$196	2%	$9,604	($396)	−3.96%
3	$9,604	$192	2%	$9,412	($588)	−5.88%
4	$9,412	$188	2%	$9,224	($776)	−7.76%
5	$9,224	$184	2%	$9,039	($961)	−9.61%

EXHIBIT 14.2 Drawdown Analysis on $10,000 Account, 5 Percent Losses

Loss #	Preloss Balance	$ Loss	% Loss	Postloss Balance	Total $ DD	Total % DD
1	$10,000	$200	5%	$9,800	($200)	−2.00%
2	$9,800	$490	5%	$9,310	($690)	−6.90%
3	$9,310	$466	5%	$8,845	($1,156)	−11.56%
4	$8,845	$442	5%	$8,402	($1,598)	−15.98%
5	$8,402	$420	5%	$7,982	($2,018)	−20.18%

As you can see, if you take a 2 percent loss on each of the trades, then your total loss from your initial balance will be slightly under 10 percent if you hit five consecutive losses.

If using the same example you risked 5 percent on each trade, then your drawdown would be much bigger. See Exhibit 14.2.

Exhibit 14.2 shows the numerical and percentage-based breakdown of what a 20 percent drawdown on a $10,000 account would look like on five 5 percent losses.

Using this simple table calculation, you can play around with the historic results or back-test of your trading system to determine how much to risk on each trade.

If you don't have any historic results for your trading system, nor have you back-tested it, then it is best to stick to the rule of thumb of 2 percent as you initiate your test and work with the numbers from there. Going over a 5 percent maximum loss risk on any trade is not a good idea regardless of the trading system.

DETERMINING POSITION SIZE

Your position size should be derived from the amount that you are planning to risk on each trade and your maximum potential loss. This section will explain how to calculate the appropriate position size when creating your trading system.

As we outlined earlier, there are various methods for exiting your position. You can use a time stop, execute a stop-loss, exit based on a certain technical indicator, exit based on a fundamental event, or simply hold an option position until expiration.

If you are using a time stop or exiting your trade based on a technical or a fundamental indicator, then you will not know the exact maximum amount that you stand to lose on a trade because your exit is going to be determined by either your interpretation of the market condition using a technical or fundamental indicator or it is going to be determined simply by time. With this approach, your loss is not capped. This can happen on even a binary option trade if you are not holding until expiration.

When faced with this situation, you have to make an estimate of what your maximum loss will be on a trade. There are a few ways to do this.

If you back-tested your system, this can actually be fairly simple. You can look at your back-test report and assess your losses. You can take the highest loss that the system had historically and multiply it by 1.5 to be on the safe side and use this value as your estimate for your maximum potential loss.

If you are going to be trading binary options and are planning to exit your trades before expiration, you can simply take the maximum collateral of your trade and multiply it by .8 or .9 and use this as an estimate.

You can also demo trade the system for a period of time. Take the maximum loss that you achieve, multiply it by 1.5 or 2 to be on the safe side, and use that.

The main idea here is that if you don't have a hard dollar stop or are not holding the position until expiration, you will have to spend some time estimating your maximum potential dollar loss per unit on your trade.

You want to be fairly conservative with this estimation. In other words, make the estimate larger than you expect it to be. Doing so will control those negative emotions of greed and fear and, most important, justification. Your greed will be telling you to get into bigger trades so that you can "get rich quicker" and you will justify this by assuming a smaller maximum loss so that you can allow yourself to get into larger positions. Your rational side has to step up and assume a larger loss per unit here to mitigate those counterproductive emotions.

If you know the exact maximum that you stand to risk on a trade per unit of the instrument that you are trading, you can use the 2 percent rule to calculate the appropriate position size. The great aspect of binary options is that you always know this maximum if you hold the position until expiration, which makes it fairly easy to determine the number of contracts that you should risk on a position.

Let's address how you are going to determine position size when you either know or have estimated the single trade maximum potential loss per unit for your trading system.

Calculating the position size can be done with some basic math. In order to do this, you first must determine the maximum dollar loss that you are willing to take on your entire account on one single trade. This is done based on your predetermined maximum percent loss (the 2 percent rule). For example, if you have a $10,000 account and the most that you can lose on a trade is 2 percent, then your maximum dollar loss on that account is $200 (2 percent of $10,000).

Once you have the maximum dollar loss that you can take on your account figured out, you need to divide this number by the maximum single-unit dollar loss to determine the maximum number of shares/contracts that you can trade on any single position.

There is a free risk management calculator available at www .traderschoiceoptions.net. With this calculator you can plug in your account size, maximum single trade loss in points/dollars, and maximum single trade percent loss of your account that you are willing to risk, and the calculator will run through the entire process and provide you a recommendation of the number of contracts that you need to trade.

Trade Example

Let's review the following trade example:

Assumptions   Let's assume that you have a $10,000 account. You see a trading opportunity to buy a binary options on gold futures. The option contract that you want to enter has a premium of $50, and you plan to hold until expiration. The maximum percentage that you are willing to lose on the account is 2 percent on any one single trade.

Position Size Calculation   Because your account is $10,000 and you are willing to risk no more than 2 percent on any one trade, the maximum dollar amount that you can risk is $200.

Since you are planning to purchase an option with a $50 per contract premium and are planning to hold until expiration, your maximum loss per contract is going to be $50.

Since the maximum single trade loss that you are willing to take on the account is $200 and the maximum loss that you can possibly sustain per contract is $50, you simply divide the two numbers out to determine the exact number of contracts that you are supposed to trade. In this case, you would divide $200 by $50. This tells you that you can enter up to four contracts on this trade.

This rule is very important, as it prevents you from getting into overly large trades where your negative emotions get the better of you. It also mitigates your losses and helps you avoid a situation when one trade wipes out a large portion of your account.

Summary   Exhibit 14.3 contains all of the data points for this trade.

The key line to remember here is "Trade small enough to trade again"!

EXHIBIT 14.3 Data Points for Binary Options Trade

Trade	Figure	Calculation
Underlying asset	Gold futures	
Expiration	1 day	
Size long	1 contract	
Price	Ask price of $50/contract	
Total collateral	$50	Collateral = ask price
Max loss	$50	Ask price × number of contracts = max loss $50 × 1 = $50
Account size	$10,000	
Risk %	2%	
Maximum risk	$200	Account size × risk % $10,000 × 2% = $200
Max trade size	4 contracts	Maximum risk / collateral = trade size $200 / $50 = 4

Now let's take a look at how you would calculate position size on a short binary options trade.

Short Binary Options Trade

Let's review the following trade example:

Assumptions Let's assume that you think that gold futures are going to go down substantially and decide to sell an option with a $90 premium. Just as in the previous example, you have $10,000 in your account when you enter the trade and you are willing to risk 2 percent of your account on any one single trade. This makes the total dollar amount that you are willing to risk on any one trade $200.

Just as in the previous trade you decide to hold until expiration. Therefore, your maximum loss on this trade is equal to your collateral, which is $10. Since the most you are willing to risk on this trade is $200 and the most you can lose on each contract is $10, all you need to do is divide $200 by $10 to determine you maximum trade size. When you do this, you end up with 20 contracts.

With this approach you are risking only $10 per contract to make $90. That is a gigantic 800 percent potential return if you are correct. Of course, your chances of winning with an out-of-the-money trade are much less than they are with an in-the-money or even an at-the-money trade.

Summary Exhibit 14.4 contains all of the data points for this trade.

EXHIBIT 14.4 Data Points for Short Binary Options Trade

Trade	Figure	Calculation
Underlying asset	Gold futures	
Expiration	1 day	
Size long	1 contract	
Price	Bid price of $90/ contract	
Account size	$10,000	
Risk %	2%	
Maximum risk	$200	Account size × risk % $10,000 × 2% = $200
Max trade size	20 contracts	Maximum risk / collateral = trade size $200 / $10 = 20

Now that you know how to determine position size on a long trade and a short, let's take a look at one trade example when you are planning to exit prior to expiration.

Exiting Prior to Expiration

Let's assume that you are purchasing an in-the-money option contract with a premium of $60, and your plan is to cut the trade if the value of the option drops by $40. Now you know that your maximum potential loss on this trade is $40.

Summary Exhibit 14.5 contains all of the data points for this trade.

Taking this into consideration, you first need to determine the maximum potential loss that you are willing to incur on the entire account.

Let's assume that you are trading a $5,000 account in this instance. And you are willing to accept risk of 5 percent of the account. This means that you can take on risk of $250 on each trade.

Since your maximum potential risk per unit is $40, you would divide $250 by this number to determine how many contracts to trade. This gives you a value of six contracts. As you can see, you always want to round down here.

It is very important to keep in mind that when exiting trades prior to expiration, the price you are going to get is not guaranteed. For example, if you are willing to take on a $30 loss per contract on a trade and are planning to cut the trade if your loss exceeds this figure, you may not always get out in time to limit this loss. Therefore, it is important to steer

EXHIBIT 14.5   Data Points for an In-the-Money Trade

Trade	Figure	Calculation
Underlying asset	S&P futures	
Market price	1250	
Expiration	1 day	
Strike price	1240	
Long/Short	Long (buy)	
Size	1 contract	
Entry price	Ask price of $60/ contract	
Max loss	$40	Cutoff at 40 point loss
Collateral	$60	Collateral = option premium
Max profit	$40	($100 − ask price) × number of contracts = max profit ($100 − $60) × 1 = $40 × 1 = $40

on the side of caution and round down with these numbers as much as possible.

RISK MANAGEMENT ON OPTION SPREADS

One of the great benefits of binary options is that you can get into spread trades where you are speculating on volatility rather than direction. In other words, you are not trying to forecast where the market will or will not go. Rather, you are trying to forecast by how much it will move.

Let's analyze how you would determine position size for both volatility long and volatility short trades.

Determining Position Size on Volatility Long Trades

As we previously discussed, in volatility long trades you are forecasting for the underlying instrument to make a move in one direction or another. You do not care where the underlying instrument goes as long as it moves by a large enough amount for you to profit. This type of trade is also referred to as a *strangle* in the option trading industry.

As you just learned, your position size here is determined by your maximum loss. When making this type of trade, you would lose if the underlying does not move by a large enough amount in one direction or another. In order to determine your position size, you need to find out what this maximum loss will be.

As you may recall, in order to make a volatility long trade, you need to purchase a binary option with a strike price above the market price of the underlying, and you need to sell the option with the strike price below the market price of the underlying.

For both of these trades you will need to put up collateral for the long trade. This will be equivalent to the premium of the option you are buying. And for the short trade, this will be equivalent to 100 minus the premium of the option that you are selling. If the underlying does not make a large move up or a large move down, you stand to lose both of the collaterals that you put up to enter this trade.

In order to figure out the number of contracts to trade for each leg of the spread, you will need to take the maximum single trade dollar loss that you are willing to risk on your account and divide this number by the maximum you stand to lose per contract if the underlying does not move by a large enough amount in either direction.

For example, if $500 is the most you are willing to risk on one trade in your account and the maximum single trade dollar loss for both legs of the trade is $100, then you would be able to get into five contracts for each leg of your strangle.

Exhibit 14.6 depicts an option chain on US 500 binary options.

So let's assume that the S&P futures are trading at 1300 and you assume that they will make a large move in one direction or another. You

Contract	Bid	Offer
Daily US 500 (Mar) > 1330	2.1	5
Daily US 500 (Mar) > 1325	4.5	7
Daily US 500 (Mar) > 1320	8	10
Daily US 500 (Mar) > 1315	17	20
Daily US 500 (Mar) > 1310	26	29
Daily US 500 (Mar) > 1305	36.1	40.1
Daily US 500 (Mar) > 1300	48.1	51.6
Daily US 500 (Mar) > 1295	60.1	63.1
Daily US 500 (Mar) > 1290	71.2	73.9
Daily US 500 (Mar) > 1285	75.8	77.4
Daily US 500 (Mar) > 1280	80	84
Daily US 500 (Mar) > 1375	90.2	93.4
Daily US 500 (Mar) > 1370	95.4	98.4

EXHIBIT 14.6 Option Chain

decide to sell the 1280 option and buy the 1320 option to get into your strangle. The 1280 option has a premium of 80, requiring you to put up a $20 collateral. And the 1320 option has a premium of $10, requiring you to put up a $10 dollar collateral.

Summary Exhibit 14.7 contains all of the data points for this trade.

EXHIBIT 14.7 Data Points for a Volatility Long Trade

Trade	Figure	Calculation
Underlying asset	S&P futures	
Market price	1300	
Expiration	1 day	
Strike price long	1320	
Strike price short	1280	
Size long	1 contract	
Size short	1 contract	
Price	Long leg: Ask price of $10/contract Short leg: Bid price $80/contract	
Max loss	$30	(Long position ask price + ($100 – short position bid price)) × number of contracts = total collateral ($10 + ($100 – $80)) × 1 = ($10 + $20) × 1 = $30 × 1 = $30
Total collateral	$30	Collateral = max loss
Max profit	$70	$100 minus total collateral $100 – $30 = $70
Account size	$10,000	
Risk %	3%	
Maximum risk	$300	Account size × risk % $10,000 × 3% = $300
Max trade size short	10 contracts	Maximum risk / collateral = trade size $300 / $30 = 10
Max trade size long	10 contracts	Maximum risk / collateral = trade size $300 / $30 = 10

Let's also assume that you have $10,000 in your trading account and you are willing to risk 3 percent on any one trade. Therefore, your maximum single trade dollar loss is $300.

The total collateral that you put up to enter this trade is $30. If you are going to be holding until expiration, you will need to divide the maximum single trade loss that you are willing to accept in your account by the collateral that you have to put up per contract in order to determine how many contracts to trade for each leg.

Therefore, in this case, you will need to divide $300 by $30. This will show you that you can trade 10 contracts in this trade. This means that you buy 10 contracts of the 1280 strike price binary option and you sell 10 contracts of the 1320 strike price binary option.

The main rule of thumb when trying to figure out the number of contracts to trade on positions that you plan to hold until expiration is always going to be as follows: Divide the max single trade loss that you are willing to accept by the total max collateral per unit of the trade or for the entire spread (if you plan to be getting into a spread position).

When getting into a volatility long spread with binary options, time is working against you. As expiration approaches, the time value of the option is going to decrease if the underlying does not make a drastic enough move in one direction or another.

Exhibit 14.8 depicts how an option's time value decreases as the contract nears expiration. The y-axis represents the time value of an option. The x-axis represents the amount of time until the option contract expires.

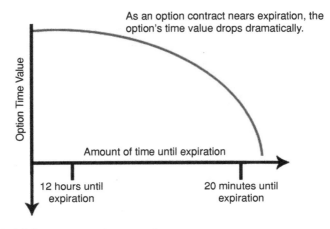

EXHIBIT 14.8 An Option's Time Value

194

Options with strike prices below the market price will all start to approach $100, as they are most likely to settle in-the-money. And options with strike prices above the market price will start to approach $0, as they are most likely to settle out-of-the-money.

Exhibit 14.9 shows option chains of the US 500 binary options strike prices. Pictured left is with 20 minutes to expiration, and right is with 12 hours to expiration.

Contract	Bid	Offer
Daily US 500 (Mar) > 1268	-	3.0
Daily US 500 (Mar) > 1265	-	3.0
Daily US 500 (Mar) > 1262	-	7.0
Daily US 500 (Mar) > 1259	-	7.0
Daily US 500 (Mar) > 1256	-	7.0
Daily US 500 (Mar) > 1253	54.00	55.00
Daily US 500 (Mar) > 1250	56.00	57.00
Daily US 500 (Mar) > 1247	70.00	71.00
Daily US 500 (Mar) > 1244	97.00	-
Daily US 500 (Mar) > 1241	97.00	-
Daily US 500 (Mar) > 1238	97.00	-
Daily US 500 (Mar) > 1235	97.00	-
Daily US 500 (Mar) > 1232	97.00	-

20 minutes to expiration, futures trading at 1250

Contract	Bid	Offer
Daily US 500 (Mar) > 1268	2.1	5
Daily US 500 (Mar) > 1265	4.9	7.8
Daily US 500 (Mar) > 1262	9.7	12.7
Daily US 500 (Mar) > 1259	17	20
Daily US 500 (Mar) > 1256	26	29
Daily US 500 (Mar) > 1253	36.1	40.1
Daily US 500 (Mar) > 1250	48.1	51.6
Daily US 500 (Mar) > 1247	60.1	63.1
Daily US 500 (Mar) > 1244	71.2	73.9
Daily US 500 (Mar) > 1241	79.9	83.4
Daily US 500 (Mar) > 1238	87.4	90.4
Daily US 500 (Mar) > 1235	92.3	95.3
Daily US 500 (Mar) > 1232	95.4	98.4

12 hours to expiration, futures trading at 1250

EXHIBIT 14.9 Option Chains

See Exhibit 14.10. Left: As the price of the underlying continues to move above the strike price, the premium approaches $100. Right: As the price of the underlying continues to move below the strike price, the premium approaches $100.

If you get into a volatility long spread, the options below the market that you sell will start to approach $100, and the options above the market that you buy will start to approach $0 unless the underlying starts to move in one direction or another.

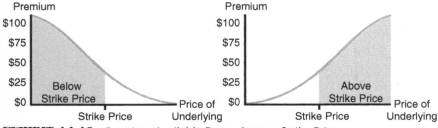

EXHIBIT 14.10 Premium Available Dependent on Strike Price

In some instances, you may decide that you want to get out of a volatility long spread before expiration. For example, you may decide that if you lose over 50 percent of your entire collateral, you will get out. Let's keep going with the previous trade example. Your total collateral is $30; this can be viewed as your cash outflow.

Once you get into the trade, you will want the 1280 option to decrease in value and you will want the 1320 option to increase in value. However, if the underlying does not move and expiration starts to approach, the 1280 strike option will approach $100 and the 1320 strike option will approach $0.

You now have to look at the exit value of your entire spread. If you stand to lose more than $15 on your spread, you should cut the trade and get out, incurring only the $15 loss rather than the $30 loss that you would take on by waiting until expiration.

Let's look at an example:

Let's assume that after you enter the trade, the underlying does not really make a significant move in either direction; the premium of the long option falls to $2, and the premium of the short option rises to $87.

In this case, your exit value for the trade is going to be $2 on the short position and $13 on the long position. This gives you a total exit value of $15. Since your initial collateral was $30, you will lose half of it on the trade. If you don't want to wait until expiration, you can decide to get out of the trade and realize the $15 loss.

When cutting off spread positions prior to expiration, it is important to keep in mind that you are incurring transaction costs on at least four trades when exiting early. Therefore, you may not want to set your cutoff points too close to entry on spread trades, as there is more spread and commission associated with a spread trade than there is with a regular direction binary option trade.

Determining Position Size on Volatility Short Trades

Another great benefit of binary options is that you can profit by speculating on market ranges. These are called volatility short spreads, and you essentially profit as long as the underlying stays within a certain range.

This position is often referred to as the short strangle in the options industry. When getting into this trade, you would purchase an option with the strike price that is below the market price of the underlying, and you would sell an option with a strike price that is above the market price of the underlying.

With this trade, you profit as long as the underlying does not fall below the long option's strike price and does not rise above the short option's strike price.

One nice aspect of this trade is that one of the legs of this trade is always going to win. The reason for this is that the underlying cannot be above the upper (short) options and below the lower (long) at expiration.

Let's look at a simple example to drive this concept home. Let's assume that the S&P futures are trading at 1300, and you purchase a 1280 option and sell a 1320 option. The S&P futures cannot be above below 1280 and above 1320 at the same time.

Exhibit 14.11 depicts the profit and loss (P&L) of going long a binary option and short a binary option. The x-axis represents the price of the underlying, and the y-axis represents the P&L. If at expiration the underlying has closed below the short position and/or above long position, the trader will profit.

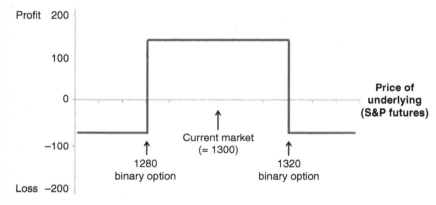

EXHIBIT 14.11   P&L Graph of a Short Volatility Spread

For this reason, your maximum risk on this type of trade is not the combined collateral of the two legs. Instead, it is the combined collateral of the two legs minus 100. The reason for this is that even though you will lose your collateral on one leg of the trade, you will still always get $100 in settlement per contract on the other leg of the trade.

The way you would calculate position size for this type of trade is the same as you would for all trades. You would divide your maximum allowable single trade loss for the entire account by the maximum single trade loss that you could expect to get per unit of the entire spread.

Here is a step-by-step breakdown of how you would determine the position size using the 2 percent rule for a binary options short volatility spread.

Step 1: Determine the maximum loss that you would be willing to take on your trading account. This is done by simply multiplying your account balance by the maximum percentage that you are willing to lose. Let's assume 2 percent here.

Step 2: Find the maximum single trade loss per one unit of the entire spread. For this you would need to determine the collateral for both legs of the spread and then simply subtract one hundred.

Step 3: Divide the maximum loss from step 1 by the maximum loss per unit from step 2.

Once you get this figure, you know how many spread positions you can put on in the account. Please keep in mind that each volatility short spread position has two trades, not one. Therefore, if you determine that you can get into six units of the trade, that means that you can buy six of the option below the market price and sell six of the binary options above the market price.

Let's look at an example for the entire spread.

Rationale   Assumption: You have $10,000 in your account and you are willing to risk 2 percent ($200) on any one trade. The S&P futures are trading at 1300, and you believe that they will stay in a range this week between 1320 and 1280.

Trade Breakdown   You decide to enter a volatility short spread by buying the 1280 in the money binary option and selling the 1320 out-of-the-money binary option.

The 1280 option has a premium of $80, and the 1320 option has the premium of $10. Please note that although the strike prices are equidistant from the market price, the option premiums are different. The reason for this is that binary options are traded on the open market and their prices are determined based on the perceptions of the participating traders and market makers.

Therefore, the collateral that you would have to put up for the long in-the-money positions is simply the $80 premium, and the collateral that you would have to put up for the short out-of-the-money position is $100 minus the $10 premium or $90.

With binary options you still have to put up the collateral for both legs, so you would need $170 ($90 for the short trade plus $80 for the long trade) to enter the spread. However, your maximum loss is only $70 since there is no possible way that you can lose on both legs of the spread at expiration.

Summary   Exhibit 14.12 contains all of the data points for this trade.

EXHIBIT 14.12 Data Points for Short Binary Option Trade

Trade	Figure	Calculation
Underlying asset	S&P futures	
Market price	1300	
Expiration	1 day	
Strike price long	1280	
Strike price short	1320	
Size long	1 contract	
Size short	1 contract	
Price	Long leg: Ask price of $80/contract Short leg: Bid price of $10/contract	
Total collateral	$170	(Ask price + ($100 − bid price)) × number of contracts = total collateral ($80 + ($100 − $10)) × 1 = ($80 + $90) × 1 = $170 × 1 = $170
Max loss	$70	Higher of: (collateral of short position − profit of long position) × number of contracts = max loss (($100− $10) − ($100 − $80)) × 1 = ($90 − $20) × 1 = $70 × 1 = $70 Or (collateral of long position − profit of short position) × number of contracts = max loss ($80 − $10) × 1 = $70
Account size	$10,000	
Risk %	2%	
Maximum risk	$200	Account size × risk % $10,000 × 2% = $200
Max trade size short	2 contracts	Maximum risk acct / Max risk/unit of spread = trade size $200 / $70 = 2
Max trade size long	2 contracts	Maximum risk acct / max risk unit of spread = trade size $200 / $70 = 2

Now that you know your maximum loss per one unit of the spread, you need to divide the maximum loss that you are willing to take on the account by it. When you divide $200 by $70, you will see that you can enter into two units of the spread. Therefore, you can buy two in-the-money 1280 options and sell two out-of-the-money 1320 options.

As you can see, we are treating the entire spread as a unit and will always use the smaller position of the two legs as the position size for both legs.

RELATIONSHIP BETWEEN POSITION SIZE AND TRADING PSYCHOLOGY

After all of the math, you have to keep a consistent theme in mind: Risk management and money management are key to mitigating the negative emotions that cause so many traders to fail. You simply cannot talk about risk management without addressing psychology and you cannot talk about psychology without tying it back to risk management.

The idea with proper position sizing is that you are trading small enough to remove your emotions from the equations. And no matter how emotionally strong you think you are, the negative emotions of fear and greed will find their way into your trading. Therefore, the newer you are, the smaller the positions you should trade. Don't worry so much about winning as a new trader; just worry about not losing. The idea is to get the technique down and the wins will come. But if you start chasing big money right away and taking on positions that are bigger than you can handle, the negative emotions will eat you alive.

HANDLING UNEXPECTED MARKET VOLATILITY

Especially when trading instruments like gold, oil, and currencies, it is extremely important to pay attention and know how you will handle unexpected market volatility cause by economic data releases and unforeseen news events. This is always something that you *must* decide before starting to trade your system with live money. And this is especially true if you are planning to trade a technical system.

Many traders start trading systems that are purely technical, and they take on bigger positions than they should be taking on. When an economic data release comes out that moves the market, the trader's systems don't account for it and the data release can literally wipe out their entire account.

So the first and most obvious practical rule to mitigating the impact of unforeseen news events on your account is proper risk management. Once you have this in place, there are a few questions that you need to answer.

First, will you hold positions while economic data releases are coming out? For example, let's assume that you are trading a binary options short volatility system. Are you going to stay in your trade during the nonfarm payroll economic data release? This is something that you have to test for and demo trade before deciding on how to proceed with live money.

However, when you are trading a volatility long system, the economic data release can work to your advantage. This is because with a volatility long system you are actually banking on a big move in one direction or another.

Certain technical traders believe that the economic data releases and news are already priced into the market and simply choose to ignore the news and economic data releases. If you choose to do this, it is even more important to maintain proper risk management and position sizing, as you can be almost certain that markets will make huge moves due to news releases.

Of course, the fact that you are trading binary options provides you with a certain safety net. This is due to the fact that with binary options, you are always fully collateralized and can never lose more than you put in. So no matter how huge a move the underlying makes in one direction or another, you are protected by the collateral that you put up on the binary option trade.

For example, if you are trading vanilla put/call options with a volatility short strategy, you are essentially selling a call and selling a put. If the market makes a huge move in one direction or another, there is no limit to how much you can lose. In fact, you can actually lose more than you originally deposited into your account since you are trading on margin.

The image on the right of Exhibit 14.13 depicts the P&L of a short volatility strangle with binary options. The image on the left depicts the P&L

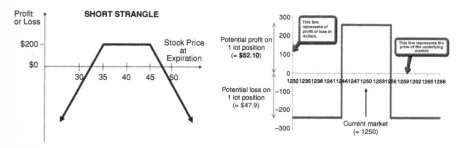

EXHIBIT 14.13 P&L Graph of a Binary Option Strangle and a Vanilla Option Strangle

of a short volatility strangle with vanilla options. The x-axis represents the price of the underlying, and the y-axis represents P&L.

Since binary options are fully collateralized, when doing a short volatility spread, you can never lose more than you allocate to a trade. For the long option, you can never lose more than the premium that you put up on the trade per contract, and for the short option, you can never lose more than $100 minus the option premium per contract.

Of course, this works against you with a volatility long strategy. When trading a volatility long strategy using vanilla put/call options, your upside is unlimited since the options are not capped at $100 at expiration. However, with binary options, no matter how much the underlying moves, your profit is limited to the option premium for short trades and to $100 minus the options premium on long trades.

The image on the right of Exhibit 14.14 depicts the P&L of a long volatility strangle with binary options. The image on the left depicts the P&L of a long volatility strangle with vanilla options. The x-axis represents the price of the underlying, and the y-axis represents P&L.

As you can see, with volatility short spreads, binary options offer quite a bit of the "disaster factor" protection due to the fact that you can never lose more than you put up to enter the trade.

Another question to ask yourself when developing any trading system is do you want to hold your position over the weekend? Typically, the market closes at the end of the day on Friday and then reopens either Sunday evening or Monday morning, depending on the trading instrument. Because a lot of things can happen between when the market closes and reopens, the market can gap. A gap in the market means that it opens either higher or lower than it closed at the end of the previous week. If you are on the wrong side of a market gap, you can lose your money very quickly.

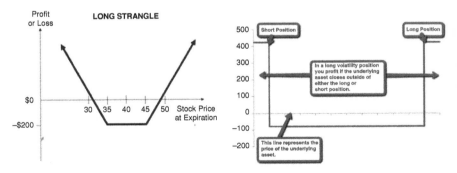

EXHIBIT 14.14 P&L Graph of a Binary Option Long Strangle and a Vanilla Option Long Strangle

Since binary options are only weekly, you cannot hold positions over the weekend when trading binary options. However, if you have an intraday system, you have to decide if you are willing to hold positions overnight. Markets do gap from day to day, so once again if you are on the wrong side of a gap between days, you can sustain a tremendous loss.

There is no right or wrong way to handle positions around economic data or hold them overnight. What you absolutely must do is back-test each approach, then test it on a demo account. Then test it on a live account with a small deposit and determine how you will handle the rule and stick to it.

It certainly sounds more exciting to just start trading, and that may be the thing to do if you are looking for a gamble and not concerned with making money. But if you want to make money, you need a very in-depth plan that takes into account every detail imaginable. That is the key to getting ahead of the game.

BENEFITS OF BINARY OPTIONS ON TRADING PSYCHOLOGY

As we covered earlier, the two biggest negative emotions that a trader has to deal with are greed and fear. When it pertains to individual trades, these two negative emotions can cause the trader to make the following two detrimental mistakes.

First, traders tend to cut their winners short and leave profit on the table. You may enter a trade, see it go in your favor, and be so fearful of losing that profit that you get out of your profitable trade earlier than you were supposed to. Second, traders tend to let their losers run. This happens because traders basically are too greedy to realize losses. They hold on to their losing trades with the hope that the trade is going to come back into positive territory for them.

Even if you cut your winners short and let your losers run by a few points, over a large enough sample of trades, these numbers will add up and eat into your profits or cause you to lose. For this very reason, binary options are a great instrument to start trading to mitigate this problem. The nature of binary options prevents traders from letting their losers run or cutting their winners short. Let's examine how this works.

As we learned, with a binary option there are two specific payouts at expiration: $100 per contract if you are correct and $0 per contract if you are wrong. If you choose to hold until expiration, there is no way that you can possibly let your losers run or cut your winners short.

For example, let's assume that you purchase a binary option and decide to stay in the trade until expiration. If you are correct on your trade and the price of the underlying ends up above the strike price, then you will win on your trade and receive revenue of $100 per contract. This will give you a profit of $100 minus the option premium. If you are incorrect, you will receive nothing and lose the collateral that you put up, which is equal to the option's premium.

When selling a binary option, it's the same scenario. If you hold until expiration and you are correct, and the price of the underlying ends up below the strike price, you will earn the premium of the option. If you are wrong and the price of the underlying ends up above the strike price, you will lose your collateral, which is $100 minus the premium of the option.

Especially when it comes to a discretionary trading strategy and beginning traders, this approach can be very effective. By waiting until expiration, you no longer have to worry about when to exit your trade regardless of whether it is winning or losing. You simply wait until expiration to see what your outcome will be.

For this reason, even if you are getting into a directional trade, you can use binary options instead of the underlying instrument and simply hold until expiration. This way, you are no longer worried about when to get out or if the price will move past your stop-loss. Of course, if you are actually trading the underlying itself, there is a possibility that you can get more of a gain than the binary option can offer. To mitigate this, you can control it with your position size. Let's examine an example of how to do this.

Using Position Size

Let's assume that you want to make directional trades on the EUR/USD cross when the rate is 1.3520. You predict that the rate will go up by 20 pips to 1.3540. And you decide to set a stop at the big figure of 1.3500.

Let's say that you have $10,000 in your account and you are willing to risk 2 percent of your account or $200 on any one trade. When entering this trade, you would put up 10 mini forex contracts. This is calculated by dividing the max loss of $200 by the max single lot loss if your trade gets stopped out—$20.

Summary   Exhibit 14.15 contains all of the data points for this concept.

If you are correct and your trade reaches its profit target, you will end up making $200. If you are wrong and you get stopped out, you will end up losing $200. Now let's consider a binary options scenario.

EXHIBIT 14.15 Data Points for Trading Concept

Trade	Figure	Calculation
Underlying asset	EUR/USD	
Market price	1.3520	
Move forecast	20 pips up	
Available cash	$10,000	
Stop loss	20 pips	
%Risk	2%	
Max loss	$200	Account size × risk % = max loss
		$10,000 × 2% = $200
Max profit	$200	10 mini lots times $20 per lot
# of contracts	10 mini contracts	Max loss / single lot loss = # of contracts
		$200 / $20 = 10

Binary Options Scenario

Exhibit 14.16 is an option chain of EUR/USD binary options.

Let's assume that you can buy an out-of-the-money binary option for $30 with a strike price of 1.3540. To find out how many contracts you can trade, you can divide your max possible loss of $200 by the option's premium (which is the most that you can lose per contract). Once you do this, you will discover that you can trade up to six contracts.

Let's examine what happens when you enter a binary options trade with this scenario. If you hold until expiration and you are incorrect, you will lose $180. However, if you are correct, you will receive revenue of $100 per contract. On six contracts that is equal to $600; once you subtract the $180 collateral from this number, you end up with a profit $420. This is actually more than twice as much of a profit as you would receive by trading spot forex.

So you may be asking yourself, what gives? I should just be trading binary options all the time. Well, here is the caveat. When trading binary options, if you are holding until expiration, the price has to reach your target by expiration. If you are making the same trade just trading spot EUR/USD, then the target can be hit at any time. Essentially, there is no time limit.

⊙ EUR/USD > 1.3545	10.00	14.50
⊙ EUR/USD > 1.3540	27.00	30.00
⊙ EUR/USD > 1.3535	50.50	56.50
⊙ EUR/USD > 1.3530	73.50	78.00

EXHIBIT 14.16 Binary Option Chain

Keeping this in mind, if you know that your strategy is short term and you do not plan to hold positions overnight or longer than a week, then binary options may be a great way to trade, especially with systems that have hard profit targets and stop-losses like those mentioned earlier.

There is even more to consider. As you know, with binary options you do not have to wait until expiration to exit your trade. Keeping this in mind, let's take another look at the same scenario described above. Let's once again assume that the EUR/USD cross is trading at 1.3520. However, now you think that it will move up 40 pips by the end of the day, rather than 20.

If you are trading spot and have the same preset stop-loss, you can get into your position with 10 contracts. If you are correct, you will earn $400 on your trade. This is $40 per contract multiplied by 10 contracts.

Summary   Exhibit 14.17 contains all of the data points for this trade.

EXHIBIT 14.17   Data Points for Binary Option Trade

Trade	Figure	Calculation
Underlying asset	EUR/USD	
Market price	1.3520	
Move forecast	40 pips up	
Available cash	$10,000	
Stop loss	20 pips	
%Risk	2%	
# of contracts	10 mini contracts	Max loss / single lot loss = # of contracts $400 / $40 = 10
Max profit	$400	Profit per contract × # of contracts = max profit $40 × 10 =$400
Max loss	$200	20 pips × 10 mini lots = $200

Out-of-the-Money 1260 Binary Option

Now let's look at what happens if you trade an out-of-the-money 1260 binary option. Let's assume that the option is priced at $10 per contract. Since the maximum loss per trade that you are willing to incur is $200, you will be able to trade 20 contracts now.

If you hold until expiration and you are correct, then you will receive $100 revenue per contract, for a total revenue of $2,000; once you subtract your $200 collateral, you will receive profit of $1800. As you can see here, by simply using an out-of-the-money binary option, your profitability just went up by four and a half times.

But it actually gets even better. Let's assume that the EUR/USD cross goes up by only 30 pips within a few hours after you enter the trade. Since binary options are a tradable instrument, the price of the option may increase from $20 per contract up to $30 per contract. You may decide to exit early and lock in profit. You will earn a total profit of $20 per contract (that is $30 at the time of sale minus $10 at the time of your entering the trade). Multiplied by 20 contracts, this will give you a profit of $400.

Exhibit 14.18 depicts a chart of the EUR/USD.

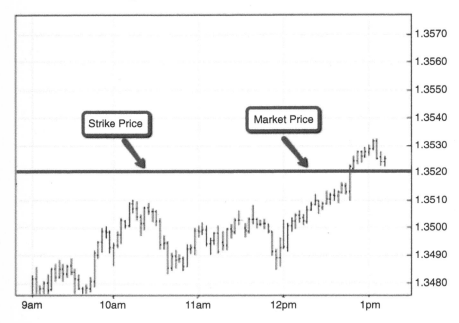

EXHIBIT 14.18   Chart Depicting Movement of EUR/USD

Summary   Exhibit 14.19 contains all of the data points for this trade.

As you can see in this case, with binary options, the underlying does not have to make as much of a move for you to earn the same dollar return, even without waiting until expiration.

DISCIPLINE OF EXPIRATION

Although based on the past example the hard expiration date is a negative, it can also be viewed as a positive. Many traders will hold open losing positions for too long and as a result eventually watch the market make an adverse

EXHIBIT 14.19 Data Points for Long Out-of-the-Money Binary Option Trade

Trade	Figure	Calculation
Underlying asset	EUR/USD	
Market price	1.3520	
Expiration	1 Day	
Strike price	1.3520	
Long/Short	Long (buy)	
Size	20 contracts	
Entry price	Ask price of $10/ contract	
Max loss	$200	Ask price × number of contracts = max loss $10 × 20 = $400
Collateral	$200	Collateral = max loss
Max profit	$1,800	($100 − ask price) × number of contracts = max profit ($100 − $10) × 20 = $90 × 20 = $1800
Exit price	Bid price of $30	
Profit or loss	Profit of $400	(Bid price when position closed − ask price when position opened) × number of contracts = profit ($30 − $10) × number of contracts = $20 × $20 = $400

move, which will negatively impact their account balance. Binary options allow the trader to get away from this negative habit simply due to the fact that they have a set expiration date. You cannot stay in your position past expiration. So whether you are profitable of not, you will have to exit the trade.

Some traders use what's known as a time stop on their strategies. They may enter based on a system or a catalyst and hold on to the trade for an hour, a day, or a week. With binary options, you can get into an options position with hourly, daily, or weekly expirations, and they will act as a natural time stop.

 KEY POINTS: PART 5

To take a quiz on this section, simply visit our companion education site, www.traderschoiceoptions.net.

- Due to their dual nature of having binary (yes or no) results but also having varied strike prices, expiration times, and underlying instruments, binary options are perfect for developing a highly profitable trading system.

- One of the most important parts of trading binary options is finding an edge for your system by employing a variety of market indicators.

- It is essential to back-test a new trading system over a long period of varied trading (not consistently up or down) to ensure profitability in real-world trading.

- Human emotions (particularly greed and fear) can be extremely harmful to trading returns.

- A trader must establish a solid trading strategy with set conditions for trade entry and trade exit in order to mitigate the effects of emotions and ensure continued success.

- The general rule in trade risk management is not to let losses on any one trade exceed some certain percentage, generally 5 percent. This helps protect you from significant losses and mitigates emotions by keeping trades small.

- Binary options are advantageous in risk management; because they are fully collateralized, you cannot lose more than you put in.

- Expiration dates on binary options can also help risk management since they keep the trader from "letting losers run," which can incur excessive losses.

PART VI

Managing Your Binary Options Account

This section will teach you proper money and account management when trading binary options.

What You Will Learn:

- At what rate should you reinvest your trading profits?
- When should you stop trading your strategy?
- How many systems should you trade in order to be successful?
- How should you deal with drawdowns and consecutive losing trades?

When you complete this section, you should know how to properly manage your binary options account.

CHAPTER 15

Proactive System Improvement

After reading the previous section, you should know how to determine the proper position size for your trade. However, there can be another small issue with your trading, and that is what happens if you hit a long streak of consecutive small losing trades.

Here, the emotions of greed and fear are very dangerous. The reason for this is that typically traders will start to interfere with their strategies and systems too soon. At the same time, you don't want to wait until it is too late and let a broken system deteriorate your account.

The fact is that practically all systems have a life cycle. A trader may find an edge in the market and start exploiting it. Then eventually other traders will catch on and the edge will disappear. For this reason, a trading system may be effective for a certain period of time (maybe a year or two) and then simply stop working. This system decay can happen with fully automated, semiautomated, and discretional trading systems.

Because most traders get impatient and the greed of not wanting to give up loss after loss after loss kicks in, they will either stop trading a system after a streak of losing trades or will start to tweak it too early.

The idea is that all modification and enhancements to a system must be proactive rather than reactive.

A simple example of a reactive change to a system is if someone has a long biased system, the instrument drops during a month, and a person changes the system to be more short biased. This is a terrible idea because you will find yourself chasing the market and never catching it.

An example of a proactive change is noticing a variable that may further improve the system and adding it to the rules without recent performance being your driving force to do so. Let's say you noticed that the system does well when trades are entered on Mondays. You can add the rule, back-test it over the robust data, and modify the system if you notice a positive result in the back-testing.

One way to distinguish between a proactive and a reactive system modification is that a proactive change should improve the system's performance on a robust data interval without overoptimizing.

SYSTEM CUTOFFS

A good trader can gauge when a system has lost its effectiveness and thus is looking for new edges in the market constantly. Ideally, you should be able to find your edge, quantify it, back-test it, effectively trade it live, monitor the system, and know when to stop trading it when it becomes ineffective.

In order to save yourself the aggravation of trying to determine when to cut a system off, you can create proactive rules that you can follow when you are trading. By having these rules, you will mitigate your negative emotions.

There are few cutoff parameters that you can use in order to decide when to stop trading a system. Let's cover some of the key ones.

DRAWDOWN

One key aspect to monitor is the system's drawdown, which is the drop from the net equity high. This can reveal key issues about your trading strategy and system and is important in back-testing and evaluating actual results.

To calculate the drawdown, start at the first losing trade for a selected time period. From the first losing trade, add every positive trade and subtract every negative trade. A positive trade reduces the drawdown, and a negative trade increases it.

Once the first losing trade takes place, count it as a negative number and subtract all the losses and add all the wins. Once you are back in the positive for the drawdown, it's considered a recovery and you start the drawdown tracking process all over following your next losing trade. You can use the spreadsheet on TradersChoiceOptions.com to track the drawdowns for your system.

Let's look at a simple example:

Let's assume that you have $100,000 in your trading account. You make five positive trades in a row, for a total profit of $20,000. This gives you a balance of $120,000. On your sixth trade you lose $3,000. You would count the $3,000 as the first negative number. Let's assume that after that trade you win $2,000. You would add the $2,000 to the negative $3,000 and see that you are still in a $1,000 drawdown. Let's assume that after that you lose $5,000. This will put you into a $6,000 drawdown (−$1,000 minus $5,000). Finally, let's say you have a winning trade and win $7,000 on your trade. This will make the net drawdown number positive $1,000, which means that you have recovered from the drawdown and will need to start tracking on the next losing trade.

Exhibit 15.1 is a spreadsheet that depicts the drawdown calculations. You will find a similar spreadsheet with all the formulas inserted on TradersChoiceOptions.com.

Another way to look at drawdown is to simply to take the net equity high for the system, which is the maximum balance on the account if you are trading one system, and subtract it from the balance after every trade. If this number is positive, then there is no drawdown as you are making new highs; if it is negative, that is your drawdown.

With these tools you learned how to calculate drawdown in dollar terms. Now let's learn how to calculate it in percentage terms.

EXHIBIT 15.1 Binary Option Drawdown Calculations

Trade #	Trade P/L	Balance	Max	Drawdown	Calculation Notes
0		$ 100,000	$ 100,000	$ -	
1	$ 5,000	$ 105,000	$ 105,000	$ -	
2	$ 5,000	$ 110,000	$ 110,000	$ -	
3	$ 5,000	$ 115,000	$ 115,000	$ -	
4	$ 3,000	$ 118,000	$ 118,000	$ -	
5	$ 2,000	$ 120,000	$ 120,000	$ -	
6	$ (3,000)	$ 117,000	$ 120,000	$ 3,000	First loss counts as first negative
7	$ 2,000	$ 119,000	$ 120,000	$ 1,000	Add gain after first loss until DD is positive
8	$ (5,000)	$ 114,000	$ 120,000	$ 6,000	Subtract loss after first loss until DD is positive
9	$ 7,000	$ 121,000	$ 121,000	$ -	Add gain after first loss; DD becomes positive

This is fairly simple. You take the net equity high/maximum account balance since inception and you simply divide the drawdown by this number and multiply by 100 to get the percentage drawdown.

Exhibit 15.2 is the same table, with the percent drawdowns also depicted.

Drawdown does not have to be calculated trade by trade; it can be done week by week or month by month. However, if you can get statistics on the maximum open drawdown, it will be extremely beneficial in seeing the historical risk of a system.

When trading an automated system or manual system, or simply a trading strategy, you can decide for yourself in advance the maximum drawdown you are willing to take before you stop trading the system.

The maximum drawdown that you are willing to take highly depends on a few factors, including:

- *Historical/Back-tested drawdown that the system has experienced.* If you traded a system in the past on a live or demo account or simply back-tested this system in the market, you should know its historical drawdown. Based on this historical drawdown, you should know when a drawdown becomes too big and a cutoff is necessary. One thing you

EXHIBIT 15.2 Binary Option Drawdown Calculations in Percentage Terms

Trade #	Trade P/L	Balance	Max	$ Drawdown	% Drawdown	Calculation Notes
0		$ 100,000	$ 100,000	$ -	0.0%	
1	$ 5,000	$ 105,000	$ 105,000	$ -	0.0%	
2	$ 5,000	$ 110,000	$ 110,000	$ -	0.0%	
3	$ 5,000	$ 115,000	$ 115,000	$ -	0.0%	
4	$ 3,000	$ 118,000	$ 118,000	$ -	0.0%	
5	$ 2,000	$ 120,000	$ 120,000	$ -	0.0%	
6	$ (3,000)	$ 117,000	$ 120,000	$ 3,000	2.5%	First loss counts as first negative
7	$ 2,000	$ 119,000	$ 120,000	$ 1,000	0.8%	Add gain after first loss until DD is positive
8	$ (5,000)	$ 114,000	$ 120,000	$ 6,000	5.0%	Subtract loss after first loss until DD is positive
9	$ 7,000	$ 121,000	$ 121,000	$ -	0.0%	Add gain after first loss; DD becomes positive

may want to do here is take the maximum or average historic draw-down and multiply it by 1.5 or even 2. Than once you start trading your system, if this multiple is exceeded by the live drawdown, you should stop trading and reevaluate your situation.

- *The potential return for the trading system.* If you are aiming for your strategy to generate you 10 percent in a year, then it will not be worth your while to take on a 50 percent drawdown. On the other hand, if you are aiming for 100 percent a month returns, then taking on a 50 or even a 60 percent drawdown may be okay. It all depends on your risk tolerance and appetite. The general rule of thumb is the greater the returns you are going for, the higher the drawdown you should plan to withstand with your system.
- *20 percent rule.* This rule is simply what it is. Many traders shy away from trading systems where the maximum historic drawdown is higher than 20 percent. Once again, here the number depends on the returns you are going for. But, ideally, you want the max drawdown to be less than the average yearly historic return for the system.

Now, based on one of the methods mentioned earlier, you need to determine the maximum drawdown you are willing to sustain. Once you determine this value, you will need to keep the drawdown spreadsheet for your trading system. In some cases, your trading platform will have this information, or you can just go to www.traderschoiceoptions.net and use the spreadsheet there.

If your strategy exceeds the maximum drawdown that you are willing to sustain on the account, you should halt trading and begin to reevaluate the system.

Once this happens, you should evaluate the market conditions, evaluate your strategy, make any necessary modifications, and possibly start trading again with a smaller position size if you feel that is appropriate.

As you can see, this is a proactive approach rather than a reactive approach. And it should deter you from blowing up your account due to negative emotions.

CONSECUTIVE LOSING TRADES

A drawdown is a great way to know when to cut off and reevaluate a trading system. The problem is that it's a bit complex and certain traders will not want to track the drawdown. There are a few simpler ways, one of which is simply tracking the number of consecutive losing trades.

The idea here is fairly simple. In your back-testing/historical data check, determine how many losing trades you had in a row. Once you get this number, multiply it by anywhere between 1.5 and 3, depending on your risk tolerance. Whatever figure you get, that is your tolerance for maximum consecutive losing trades. If this number is breached, you will want to cut and reevaluate your trading system; if not, you can continue trading.

Let's go over a simple example. Let's assume that your back-testing results show you the maximum number of seven consecutive losing trades. You can decide to multiply this number by 2 to get 14 and set this as your reevaluation point. When you start trading your system in a live account, if you hit 14 consecutive losing trades, you will have to stop trading and reevaluate your system.

The key here is not so much what number to multiply the historic or back-tested consecutive losing trades by; rather, the key is to predetermine this number before you start trading. This will take negative emotions out of the equation.

One negative aspect of the consecutive trade cutoff is that loss magnitude is completely taken out of the equation. With the consecutive trade cutoff approach, you don't take into account how much you lose on a trade. So, for example, if you have a cutoff point of 15 trades and you lose 50 percent of your account on the second consecutive losing trade, you would need another 13 trades to determine that you need to stop and reevaluate your system. Of course, binary options help here, as the collateral that you put up on each trade acts as a natural stop-loss, which prevents you from letting trades go extremely far against you if you manage your position size properly.

A good idea may be to use a combination of the drawdown approach and max consecutive trade approach. This way, you are protected from both scenarios: a few huge losing trades and several small losing trades in a row. Of course, with this approach there is a little more work for you, as you have to keep track of both the drawdown and consecutive losing trades while trading your system.

REINVESTMENT RATE

Another important component of money management is the reinvestment rate. This basically means how much of your trading profits you want to plug back into your system.

Some people take a portion of their profits out from their trading every month. Sometimes people even take out a portion of the profits from every winning trade. This is not a good idea for many reasons. The two most important ones are as follows. First, depending on the money that you make from trading to live on is very dangerous. If you are an inexperienced trader and you depend on the money you make from trading to live on, the negative emotions of greed and fear will almost certainly eat you alive. Another key component here is that when you lose, you essentially "keep" 100 percent of your loss. If you have a system where you are reinvesting only 50 percent of your wins and losing 100 percent of your losses, you are also pretty much doomed.

This also works with losing months. If you are taking out 50 percent of your profits on losing months and yet incurring 100 percent of your losses, then you are facing a major uphill battle. Let's look at some numbers to drive this concept home.

Let's take an example of trading with a $5,000 account. Let's say you have a sample of 100 trades. On each winning trade you make $300, on each losing trade you lose $200, and you have a 50 percent success rate. This sounds like a good system. Over a large sample size, you should have approximately the same number of winning and losing trades, and your expectancy should be $50 on each trade.

$$[(50\%)\$300 - (50\%)\$200] = \$50$$

So over the 100 trades, ideally you should have 50 winning trades, 50 losing trades, and make $15,000 on your winners and lose $10,000 on your losers, giving you $5,000 in profit (which is, by the way, $50 × 100, just to show you how expectancy works). Not bad, you say! Well, here is the issue. The trades are not distributed evenly, meaning you will not have one winner then one loser, then another winner and another loser. For all you know, you can have your first 50 trades winners and your next 50 trades losers.

The problem with this is that by taking money out, you increase your chances of going bust and increasing your drawdowns. To make this dramatic, let's look at how you go bust quicker by taking money out of a system. Let's say your first 10 trades are winners. This means that you earn $3,000 (10 × $300 = $3,000).

Example 1

Take $1,500 out, leaving you with $7,500 in the account. Let's say your next 38 trades lose (38 × 200 = $7600). This leaves you broke and out of the system with only a nice watch that you bought for the $1,500 you took out! If the remaining trades stayed on pace for the 50-50 ratio, you would have 40 winners and 12 losers. If you reinvested your profits at 100 percent—in other words, kept them in the system—you would have stayed alive and been able to take profit from the system at the end.

Another reason to reinvest your profits is the power of compounding. If you reinvest your profits, your account will grow and you will be able to trade bigger lot sizes. For example $25,000 compounded annually for eight years at 20 percent turns into $107,495.

Yes, you could run into issues with your trades being distributed unevenly and most of your losing trades coming at the end when your positions are bigger, but that's what drawdown analysis is for and that's when a good trader will know to walk away from a system, take his stop-loss, and start looking for another edge to test out and possibly use.

So how do you actually reap the financial reward from a trading system or strategy? Here is one practical way.

It may be a good idea to look at a trading system like a stock. Set your holding period up front, determine your maximum sustainable drawdown, and keep track of the portfolio equity graph as you trade and keep your accounting.

You should know in advance that if the system has a drawdown greater than X percent from a net equity high, you will stop trading it and either take your profits from the system or cut your losses.

You can basically use the maximum drawdown cutoff as you set the aggregate trailing stop-loss for your entire system. Remember that all drawdowns are calculated from a net equity high. So your system can make a ton of money, then hit the max drawdown cutoff, which would cause you to stop trading it, and you can walk away with a profit.

Let's look at an example to illustrate this point.

Example 2

Let's assume that you start with a $100,000 account and you set your maximum sustainable drawdown to 20 percent.

Let's assume that over the first 20 trades you make a profit of $100,000. This will give you a total account balance of $200,000. Now let's say that over the next 10 trades you hit a series of losses and lose $40,000.

Forty thousand dollars is 20 percent of $200,000, which means that you need to stop trading your system. As you can see, you still come out $60,000 ahead. Now you can pocket the $60,000 and look for other edges or a variation of the system that you were just trading in the market.

Exhibit 15.3 is a table depicting a trader starting with $100,000 and driving his/her account all the way up to $200,000 before the max drawdown cutoff kicks in and forces him/her out of the system. As you can see, the trader still makes $60,000, a 60 percent return, even after the max drawdown cutoff.

In addition to having a max drawdown cutoff, you need to determine in advance when you will finally take the profits of the system and reevaluate if it is doing well. After all, you are trading to make money.

If you are depending on the money from trading to live on, you may want to set a specified percentage return on your investment. Once you reach your goal, you can stop trading altogether and take the money you

EXHIBIT 15.3 Max Drawdown Cutoff Example

Trade #	Trade P/L	Balance	Max	$ Drawdown	% Drawdown	Net Profit $	Net Profit %
0		$ 100,000	$ 100,000	$ -	0.0%		
1	$ 20,000	$ 120,000	$ 120,000	$ -	0.0%	$ 20,000	20%
2	$ 30,000	$ 150,000	$ 150,000	$ -	0.0%	$ 50,000	50%
3	$ 25,000	$ 175,000	$ 175,000	$ -	0.0%	$ 75,000	75%
4	$ 25,000	$ 200,000	$ 200,000	$ -	0.0%	$ 100,000	100%
5	$ (10,000)	$ 190,000	$ 200,000	$ 10,000	5.0%	$ 90,000	90%
6	$ (20,000)	$ 170,000	$ 200,000	$ 30,000	15.0%	$ 70,000	70%
7	$ (10,000)	$ 160,000	$ 200,000	$ 40,000	20.0%	$ 60,000	60%

need out and then decide whether to start trading this system or a variation of it from the beginning.

Of course, you should keep track of how you perform on all of your systems, and you should compare and contrast to find what works best for you. Many books recommend evaluating each of your trades. That may get too time consuming in the practical world. A much better approach is to simply evaluate each for the trading systems that you have.

You also may decide to trade a system for a certain period of time, stop trading it after that time, and take out your balance regardless of whether you are up or down. Once your holding period expires, you can consider the original system trade over. Now, based on the actual live performance and analysis, it is up to you to decide whether to enter the same system again or to look for another edge.

Once you do hit your profit target, you may also consider an aggregate trailing stop approach. This will help you squeeze all the last juices out of a trading system before you finally stop. To do this you would simply tighten up your cutoff parameters and let the system run. For example, if you had a max drawdown tolerance of 20 percent, you may decide to drop it down to 10 percent. This way, if the system keeps on winning, you will lock in more and more profits. And if it goes against you, you will cut the system quicker, which will allow you to keep more of what you made.

The main theme here is that the preset commitment to a system is critical to a trader's success. Many times traders will walk away from a system and give up because of a drawdown or cold streak when the system could in fact have been successful. It is imperative to success that the commitment be there, as well as the cutoff aggregate portfolio stop-loss in place, so you know when to reevaluate and/or give up on a system and when to stick with it.

Being able to spot edges is part art, part science, and part education, but sticking with the rules of the system and following them as described earlier or with your own modifications is essential for system trading success.

DIVERSIFICATION AND ACCOUNT DISTRIBUTION

Diversification is another essential component to the longevity and success of a system trader. Diversification exists among systems and within a system. For example, you may want to be trading multiple trading systems at the same time. And within each trading system you may want to trade multiple trading instruments.

INTERSYSTEM DIVERSIFICATION

If you are trading only one system and it starts to go against you, you will obviously be losing money, and it will have a greater negative impact on your psychological and mental state. If you have three active systems and one starts performing poorly, one does okay, and one does very well, you are still okay.

You may want to diversify among asset classes like stocks, futures, options, currency, and more. It is best to trade each system in a separate account. This way, there is no confusion when tracking performance and drawdown.

It is also important that each of the systems that you are trading is compatible with a specific type of market. For example, one strategy can be more of an overbought, oversold strategy like a CCI approach, and the other one can be more of a trend-following strategy like a moving average system. If both systems back-test well over a robust and sufficient sample size, you should hope for them to be successful. This way, if the market starts to trend, your trend-following system will do well, while the range system does not give up too much of your winnings. If the market gets into a range, then you should hope for the opposite to happen.

Of course, you should still have the maximum drawdown and cutoff points for each system separately. This way, if any system breaks, you can stop trading it based on your predetermined criteria. See Exhibit 15.4.

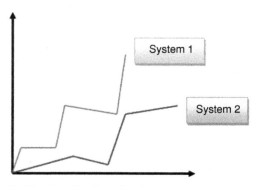

EXHIBIT 15.4   Multisystem Trading Graph

ACCOUNT BREAKDOWN

Another critical issue about systems is that a system with a higher historic drawdown should not be as well capitalized as a system with a lower drawdown. This seems simple, but the one counterintuitive concept here is that the system with the higher drawdown will usually have a higher back-tested profit to go with it, and the system with the lower drawdown will have a lower back-tested profit. A lot of people would take the system that tests for a better profit and put more money in it.

Drawdown and expectancy are far more important statistics in system results than simple profit. You may want to consider a pyramid approach, meaning more money goes into the more stable systems that generate lower returns and have lower drawdowns. Smaller capital should be allocated to the more aggressive systems that have higher potential returns but also have higher drawdowns. This is a good method of capital preservation. See Exhibit 15.5.

High Volatility

Medium
Volatility

Low Volatility

EXHIBIT 15.5 Pyramid Collateralization of Trading Systems

KEY POINTS: PART 6

To take a quiz on this section, simply visit our companion education site, www.traderschoiceoptions.net.

- Over time, trading edges tend to disappear, leading to systems becoming ineffective.

- In order to remain profitable, it is essential to be on the lookout for proactive changes to your system that could make it more effective. Reactive changes should generally be avoided.

- One way of determining when to stop using a trading system is by deciding on a maximum acceptable drawdown (dependent on the returns you are seeking) and then ceasing to use the system if it results in a drawdown exceeding that maximum value.

- Another way of determining when to stop using a trading system is by selecting an acceptable number of consecutive losing days (based on how much risk you are willing to carry), which, if exceeded, will determine that your system must be reevaluated.
- Regularly taking profits from your trading portfolio rather than reinvesting is detrimental because it both results in your portfolio's gaining a higher percent of losses than profits and prevents your money from compounding and growing over time.
- One way to take profits from trading is to wait until drawdowns exceed allowable levels, then cease to use your trading system and take profits.
- Another way is by trading with a system for a set period of time and at the end of that period shutting down the system and taking the balance, regardless of profit or loss.
- One last way (and most useful if you rely on trading returns to live on) is to decide on how much profit you seek and shutting down the system when that level is reached.
- Diversification is essential in trading, both in using diverse trading systems and in trading diverse instruments.
- It is best to have systems with higher historical drawdowns less well capitalized and vice versa.

PART VII

Profiting with Volatility

This section will give you all the tools you need to help you build a volatility short trading strategy.

What You Will Learn:

- What is premium collection?
- What are the advantages and disadvantages of selling volatility?
- What are the key components to a volatility short trading system?
- How can you put everything you learned together into an effective volatility short trading system?

When you complete this section you will be armed with a powerful binary options trading strategy.

CHAPTER 16

The Volatility Short Trading Rules

T here are thousands, if not hundreds of thousands, of books and courses available that teach various trading strategies. Many of these strategies are technical and some are fundamental. The purpose of this book is to get you comfortable with binary options so that you can use them together with various technical and fundamental strategies.

There is no perfect strategy for trading any instrument. Sometimes edges become available and successful traders start to exploit them until they disappear. With proper risk management, traders can take advantage of certain market edges for periods of time. It is highly unlikely that anyone will ever sell you or tell you the exact rules for their trading system that is very profitable. Even if they had a great system, they would most likely prefer to trade it rather than sell it or write about it in a book.

Premium collection is a strategy of speculating on an underlying instrument to stay within a range. During high volatility, you are speculating on its staying in a wider range, and during low volatility, you can speculate on narrower ranges. This strategy is fairly widely used with vanilla put/ call options. One of the greatest appeals of this strategy is the principle of normal distribution. The idea is that any underlying instrument is most likely to end up where it started after any period of time based on normal distribution.

Binary options also allow you to create a volatility short system. In this section, we will go over some basic principles that you can use to create your own volatility short binary options trading system. Please keep in mind that these are only principles; you will need to use them to put

together a system for yourself based on your desired profits and risk tolerance and preferred method of market analysis.

PREMIUM COLLECTION

According to the principle of normal distribution, when you exit a trade,
the price of an instrument is most likely to end up where it was when you
entered your trade.

Exhibit 16.1 is an image of a normal distribution curve. Due to the principle of normal distribution, the price of a tradable instrument has a higher
probability of eventually ending up where it started. To get a realistic picture
of how much the Standard & Poor's (S&P) moves in a given day or week, you
can check out our distribution tool on www.traderschoiceoptions.net.

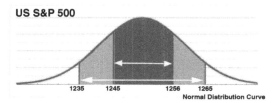

EXHIBIT 16.1   Normal Distribution Curve

This obviously does not mean that the price will always end up where
it started, but it is where the price has the highest probability of ending up.

There is a study that supports the normal distribution theory. According
to a Chicago Mercantile Exchange (CME) study of expiring and exercised vanilla put/call options for the years 1997, 1998, and 1999, 76 percent of all out-
of-the-money options purchased expire worthless rather than get exercised.

Naturally, you would think that selling options is the way to go based
on these numbers. However, this gets a bit tricky since when you are selling
an out-of-the-money option you are only pocketing its small premium, and
your loss can be unlimited with vanilla put/call options.

Binary options can be slightly better when doing a volatility short
spread, since your downside is limited if you hold until expiration. But you
are also picking up a small amount on each leg and have the potential of
losing much more.

So can a volatility short strategy work? It is possible but you need to
have certain rules in mind when trading it.

First, let's review what happens in a volatility short strategy. When entering a volatility short spread, you are speculating on the fact that the
underlying instrument will stay in a range. In order to do this, you would
sell a deep-in-the-money option and buy a deep-out-of-the-money option.

Exhibit 16.2 depicts the profit and loss of going long a binary option and short a binary option. The x-axis represents the price of the underlying, and the y-axis represents the profit and loss (P&L). If at expiration the underlying has closed below the short position or above long position, the trader will profit.

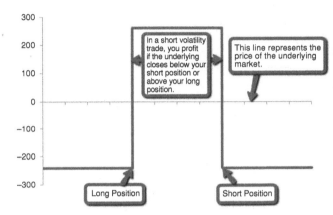

EXHIBIT 16.2   P&L Graph of a Long Volatility Trade

As long as the price of the underlying stays above the strike price of the contract that you purchased, you will earn $100 minus the premium of the option that you purchased. And as long as the price of the underlying stays below the premium of the option that you sold, you will earn the premium on the out-of-the-money option that you sold. Essentially, you want the underlying to stay in a range.

Trade Example

Let's take another look at an example of a volatility short trade and then provide you with some pointers in order to trade this strategy more effectively.

Rationale   Let's assume that the market price of the S&P futures (US 500) is 1250. You speculate that the S&P futures will remain in a range, staying above 1244 and below 1256.

Entry Breakdown   In order to do this, you decide to sell one contract of the US 500 > 1256 binary option for $10, and also buy one contract of the US 500 > 1244 binary option for $93. The collateral for this trade is $183, which is the collateral of the long position, $93, added to the collateral of the short position, $90 ($100 − $10).

Long Trade Logic   Since you are assuming that the S&P 500 futures will stay within your desired range, you would put up 93 for the "> 1244" option and hope that the price would indeed close greater than 1244, which would give you a $100 total payout on the 1244 option for a potential profit of $7 per contract ($100 − $93).

Short Trade Logic   With the short position, you are assuming that the underlying will stay in the desired range and therefore it will not cross above 1256. So you sell short (sell) the ">1256" option. You would put up $90 in collateral (this is the difference between $100 and the $10 premium of the option you sell). As long as the market does not go above 1256, you will receive the settlement of $100, for a profit of $10 ($100 − $90).

Total Collateral   Your total collateral on the spread is $183. This is $93 option premium for the long trade plus $90 collateral for the short trade ($100 − $10).

Exit Breakdown

Maximum Risk   If the S&P futures move outside of either strike price, the traders will lose $83. The calculations for these numbers are explained later.
   When going short volatility you cannot lose on both legs of your position at the same time if you hold until expiration. The futures cannot be both below 1244 and above 1256 at the same time. Therefore, you have to win on at least one of your positions if you hold until expiration.

Upper Strike Price Breach   Your maximum risk if the S&P 500 futures close above 1256 at expiration is equal to the $7 gain from the ">1244" option that you bought minus the $90 loss on the ">1256" option that you sold; $7 minus $90 equals a total loss of $83.

Lower Strike Price Breach   Your maximum risk if the S&P 500 futures close below 1244 at expiration is equal to the $10 profit that you take in on the ">1256" option minus the $93 loss that you will incur with the ">1244" option. This also equals a total loss of $83.
   Now let's look at what happens if the underlying stays between 1244 and 1256 by expiration.

Maximum Reward   If the US 500 stays between 1244 and 1256 at expiration, your cash inflow would be $100 on both the long and the short options. So you would collect a total of $200 at expiration. To find out your profit, simply subtract the collateral that you put up from your cash inflow at expiration.

As you recall, your total collateral is $183. Subtract that number from the $200 revenue at expiration, and you arrive at a maximum profit of $17.

Reward Risk Ratio   Your reward/risk ratio on this trade is simply equal to $17 (max profit at expiration) divided by $83 (max risk at expiration) or .2:1.In other words, you are risking $4.88 for every $1 you make.

Exhibit 16.3 depicts the P&L of going long the 1244 binary option and short the 1256 binary option when the underlying instrument is trading at 1250. The x-axis represents the price of the underlying, and the y-axis represents the P&L. If at expiration the underlying has closed below 1256 and above 1244, the trader will profit.

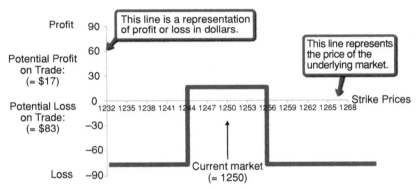

EXHIBIT 16.3   P&L Graph of a Short Volatility Binary Option Trade

Summary   Exhibit 16.4 contains all of the data points for this trade.

EXHIBIT 16.4   Data Points for Short Volatility Binary Option Trade

Trade	Figure	Calculation
Underlying asset	S&P futures	
Market price	1250	
Expiration	1 day	
Strike price long	1244	
Strike price short	1256	
Size long	1 contract	
Size short	1 contract	
Price	Ask price of > 1244 contract: $93	
	Bid price of > 1256 contract: $10	*(Continued)*

EXHIBIT 16.4 (*Continued*)

Trade	Figure	Calculation
Total collateral	$183	(Ask price + ($100 – bid price)) × number of contracts = total collateral ($93 + ($100 – $10)) × 1 = ($93 + $90) × 1= $183 × 1 = $183
Max loss	$83	Higher of: (collateral of short position – profit of long position) × number of contracts = max loss (($100 – $10) – ($100 – $93)) × 1 = ($90 – $7) × 1 = $83 × 1 = $83 Or (collateral of long position – profit of short position) × number of contracts = max loss ($93 – $10) × 1 = $83
Max profit	$17	Revenue – total collateral = max profit $200 – $183 = $17
Risk vs. reward	1:4.88	Max profit / max loss = risk vs. reward $17 / $83 = 1:4.88

Exhibit 16.5 depicts the maximum loss and maximum gain for each leg of the short volatility trade above. The light grey shaded area represents the maximum profit for each position, and the dark grey shaded area represents the maximum loss for each position.

It's pretty certain by now that you see the big issue with this type of strategy. You are risking $4.88 dollars for every $1 that you make. So the

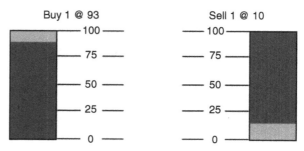

EXHIBIT 16.5 Graphical Representation of the P&L on Both the Long and Short Positions

key to success with a premium collection strategy is to find a way to mitigate the risk.

Let's look at some way that you can do this.

RULE 1: CUT OFF YOUR LOSING TRADES

Let's use Exhibit 16.6 to analyze the magnitude of the price movement of S&P futures.

Exhibit 16.6 depicts the magnitude of weekly moves by S&P futures. It shows the percentage of the weeks during each of the five-year intervals that the S&P futures moved by more than a certain percentage. A greater detailed interactive graph is available at www.traderschoiceoptions.net.

For example, if there were 100 trading days and the SPX moved by more than 3 percent 10 times, the table would show 10 percent.

As you can see from Exhibit 16.6, the S&P index moved down by more than 3 percent 15.06 percent of the time and moved up by more than 3 percent 11.58 percent of the time. In total, the S&P futures moved by more than 3 percent 26.64 percent of the time.

This means that if you were to speculate that the S&P futures will stay within a range of 3 percent above market price and within a 3 percent range below market price, you would be correct roughly three out of four times. Let's do a basic calculation to figure out how much you needed to make on your winning volatility short spreads in order to compensate for your losing short spread.

Here is the formula for volatility short spread compensation:

$$3 \text{ (winning trades)} - 1 \text{ (losing trade)} = 0$$

Based on this formula, you can lose up to 3 times your potential gain on winning trades on your losing trades and still break even. So if you win $1 on your winning trades, you can lose up to $3 on your losing trades.

The issue is that based on the last example and this approach, the amount that you will collect in premium on the spreads will be much less than one third of your maximum risk. Based on the trade example provided earlier, your reward/risk ratio was 1:4.88. If you win only $1 on three winning trades and lose $4.88 on your one losing trade, you will actually end up behind by $1.88.

In order to avoid this pitfall, you need to make sure that you cap your loss on each spread to a specific percentage of your win. The way to do this is not to wait until expiration if the trade is going against you, but instead to cut the trade off.

EXHIBIT 16.6 Weekly S&P 500 Futures, Five-Year Intervals

		-6+% changes	-5% changes	-4% changes	-3% changes	-2% changes	2% changes	3% changes	4% changes	5% changes	6+% changes
1/9/2012 – 1/9/2007	# of weeks:	10	14	27	39	58	57	30	19	13	8
	percentage:	3.86%	5.41%	10.42%	15.06%	22.39%	22.01%	11.58%	7.34%	5.02%	3.09%
1/8/2007 – 1/8/2002	# of weeks:	2	3	5	10	28	26	11	4	2	1
	percentage:	0.78%	1.16%	1.94%	3.88%	10.85%	10.08%	4.26%	1.55%	0.78%	0.39%
1/7/2002 – 1/7/1997	# of weeks:	3	5	13	19	41	51	24	13	3	2
	percentage:	1.16%	1.94%	162.50%	7.36%	15.89%	19.77%	9.30%	5.04%	1.16%	0.78%
Total:	# of weeks:	15	22	45	68	127	134	65	36	18	11
	percentage:	1.94%	2.84%	5.81%	8.77%	16.39%	17.29%	8.39%	4.65%	2.32%	1.42%
1/7/1997 – 1/9/2012	0										
Grand Total:	# of weeks:	15	22	45	68	127	138	65	36	18	11
	percentage:	1.71%	2.50%	5.12%	7.74%	14.45%	15.70%	7.39%	4.10%	2.05%	1.25%

Note: Calculated only for five-day and four-day weeks. Open intervals (i.e., 3% changes = 3+%)

Here is how you would do this. Let's assume that based on your analysis of historical data you decide that you are willing to lose no more than three times what you stand to make. So if you stand to collect a total of $17 on a volatility short spread, you are willing to give up no more than $51.

Let's use our previous example to discuss how to implement this strategy. As you know, the trade can only go against you in one direction or the other. Therefore, one leg of your spread will be positive while the other leg will be negative.

To reiterate, you stand to collect $7 on your long leg and you stand to collect $10 on your short leg if you are correct.

Cutoff on the Long Leg Potential Breach

If the price starts to make a significant move toward the bottom barrier of the range, your short > 1256 option will be fine and you will lock in that premium. Therefore, you can leave this leg alone and will need to focus on your long 1244 leg. In order to do this, as the price is moving down, you simply watch the premium until it drops by more than $61.

The reason the number is $61 and not $51 is that you already stand to collect the $10 on the upper > 1256 leg of the spread. So you can lose $61 on the lower leg and still have only a $51 loss on the entire spread.

Therefore, you can stay in your trade until the bid price of the > 1244 option goes below $32. This is calculated by subtracting $61 from the $93 premium that you paid to get into the lower leg of the spread.

As you can see, the option still needs to move quite a way against you in order for you to have to cut off, but this way you still maintain the needed reward/risk ratio.

Cutoff on the Short Leg Potential Breach

Let's analyze how this scenario plays out on a potential breach of the long leg. If the price of the underlying starts to move up and heads toward the > 1256 strike price, you will need to think about cutting the > 1256 option; however, you stand to lock in your $7 profit on your 1244 option.

As you recall, based on our desired reward/risk ratio, you decided that you are willing to give up only $51 on the entire spread; this is the $17 premium collected multiplied by 3. Since you stand to lock in $7 on the bottom > 1244 leg, you need to add this number to $51 in order to calculate your maximum acceptable loss on the > 1256 position. Based on this calculation, your maximum acceptable loss on the > 1256 position is $58. Since you put up $90 collateral to potentially collect your $10 premium, you can wait until the ask price of the > 1256 option climbs all the way up to $68 before cutting your trade off.

When you do this, you will lose $58 on your short trade and still gain $7 on your long trade, which will give you a net loss equivalent to your maximum threshold of $51.

There are a few things to keep in mind when implementing a cutoff rule on a volatility short strategy. First, you do not want to calculate the cutoff number with the intention of breaking even. After all, you are trading the system to make money. So when you do your historical analysis and calculations to determine your breakeven cutoff multiple, you need to make the actual multiple lower than the one you come up with.

For example, if you decide that the maximum reward/risk ratio that you can sustain on a short volatility system to break even is 1:3, you need to make the actual cutoff ratio 1:2 or 1:2.5.

Of course, having a cutoff ratio will decrease your trade accuracy. The reason for this is that now, instead of waiting all the way until expiration to see if the price of the underlying will come back within your range, you are cutting your trade off before and locking in a loss. Therefore, you will miss out on times when the underlying comes back, and this will cause you to have more losing trades. Additionally, there may be extreme times when the underlying not only comes back but also crosses your other option leg's strike price, causing you to lose on both positions. Of course, this will be a rare occurrence, but once again, sticking with the common theme of this section, you need to plan for everything.

These two aspects don't mean that you have to give up on a volatility short trading system. They simply mean that you need to add more parameters in order to try to put the odds in your favor.

RULE 2: COLLECT ENOUGH PREMIUM

The available premium to collect when trading a volatility short strategy greatly depends on market volatility. If the volatility is high, the out-of-the-money options above the market price of the underlying will be priced higher. This is due to the fact that there is a higher chance of the underlying's reaching those levels.

Let's look at an example to illustrate this point. Let's assume that the S&P futures are trading at 1300. A 1320 option may cost only $4 during low volatility, while the same 1320 option may cost $15 during higher volatility. Since you are selling the option, you are aiming to collect the premium on the trade. The more you collect, the more advantageous it is for you. See Exhibit 16.7.

US 500 (Jun) >1323	5.00	7.50	US 500 (Jun) >1323	2.00	5.00
US 500 (Jun) >1320	15.00	18.00	US 500 (Jun) >1320	4.00	7.00
US 500 (Jun) >1317	20.00	23.50	US 500 (Jun) >1317	18.00	21.00
US 500 (Jun) >1314	31.50	35.00	US 500 (Jun) >1314	31.00	33.00
US 500 (Jun) >1301	47.00	51.50	US 500 (Jun) >1301	56.00	58.00
US 500 (Jun) >1298	61.00	65.00	US 500 (Jun) >1298	68.00	72.00
US 500 (Jun) >1295	74.00	77.50	US 500 (Jun) >1295	75.50	78.00
US 500 (Jun) >1292	88.00	90.00	US 500 (Jun) >1292	88.00	91.00

Binary option pricing during high volatility   **Binary option pricing during low volatility**

EXHIBIT 16.7   Option Chains during High and Low Volatility

The drawback is that during periods of higher volatility, the underlying is more likely to make a bigger move. The subsequent section will address how far away you need to sell options with a volatility short strategy. In the meantime, let's drive home the concept of collecting enough premium.

In the previous example, the S&P futures are more likely to close above 1320 when the volatility is higher than they are to close above 1320 when the volatility is lower. This is the reason you can collect a higher premium.

When it comes to the long leg of the trade, you also stand to make more money on the same strike price option during periods of high volatility than you do during periods of low volatility. When there is high volatility in the market, there will be a higher chance that the price of the underlying will drop below the strike price of the in-the-money option. Using the same example, if the S&P futures are trading at 1300, they will be more likely to close below 1280 at expiration during periods of high volatility than during periods of low volatility.

However, during periods of low volatility, the S&P futures will be less likely to drop below the 1280 strike price. Since there is a higher chance of the underlying's staying above the strike price of the option at expiration and the option's expiring in-the-money, the price of the option will be higher during periods of low volatility than during periods of high volatility.

Another way to look at it is to think of fair market. Since the premium of a binary option is a fair market price during periods of high volatility, there is less chance that an in-the-money option will stay in-the-money, so fewer people are going to want to buy it. And during periods of low volatility, more people will think that the option will end up in-the-money and more people will want to buy it. Since more people are buying, the price will go up and be higher. Therefore, the price of in-the-money options is higher during periods of low volatility. See Exhibit 16.8.

Since you stand to collect $100 per contract minus the option premium on your long trade, if you are profitable at expiration, then you would collect more during periods of high volatility than you would during periods of

US 500 (Jun) >1323	5.00	7.50
US 500 (Jun) >1320	15.00	18.00
US 500 (Jun) >1317	20.00	23.50
US 500 (Jun) >1314	31.50	35.00
US 500 (Jun) >1301	47.00	51.50
US 500 (Jun) >1298	61.00	65.00
US 500 (Jun) >1295	74.00	77.50
US 500 (Jun) >1292	88.00	90.00

Binary option pricing during high volatility

US 500 (Jun) >1323	2.00	5.00
US 500 (Jun) >1320	4.00	7.00
US 500 (Jun) >1317	18.00	21.00
US 500 (Jun) >1314	31.00	33.00
US 500 (Jun) >1301	56.00	58.00
US 500 (Jun) >1298	68.00	72.00
US 500 (Jun) >1295	75.50	78.00
US 500 (Jun) >1292	88.00	91.00

Binary option pricing during low volatility

EXHIBIT 16.8 Graphical Representation of Option with High Premium

low volatility. One hundred dollars minus a smaller number is going to be more than $100 minus a bigger number.

Exhibit 16.9 depicts the price and profit potential of a long in-the-money option during high volatility.

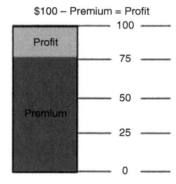

$100 – Premium = Profit

EXHIBIT 16.9 Graphical Representation of P&L on Both the Long and Short Positions

Taking all this into consideration, you have to weigh out two options. During periods of low volatility, there may not be enough premium for you to collect. And during periods of high volatility, you can pick up substantial premium but the underlying is more likely to move outside of your predefined range.

The way to address this issue is to first determine how much you need to collect from each trade. This can be determined by your reward/risk ratio. If based on historical analysis you determine that you need to have a 1:3 reward/risk ratio, you can calculate the amount that you need to collect in order to maintain this ratio with your trading system.

First, you need to consider the transaction costs. When you are buying or selling a binary option, you are buying at the ask price and selling at the bid. Typically binary options will have a two- to three-point spread where every point is worth $1 per contract. Additionally, there is a commission to enter the trade and exit the trade and a settlement fee that you have to pay if you are profitable at expiration. Altogether, you should assume that you will end up paying at least $3 per leg in transaction costs if you are profitable. Exhibit 16.10 shows the commission and settlement variables for binary options.

EXHIBIT 16.10 Transaction Costs

Trade	Win	Loss
Entry	Commission	N/A
Exit prior to settlement	Commission	Commission
Settlement	Settlement fee	Nothing

Therefore, if you hold either leg of your binary option spread until expiration and you collect $4 in premium revenue, your actual profit will be only $2, since $1 went to commission to enter the trade and another $1 went to settlement fee when your trade settled in profit.

For example, when you enter a long in-the-money trade, you pay $96 per contract. If you are correct on your trade and you hold until expiration, you will make only $4 per contract revenue. Once you subtract transaction costs, your revenue will be cut in half to at the most $2.

For a short trade, it's a similar scenario. If you want to sell an out-of-the-money option for $4, then you will put up $96 in collateral. You will end up paying $2 in transaction costs if you hold until expiration, and at least $3 if you decide to get out early.

Although it may seem like a lot of transaction costs, even a $2 return on a $96 collateral is not that bad. It comes out to 2.08 percent per week. If you make just one trade per week like this, you can earn over 100 percent per year on your deposits. That is, of course, if you don't lose.

So the first rule of collecting enough premium is to make sure that you collect enough to cover transaction costs. Three to four dollars per leg should be the minimal number with binary options. Even if you hold until expiration, if you collect less than $3 in transaction costs, the entry commission and settlement fee will simply eat away your profits.

Now you need to look at your reward/risk ratio. A good way to determine reward/risk ratios for volatility short spreads is to analyze historical data to see how many times certain levels were breached. Past price data are not an indication of future movements, but it should give you a ballpark idea of what can be expected. So let's look at the data for the S&P 500 futures again.

As you can see (Exhibit 16.11), from 2007 to 2012 the S&P moved by more than 3 percent up or down 26.64 percent of the time. This means that for every four volatility short spreads that you will put on with strike prices at least 3 percent away, you will be correct three times and wrong once.

EXHIBIT 16.11 Weekly S&P 500 Futures, Five-Year Intervals

	-6+% changes	-5% changes	-4% changes	-3% changes	-2% changes	2% changes	3% changes	4% changes	5% changes	6+% changes
1/9/2012 – 1/9/2007 # of weeks:	10	14	27	39	58	57	30	19	13	8
percentage:	3.86%	5.41%	10.42%	15.06%	22.39%	22.01%	11.58%	7.34%	5.02%	3.09%
1/8/2007 – 1/8/2002 # of weeks:	2	3	5	10	28	26	11	4	2	1
percentage:	0.78%	1.16%	1.94%	3.88%	10.85%	10.08%	4.26%	1.55%	0.78%	0.39%
1/7/2002 – 1/7/1997 # of weeks:	3	5	13	19	41	51	24	13	3	2
percentage:	1.16%	1.94%	162.50%	7.36%	15.89%	19.77%	9.30%	5.04%	1.16%	0.78%
Total: # of weeks:	15	22	45	68	127	134	65	36	18	11
percentage:	1.94%	2.84%	5.81%	8.77%	16.39%	17.29%	8.39%	4.65%	2.32%	1.42%
1/7/1997 – 1/9/2012 Grand Total: # of weeks:	15	22	45	68	127	138	65	36	18	11
percentage:	1.71%	2.50%	5.12%	7.74%	14.45%	15.70%	7.39%	4.10%	2.05%	1.25%

Note: Calculated only for five-day and four-day weeks. Open intervals (i.e., 3% changes = 3+%)

This means that you can lose three times as much on your losing spreads as you make on your winning spreads and still break even. Now remember you cannot lose on both legs of your spread, so it may be a good idea to look at each leg individually. Based on the same table, a breach 3 percent above market price happened only 11.06 percent of the time, and a breach 3 percent below market price happened 15.06 percent of the time. Let's use the higher number of the two for simplicity and to be on the safe side. Since the price will breach one leg 15 percent of the time, then you can lose as much as six times what you make on the trade and still break even.

This is where the system starts to get exciting; let's look at how this number is derived. According to Exhibit 16.11, over the past five years you would lose 15 percent of the time when you bought an in-the-money option with a strike price 3 percent away from the market price. That means that you would lose one time for every 6.67 trades that you make. Let's use six to be safe. That means you can lose six times as much as you win on your losing option trade and still break even.

For the upper strike price breach, the percentage is 11.06 percent that the price will move up by more than 3 percent in one week. To be on the safe side, we will use the higher of the two scenarios and will carry over the six from the down move.

Now we have our minimum reward/risk ratio of 1:6. Knowing this, we can now determine that we will cut off our trade at six times the premium we stand to collect. Since we want to more than break even, we can start by setting this reward/risk ratio to four.

With this in mind, if we sell an out-of-the-money option for $4, we will cut if the value grows to $16. And if we buy an in-the-money option for $96, we will cut if the value falls to $80. This creates another issue. Moves of 16 points are fairly likely to happen in the market, and since we are collecting such a small premium, we need to make sure that the cutoffs don't happen too often.

So now you as a trader will need to analyze price data and demo trades to determine minimum premiums to collect and minimum cutoff amounts.

As you can see, your cutoff rule is based on the premium that you collect before transaction costs. Ideally, you want to be able to collect at least $5 to $6 in premium. This will give you enough cushion to have normal cutoff rules.

In some instances, there simply will not be options far enough away available where it's worth your while to sell. So in the next sections we will address minimum selling distance and time until expiration, which is another critical component of building a proper premium collection system.

RULE 3: SELL FAR ENOUGH AWAY FROM MARKET PRICE

Now that you know how much premium you want to collect on both of your option legs, you need to determine how far away the strike prices should be from the market price when you enter the trade.

The easiest way to look at it is on a percentage basis, rather than a point basis. Let's use the S&P futures and the S&P data as an example. See Exhibit 16.12.

Let's first analyze strike prices 2 percent away. Both moves 2 percent above market and 2 percent below market happened roughly 20 percent of the time. That means that to break even, you need to make at least one fifth as much as much on your winning trades as you would on your losing trades.

Therefore, your cutoff here will be five times as much as the potential premium you stand to make on the trade. The premium that you stand to make is always going to be equal to $100 minus your collateral times the number of contracts.

It is hard to determine how big the cutoff should be. If it's too small, then slight fluctuations in the price of the underlying will cause you to have to cut off your trade. If the cutoff value is too big, then you will lose a lot more on your losing trades than you make on your wining trades.

A good rule of thumb is to cut off the trade only when the strike price is breached. Typically, when this happens, the price of the option will be around $50 per contract, since most at-the-money binary options are priced around $50. Knowing this can help you determine how much premium to collect and how far away to sell.

Let's assume that you are selling an option for $7, 2 percent away from the market price of the S&P futures. This means that your collateral is $93. Based on the theory mentioned, the price of the option will be around $50 when the price of the underlying is equal to the option's strike price. That means that the option price will make roughly a 43-point move against you.

In this case, you can see that your cutoff here will be six times the premium on the option. Knowing this, you can now look back at the historical data and see if this trade makes sense. Based on options 2 percent away from market price, your minimum allowable cutoff is five times the premium. The premium may be too small to sell 2 percent away.

Let's look at another example, but this time we will look at a long in-the-money option purchased 3 percent away. A 3 percent drop in the price of the S&P futures happened 15 percent of the weeks in the last five-year period. Based on this, you need to make at least one sixth as much on your winning trades as you lose on your losing trades. Let's assume that an in-the-money option 3 percent away from market price is priced at $90.

EXHIBIT 16.12 Weekly S&P 500 Futures, Five-Year Intervals

		-6+% changes	-5% changes	-4% changes	-3% changes	-2% changes	2% changes	3% changes	4% changes	5% changes	6+% changes
1/9/2012–1/9/2007	# of weeks:	10	14	27	39	58	57	30	19	13	8
	percentage:	3.86%	5.41%	10.42%	15.06%	22.39%	22.01%	11.58%	7.34%	5.02%	3.09%
1/8/2007–1/8/2002	# of weeks:	2	3	5	10	28	26	11	4	2	1
	percentage:	0.78%	1.16%	1.94%	3.88%	10.85%	10.08%	4.26%	1.55%	0.78%	0.39%
1/7/2002–1/7/1997	# of weeks:	3	5	13	19	41	51	24	13	3	2
	percentage:	1.16%	1.94%	162.50%	7.36%	15.89%	19.77%	9.30%	5.04%	1.16%	0.78%
Total:	# of weeks:	15	22	45	68	127	134	65	36	18	11
	percentage:	1.94%	2.84%	5.81%	8.77%	16.39%	17.29%	8.39%	4.65%	2.32%	1.42%
1/7/1997–1/9/2012 Grand Total:	# of weeks:	15	22	45	68	127	138	65	36	18	11
	percentage:	1.71%	2.50%	5.12%	7.74%	14.45%	15.70%	7.39%	4.10%	2.05%	1.25%

Note: Calculated only for five-day and four-day weeks. Open intervals (i.e., 3% changes = 3+%).

Once again, you should assume that the at-the-money value will be $50. Based on the option premium, there is a 40-point drop between the current price of the option and the at-the-money value.

If you are correct, you stand to collect $10 per contract at expiration. If you are wrong, you can cut at up to six times the potential premium that you stand to collect. Therefore, you can let the option drop all the way down to $30. Since the at-the-money value is $50, this looks like a reasonable trade. And you can see that there is enough premium to buy the in-the-money option 3 percent away.

As you can see, the distance that your strike prices should be from the market price is a function of many things, including your cutoff parameters, market volatility, and option premiums.

One key aspect to keep in mind is that there are professional institutional traders with teams of risk managers and mathematicians behind them that are trading against you. Therefore, you cannot assume that you will beat them by doing just these basic mathematical calculations. In order to have true success with a volatility short system, you need to find and exploit some kind of an edge that works for you. This could be technical, fundamental, contrarian, or a combination of all three. Before allocating serious money to the system, you need to test this edge and demo trade it, and even trade it in a smaller live account. The next section will give you some ideas of how to develop this edge.

RULE 4: USE UNDERLYING INSTRUMENTS THAT REVERT TO THE MEAN

Binary options are available on more than 20 underlying instruments. These include currency pairs, gold, silver, oil, index futures from all over the world, and even natural gas. How do you decide which underlying instrument to use a volatility short strategy on?

This is going to seem very counterintuitive, but when trading a volatility short system, most of the money that you make for the year is during periods of high volatility. The reason for this is that during these periods premiums of out-of-the-money options above the market price go up and premiums of in-the-money binary options farther below market price go down. This allows the trader to collect enough premium in order to make good returns with the system.

Many traders believe that volatility is cyclical. Therefore, periods of high volatility are usually followed by periods of low volatility. However, prices of binary options usually do not adjust as quickly. Therefore, you can get into trades really far away from market price and stand to collect sufficient premium.

Conversely, periods of extreme low volatility are when you should be the most careful. There is usually very little potential premium to collect. Many volatility short traders are tempted to get into their positions closer to market price during these times. But this is a big trap since markets are likely to make a substantial move in one direction or another at any time. See Exhibit 16.13.

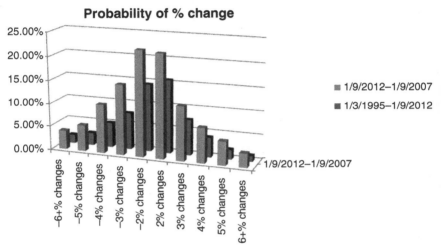

EXHIBIT 16.13 Option Chain during High Volatility and Low Volatility

The key here is to analyze historical data for your underlying instrument and demo trade your strategy enough to get a good feel for how the instrument is going to behave. For example, for S&P futures, as a rule of thumb, it is a good idea for your strike prices to be at least 2.5 percent away from market price on weekly volatility short trades.

Some traders will look at multiple underlying instruments and seek out areas of high volatility. This is a good idea as long as you are picking underlying instruments that historically have been more likely to revert to the mean than to trend.

S&P futures are a great underlying instrument to use with a volatility short strategy, since they historically have reverted to the mean. Instruments like gold, oil, and certain currency pairs usually don't fare as well since they are more trending instruments. Typically, these instruments will have higher-priced out-of-the-money options and lower-priced in-the-money options, which can provide you with better profitability if you are correct. The problem is that they are more likely to move outside the strike prices than an instrument like S&P futures. See Exhibit 16.14.

US 500 (Jun) >1323	5.00	7.50
US 500 (Jun) >1320	15.00	18.00
US 500 (Jun) >1317	20.00	23.50
US 500 (Jun) >1314	31.50	35.00
US 500 (Jun) >1301	47.00	51.50
US 500 (Jun) >1298	61.00	65.00
US 500 (Jun) >1295	74.00	77.50
US 500 (Jun) >1292	88.00	90.00

Binary option pricing during high volatility

US 500 (Jun) >1323	2.00	5.00
US 500 (Jun) >1320	4.00	7.00
US 500 (Jun) >1317	18.00	21.00
US 500 (Jun) >1314	31.00	33.00
US 500 (Jun) >1301	56.00	58.00
US 500 (Jun) >1298	68.00	72.00
US 500 (Jun) >1295	75.50	78.00
US 500 (Jun) >1292	88.00	91.00

Binary option pricing during low volatility

EXHIBIT 16.14 Option Chains on Gold Futures and US 500

In order to build the best volatility short strategy for yourself, you will need to analyze all the possible underlying instruments on which you can trade binary options and decide which ones you will use. You should perform an analysis of what percentage of the time the price moved by x percent over the past 5 to 10 years, as it was done for the S&P in Exhibit 16.12.

Typically, you are most likely to find that indexes tend to revert to the mean and commodities and currencies tend to trend. Therefore, volatility short strategies should work better on indexes than commodities. This, of course, is just a theory, and once again the correct answer depends on your risk tolerance and preference. Are you okay with having to cut trades off more often in exchange for collecting a higher premium on your correct trades? This data has to be determined by you before analyzing various underlying data.

Once you decide which underlying instruments to use, you can assess the option premiums each week and enter what you believe to be the most favorable trading opportunity based on the methods described in the sections above.

RULE 5: SELL OPTIONS WITH PROPER DURATION UNTIL EXPIRATION

Binary options are available with weekly, daily, and even hourly expirations. Typically, with shorter-term options, there is not enough potential profit to be made. Once again, it becomes a question of numbers. Exhibit 16.15 shows the distribution data for S&P futures daily percent moves.

As you can see, in the past five years the S&P futures move more than 1 percent in a day 8 percent of the time. This means that you could have lost as much as 12 times your average win and still would be able to break even on the system. This is a very favorable breakeven accuracy. The question is: Are there options available outside the 1 percent range that would yield you enough potential premium to justify the trade? This, of course, is something that you would need to look for in your option chain.

EXHIBIT 16.15 Daily S&P 500 Futures, Five-Year Intervals

		1% changes	2% changes	3% changes	4+% changes
1/9/2012–1/9/2007	number of days:	106	98	55	40
	percentage:	8.41%	7.78%	4.37%	3.17%
1/8/2007–1/8/2002	number of days:	215	39	12	5
	percentage:	17.09%	3.10%	0.95%	0.40%
1/7/2002–1/7/1997	number of days:	285	67	13	7
	percentage:	22.66%	5.33%	1.03%	0.56%
Total:	number of days:	606	204	80	52
	percentage:	16.05%	5.40%	2.12%	1.38%
1/7/1997 – 1/9/2012					
Grand Total:	number of days:	827	204	80	52
	percentage:	19.29%	4.76%	1.87%	1.21%

Note: Closed intervals (i.e., 3% changes = 3–4%).

If there are no sufficient premiums available far enough on the daily options, you would want to move up to weekly options. When it comes to weekly options, you need to determine the best day of the week to enter your trade.

Some traders like to get in as soon as the option becomes available; this happens on Monday morning for the S&P futures options. Other traders prefer for market direction to be established and wait to get in on Tuesday. There are positives and negatives to entering your trade later in the week. Premiums are a function of time until expiration and price of the underlying. If the underlying were to stay in one place, as expiration approached, in-the-money options would start to increase in value since there is less time for the underlying to fall below the option's strike prices. At the same time, the out-of-the-money options would decrease in value, as the amount of time for the underlying to cross above their strike prices would decrease.

The upside to selling options with less time until expiration is that your exposure decreases. The longer you are in a volatility short trade, the more chance there is that the underlying instrument will cross one of your options strike prices.

Therefore, if there is enough profitability available based on the options premiums, it makes sense to sell a few days closer to expiration than right at the beginning of the week. For example, you can use Monday to determine the overall direction of the market and then make your trade on Tuesday.

Just as with all trading systems, having a feel for what the underlying instrument is doing is very beneficial to your trading. For example, if you see an upward bias in the market, you can buy your in-the-money options a bit closer to market price than you sell your out-of-the-money options. Or you may want to skew the number of contracts for each leg of the trade. The great aspect of volatility short spread trading is that you don't have to be right on the direction of the market; you just have to be not extremely wrong. In the next section, let's look in what additional analysis you can do in order to get a feel for the market.

RULE 6: PERFORM ADDITIONAL ANALYSIS IN ORDER TO GET A FEEL FOR MARKET DIRECTION

Binary options market makers use advanced mathematical principles to determine the fair prices of the available options. If the market deems the option to be cheaper than their fair price, they buy, and if the market deems the option to be more expensive, they sell.

There are option pricing calculators and formulas, such as the Black-Scholes Model, that traders and market makers use to price the options. Typically, institutions will have entire research teams behind option traders. There are institutions trading all instruments including stocks, options, futures, and forex. So as a retail trader, you are always competing with an entity that has more resources than you have.

In order to be successful, you should not try to beat the competing entities as most directional systems do. Instead, you should understand the dynamics in the market and work in line with those dynamics. The best way to put it is that you should go with the flow of the major market participants.

For example, with vanilla put/call options, major market participants such as mutual funds and portfolio managers purchase puts far away from the market price in order to protect their long only portfolios. They are perfectly fine with these put options expiring worthless because it means that their overall portfolio has gone up in value. As an options trader, you can sell puts with the intent of taking advantage of this and act like an insurance company in a sense.

Most retail traders are going to be using binary options with an attempt to predict direction. This is just the nature of the retail trader. Most of them are looking to make a large return with a small investment in a short period of time. When using a premium collection strategy, you are essentially taking the opposite side of these retail traders by forecasting where the underlying instrument will not go.

The beauty behind a range volatility short strategy is that you don't have to predict where an instrument will go. You simply need to predict where it will not go. This gives you many more opportunities to be correct.

For example, when making a directional trade using the underlying instrument, time is not an issue but you have to predict where the instrument will go. If the instrument stays where it started out, you will lose; if it goes against you, you will also lose.

With a directional option strategy, all of the above parameters are also true but now time is also working against you. So not only do you have to predict where the underlying instrument will go, but also you have to predict when it will get there.

With short volatility trading, you simply need to predict where an instrument will not go. So if the instrument goes in your favor, you win; if it goes a little bit against you, you also win; and if it stays where it is, you also win. The only time you lose is when the instrument goes into an area where you forecasted that it would not go.

This means that your directional analysis does not have to be nearly as accurate with volatility short trading as it does with directional trading. And this is a good thing since most directional analysis is not accurate in general.

Having a feel for the general direction of the market is a good idea no matter what type of volatility strategy you are trading. If you have this feel, you can skew your trades or stagger into your trades in a way that can coincide with the market trend and attempt to put the odds in your favor. Let's take a look at some basic technical and fundamental strategies that you can use to get an idea of market direction when trading a volatility short strategy and discuss how you can modify your volatility short binary option spreads based on your analysis.

Support/Resistance Analysis

The first type of analysis that you can do is basic technical analysis. This includes trend lines, support/resistance, big figures, Fibonacci levels, or chart patterns such as head and shoulders, double bottoms, and double tops.

You don't have to do high-end analysis here, and we are not going to get into in-depth discussion of the technical concepts. They all can be found in virtually any technical analysis book. The idea is that you can use basic technical analysis to fine-tune your volatility short binary option spreads.

Let's look at some examples:

Let's assume that you are planning to make a volatility short spread with strike prices at least 3 percent away from market price when the S&P futures are trading at 1320.

Exhibit 16.16 depicts a key support level at the critical 1300 price zone. This support level has been heavily respected and will most likely continue to repel price.

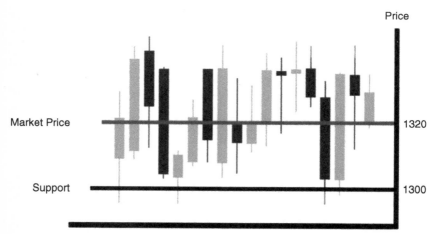

EXHIBIT 16.16   Key Support Levels and the Probability of Change

You notice that there is a strong support level at 1300. You also know that 1300 is a big figure, which acts like a tougher level to breach. Big figures are simply round number prices ending in zero or five. Psychologically, they are tougher to breach than regular numbers.

Under normal conditions, you would be buying your in-the-money option 3 percent away from market price. Three percent from 1320 is 39.5 points away. Therefore, you would be looking to buy the 1280.5 strike price. However, since you see a support level at 1300, you can decide to buy a bit closer and collect more profit if you are correct. For example, you can decide to buy the 1290 strike price instead of the 1280.

There are other ways to handle this situation. For example, if you decide to enter both legs of the trade anyway you may want to enter more contracts on the long leg than the short leg. This is called *skewing the trade*. If you typically enter five contracts per leg, you may consider doing six on the long side and only three on the short side.

Another way to handle this situation is to enter the long leg sooner than entering the short leg. If you plan to be trading weekly binaries with this approach, you would buy the long contracts on Monday and wait to see what will happen to the underlying, and then only enter the short leg once market direction is established.

These similar tactics can be performed with other technical studies such as trend lines, Fibonacci levels, and even moving average support areas. The level of aggressiveness in moving your option strike prices, selling earlier, or skewing the number of contracts that you plan to trade depends on you and your risk appetite.

Contrarian Analysis

As you may recall from the previous section, you need to trade underlying instruments that are likely to revert to the mean. Reverting to the mean means that when an instrument makes a significant move in a specific direction, it bounces back in the other direction.

With an instrument that tends to revert to the mean, a large move in one direction is usually followed by a large move in the other direction. If you get into a volatility short spread on the wrong side of one of these moves, you can get yourself into trouble fairly quickly. At the same time, you can use these moves to skew your trades to your advantage.

Let's look at some examples to further clarify this contrarian concept:

Let's assume that the S&P futures are trading at 1310, but they have gone up by 3 to 5 percent for the past three weeks in a row. You also realize that the S&P futures are below the 200-week moving average and the overall trend and market sentiment are down. You may decide that the market is overextended to the upside.

Exhibit 16.17 depicts an extended upward move below the 200-period moving average.

Let's say that once again your volatility short strategy is designed for you to take binary option trades 3 percent away from the market price of the underlying. Therefore, at 1310 you would be looking to make trades at

EXHIBIT 16.17 Upward Movement

least 39.3 points away from the market price. The option that you would sell would have a strike price of at least 1349.3, and the options that you would normally buy should have a strike price of 1279.7 or lower.

Based on the fact that you are seeing the market overextended to the upside, you may decide to sell the out-of-the-money a little closer to the market price. Since you are expecting a drop in the price of the underlying, you may decide to either not buy the in-the-money option at all or to buy it a bit farther away if there are strike prices available.

For example, if the S&P futures are trading at 1310, you can sell the out-of-the-money option at 1340 instead of 1349 and buy the in-the-money option at 1270 or 1280 instead of 1279.

Exhibit 16.18 depicts the P&L of going long a binary option and short a binary option. The x-axis represents the price of the underlying, and the y-axis represents the P&L. If at expiration the underlying has closed below the short position and/or above long position, the trader will profit.

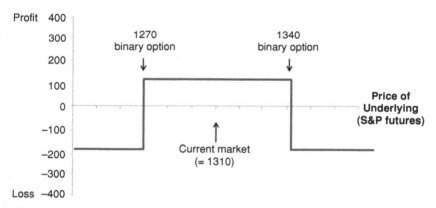

EXHIBIT 16.18   P&L Graph of a Short Volatility Binary Option Trade

Another thing you can do is to wait for the market to establish direction before entering the option position of where you think the market will go. For example, in this case you can sell the out-of-the-money option right away but wait for the market to drop and establish clear direction before buying the in-the-money option.

You can also skew these trades with the number of contracts that you trade. In the example mentioned here, you would sell more out-of-the-money option contracts than you would buy in-the-money option contracts.

Here are a few key theories to keep in mind about this type of analysis. First, this analysis works in both upward and downward moves. So you can implement it if you feel that the market is overextended to the upside or to the downside.

Additionally, it is very important to be careful with this approach. You don't want to buy or sell options really close just because you feel the market is extended. With the S&P futures, it's a good idea for the moves in a specific direction to be during multiple periods on the chart. For example, if you are looking at daily moves, you will want to see three to five days of a move in the same direction. With weekly charts, a move over two to four weeks in a row may be sufficient.

Another key aspect here is that you want to pay attention to news announcements and economic data releases that will affect the underlying instrument. If there is a major announcement like the federal funds rate or the nonfarm payroll during the week, you should be more careful and not modify your trade based on just technical analysis. At the same time, option profitability will be available farther away from the market during those times, so you will be able to buy in-the-money options and sell out-of-the-money options farther away from market price and still stand to collect sufficient returns on your trades.

Rolling Out

The contrarian analysis can be taken even one step further when you implement the principles of rolling out. Rolling out is an approach where you basically always expect the underlying instrument to snap back and revert to the mean in a short time frame.

The way to roll out is to actually not cut your trades and take on a loss. But once you take on the loss, you will enter the same trade for the following time period without changing the strike price.

Let's look at an example to clarify this concept. Let's assume that the S&P futures are trading at 1350 and you sell a 1360 out-of-the-money options with the hope to collect a $20 premium. The collateral that you will put up on the trade is $80.

Exhibit 16.19 is an option chain of US 500 binary options.

Let's assume that as soon as you enter the trade the price of the S&P futures shoots up toward 1360 and actually closes the week out at 1375.

With a rolling-out strategy, you would not cut the trade. Instead, you would simply sell the 1360 option again next week. Now this option will be in-the-money and the premium on it may be $70. You would need to put up collateral of $30 to enter the trade. If the market snaps back and moves down now, you would collect $70 on the 1360 option and this would make up for part of the $80 loss that you incurred.

You can even combine a cutoff strategy with a rolling-out strategy. Let's demonstrate how this works with the same example. Now as the market moves against you, let's assume that you decide to cut your trade rather than stay in it all the way until expiration. Let's assume that you cut your trade when the S&P futures are at 1360 and the price of the binary option that you sold is at $50. You would lose $40 on the trade when you cut your trade off.

Now you can wait for next week and sell your option again. Let's once again assume that the S&P futures will be trading at 1375. You would sell

Contract	Bid	Offer
Daily US 500 (Mar) > 1380	2.1	5
Daily US 500 (Mar) > 1375	4.5	7
Daily US 500 (Mar) > 1370	8	10
Daily US 500 (Mar) > 1365	17	20
Daily US 500 (Mar) > 1360	20	24
Daily US 500 (Mar) > 1355	36.1	40.1
Daily US 500 (Mar) > 1350	48.1	51.6
Daily US 500 (Mar) > 1345	60.1	63.1
Daily US 500 (Mar) > 1340	71.2	73.9
Daily US 500 (Mar) > 1335	75.8	77.4
Daily US 500 (Mar) > 1330	80	84
Daily US 500 (Mar) > 1325	90.2	93.4
Daily US 500 (Mar) > 1320	95.4	98.4

EXHIBIT 16.19 Binary Option Chain

the 1360 option for a premium of $70. If the market does move down, you can collect the $70 premium on the 1360 option and actually more than make up for your loss from the previous week.

Needless to say, you should be extremely careful with this approach. If the market makes a strong move in one direction, you may end up experiencing loss after loss, which can eventually eat up your account. Once again, the decision of whether to implement this strategy should strongly depend on your risk appetite and tolerance.

Overall Trend Analysis

Unlike other trading systems, when using a volatility short approach, you do not need specific technical or fundamental parameters in order to enter your trade and predict direction. The key with a volatility short system is to put every possible edge on your side.

One way to do this is to determine the overall market trend. This should not be a subjective analysis since you do not want to get into a situation when you are justifying an emotional trade. Instead, this should be an objective analysis. With an objective analysis, you need to determine how you will determine trend.

A simple way to do this would be to use a moving average. You can incorporate a moving average filter into your historical analysis of the magnitude of the moves of the underlying instrument. Let's look at the table again. See Exhibit 16.20.

EXHIBIT 16.20 Daily S&P 500 Futures, Five-Year Intervals

	-6+% changes	-5% changes	-4% changes	-3% changes	-2% changes	2% changes	3% changes	4% changes	5% changes	6+% changes
1/9/2012–1/9/2007 # of weeks:	10	14	27	39	58	57	30	19	13	8
percentage:	3.86%	5.41%	10.42%	15.06%	22.39%	22.01%	11.58%	7.34%	5.02%	3.09%
1/8/2007–1/8/2002 # of weeks:	2	3	5	10	28	26	11	4	2	1
percentage:	0.78%	1.16%	1.94%	3.88%	10.85%	10.08%	4.26%	1.55%	0.78%	0.39%
1/7/2002–1/7/1997 # of weeks:	3	5	13	19	41	51	24	13	3	2
percentage:	1.16%	1.94%	162.50%	7.36%	15.89%	19.77%	9.30%	5.04%	1.16%	0.78%
Total: # of weeks:	15	22	45	68	127	134	65	36	18	11
percentage:	1.94%	2.84%	5.81%	8.77%	16.39%	17.29%	8.39%	4.65%	2.32%	1.42%
1/7/1997–1/9/2012 Grand Total: # of weeks:	15	22	45	68	127	138	65	36	18	11
percentage:	1.71%	2.50%	5.12%	7.74%	14.45%	15.70%	7.39%	4.10%	2.05%	1.25%

Note: Calculated only for five-day and four-day weeks. Open intervals (i.e., 3% changes = 3+%).

As an example, let's analyze a 3 percent downward move. Based on Exhibit 16.20, this move happened 15 percent of the time. If you pull up historical data, you can determine what percent of the time the move happened when the market was above the 50-week moving average and what percentage of the time such a move happened when the market was below the 50-week moving average.

The in-depth data for the S&P 500 moves can be found on www.traderschoiceoptions.net. This research was purposely omitted from the book as you should do it on your own and test various instruments and moving averages. Once again, the level of a filter really depends on your risk appetite. Some people are perfectly fine using very strict filters and entering 5 to 10 trades per year to capture only a 5 percent annual return. At the same time, other people want to trade every day and earn 100 percent per year. Of course, the latter option has a higher risk than the former one.

There are two factors to consider when performing this test. First, don't overoptimize the data; test only major moving averages. Overoptimization works well only with historical data. It is best to use the major averages like the 50, 100, and 200 exponential moving averages (EMA) or simple moving averages (SMA). Test them out and see which ones work best. Once again, the idea here is not to find the perfect entry but to put the odds in your favor.

Once you determine what you believe to be the overall trend, you can implement the same principles in your trading. You can modify the distance from the market price, the number of contracts, and the time from expiration when you make your trade.

Staggering Into Your Trade

Many traders like to base their initial decision on some kind of a catalyst and start their trade with only one leg in a volatility short spread.

For example, when trading weekly options on Monday or early on Tuesday, you may first enter the trade based on what you believe to be your forecasted direction. For example, if you see a strong resistance area in the market that the underlying is approaching, then you would sell only out-of-the-money options initially. Once a day passes and the market adjusts, you would enter both legs of the trade based on the proper distance of your trading system, that is, 3 percent. Once another day passes, you would enter your trade again. The idea here is to stagger into your trade over the course of the week rather than enter all at once.

Let's look at an example of how you would do this. Let's once again assume that you are trading the S&P futures and that they are trading at 1320. Let's also assume that you notice a strong support area at 1300. Finally, let's assume that your account and risk management settings allow for you to trade 10 contracts per leg and you plan to sell options at least 3 percent away from market price. See Exhibit 16.21.

EXHIBIT 16.21 Staggered Trade Entry

Day of the Week	Leg 1	Leg 2	Strike Price
Day 1	50% (catalyst)	0%	3% away from market if available
Day 2	50%	100%	3% away from market if available
Expiration	Expiration	Expiration	N/A

A way to handle this strategy is to get into only the long leg of your trade on Monday with only three contracts. Let's assume that on Monday the price of the S&P futures moves down to 1310. Now you would enter into more contracts on Tuesday but this time you want to be 3 percent away from 1310 rather than 1320. So on Tuesday you would get into three more contracts at 1270, and now you can also sell three contracts above 1310 at 1349. Of course, you would enter the trade only if there are options available at those price points.

Let's assume that on Wednesday the S&P futures move up in price to 1340. Now you can buy the remaining four in-the-money contracts at 1299 (3 percent below market price) and you can sell two to three more contracts at 1380. Notice that you should be more careful with the out-of-the-money options since your initial analysis forecasted an upward move.

If all goes well, by expiration none of the strike prices will be breached. If they are breached, you will not have to cut your entire position and still may end up being profitable on your trade.

The advantage to this kind of approach is that you are more fluid with the market when setting your strike prices. The disadvantage is that there may not be enough premium/profit available on your latter entry days. Therefore, the system is a bit more conservative than just getting into your trade all in one day.

RULE 7: ATTEMPT TO MAKE YOUR MARKET

As previously discussed, binary options have an entry commission cost, an exit commission cost, and a settlement fee that will be charged only if you are profitable. Additionally, binary options will have a spread between the bid and the ask price of each option.

Also, as we previously discussed, the idea when trading binary options is to put all of the odds in your favor. One way to do this is to consistently try to get a better fill than what's available on the options chain. For example, if you are trying to buy an in-the-money option and the bid/offer pricing is 77.25 by 79, try to get in the middle of that spread and purchase at 78.

The way to do this is by placing a limit order when you enter the trade. This is especially effective when you are not in an extreme hurry to get in. You can throw a few limit orders up and hope to get filled.

For example, if you are trading a weekly strategy on Monday, you can be very aggressive with your limit orders. Your buy orders can be on the bid, and your sell orders can be on the offer. If you don't get in by Tuesday, in the morning you can get a little less aggressive with your orders. For example, you can place them right in between the spread.

If you still don't get in by Tuesday afternoon, you can fully ease up and do whatever it takes to get into the trade. If you need to, you can buy at the ask and sell at the bid.

Although this approach will take a little more time, it can really add up over a substantial number of trades, especially when the binary option spreads are high. Whether to implement this strategy is really a question of how much time you have to allocate to this approach.

CONCLUSION

Are you ready to step into the binary options trading world? At the very least, now you should know the basics, such as what instruments the options are traded on and how they work. You should be able to make basic directional trades and understand how the concepts of collateral and settlement work. To take things up a level, you should know how volatility long and short spreads work and how to combine them with basic market analysis.

Finally, it is time to create your own strategy. Hopefully, this book has laid out the ground rules. As you can see, you need to plan for your trading, know yourself, and design your system with yourself in mind. With all this said, you absolutely must have and adhere to a strong risk and money management plan.

If this is not enough, by reading the last section, you should get the idea of the basics of volatility short trading. Known as premium collection in the vanilla option world, this approach can be carried over to binary options. Of course, there are advantages and disadvantages of volatility short trading with binaries. The biggest advantage is that the disaster factor risk is gone since binary options are fully collateralized and you can never lose more than you put in no matter how drastically the market moves against you.

If you don't like volatility short trading, there are plenty of other strategies that you can implement with binary options. Did you ever try to look for technical trends in economic data releases? The possibilities are literally endless. And with only as small amount of money necessary to start trading this product, just about anyone can dive right in and enjoy the exciting ride.

KEY POINTS: PART 7

To take a quiz on this section, simply visit our companion education site, www.traderschoiceoptions.net.

- Premium collection is a method of trading in which you bet on an underlying instrument staying within a certain range. This strategy is based on the idea of normal distribution, which suggests that an instrument is most likely to be at the same price at the beginning and end of a time interval.

- Binary options make this strategy more effective by limiting the potential losses.

- In order to manage risk, it is best to cut any losses at a certain percentage of potential gains.

- It is also essential to ensure that the range that you speculate the instrument will stay within is wide enough that you collect enough premium to cover commissions, bid-ask spreads, and risk of losses.

- The distance that your strike prices should be from the market price is a function of many things, including your cutoff parameters, market volatility, and option premiums.

- When using premium collection strategies, it is best to speculate on underlying instruments that have a tendency to hold toward a mean price rather than trend.

- It is best to use binary options with less duration in volatility short trading, as this minimizes exposure to extreme movements in the market.

- When using volatility short trading systems, it is in your interest to do extra research to get an idea of where it is going/where it is not going in order to increase profitability.

- You can use basic technical analysis (identifying trends, resistance or support levels, patterns, etc.) to adjust your volatility short spreads and increase returns.

- Contrarian analysis (betting on the market reversing a recent trend) can also be used to adjust volatility short spreads and boost returns.

- Staggering into trades involves entering each leg in your volatility short spread separately (and possibly even with multiple trades per leg) over the first few days of a week. This conservative approach decreases risk by making your trade more fluid with the market but can also reduce your returns.

- A final way to increase profitability on volatility short spreads is to use limit orders to attempt to buy in-the-money at a price lower than the ask and sell out-of-the-money at a price higher than the bid.

Glossary

At-the-Money The strike price of an option contract and the price of the underlying asset on which the option is based are at the same level.

Bid The current price to sell an option.

Binary Option Also known as digital options or all-or-nothing options. They are a type of options derivative. Binary options can be considered a yes-or-no proposition—either the event happens or it does not.

Buying Volatility Speculation that the underlying asset will make a large move without necessarily picking direction.

Call A call option gives the owner the right to purchase the underlying instrument at a particular price (known as the strike price) any time before expiration.

Ceiling Also known as the maximum gain, or the most you can profit on a binary option trade.

Collateral The amount of money a trader will need to provide in order to trade a binary option. If the trader's assumption is correct, the trader will be given back the collateral plus profit.

Commission Fees charged by a broker or exchange to trade.

Commodity Physical goods, such as oil, corn, or gold.

Commodity Future Futures contracts that can be used to speculate or hedge on various physical commodities.

Contract A trading unit for a derivative instrument. Binary options are traded in contracts.

Currency Pair Currencies are always quoted in pairs, such as GBP/USD or USD/JPY. The reason they are quoted in pairs is that in every foreign exchange transaction, you are simultaneously buying one currency and selling another.

Daily Expiration Contracts that expire at the end of the trading day. Daily binary options expire each day at 4:15 P.M. EST.

Directional Trading Speculating on whether an underlying market will go up or down.

Economic Event A report released by a government agency that depicts a specific part of the economy.

Expiration The point at which a contract is no longer tradable.

259

Floor   Also known as the maximum risk, or the most you can lose on a binary option trade.

Futures   A contract that says that the buyer or seller will purchase or sell a specific asset for a specific price at a specific time in the future.

Hedging   Using options, futures, or binary options to protect the value of a corresponding asset class that is either owned or currently being traded.

Historic Volatility   The actual volatility of a financial instrument over a given period of time.

Implied Volatility   The estimated volatility of a security's price. In general, implied volatility increases when the market is bearish and decreases when the market is bullish.

In-the-Money   In-the-money means that an option contract is worth money. If a trader buys a binary option and the underlying asset is above the strike price of the binary, the binary is in-the-money. If a trader sells a binary option and the underlying asset is below the strike price of the binary, the binary is in-the-money.

Intraday   Contracts that expire throughout the day. With intraday binary options you can choose from binaries that expire at 11 A.M., 12 P.M., 2 P.M., and 4:15 P.M. EST. These options expire within a trading day.

Leg   An options term that refers to one side of a spread transaction. For instance, a trader might buy a call option that has a particular strike price and expiration date, then combine it with a put option that has the same strike price and a different expiration date. The two options are called legs of the spread.

Limit Order   A type of pending order.

Long Position   Buying a particular asset class. With binary options trading, taking a long position means speculating that an underlying asset will settle above the binary option's strike price.

Long Volatility   A binary option strategy that consists of buying a binary option with a strike price above an underlying asset's market price and also selling a binary option with a strike price below the underlying asset's market price. Long volatility strategies are used when an assumption is made that an underlying asset will move in one direction or another.

Margin   Funds that are required to trade vanilla options and futures. Typically, the amount of margin required is a small percentage of the overall contract cost. When trading on margin, a trader is using a small amount of money to control a larger amount of an asset class.

Maximum Loss   The most money that can be lost on a binary option trade.

Maximum Profit   The most money that can be made on a binary option trade.

Natural Market Consensus   The general consensus of all market participants currently trading in a particular asset class.

Offer   The current price to buy an option. Also known as the "ask" price.

Option Chain   A list of the available option strike prices on a particular underlying asset.

Option Delta   A parameter of the option that depicts its sensitivity to the price movement of the underlying market on which the option is based.

Option Spread   An option strategy that involves buying and selling multiple options.

Out-of-the-Money   Out-of-the-money means that an option contract is not worth money. If a trader buys a binary option and the underlying asset is below the strike price, the binary is out-of-the-money. If a trader sells a binary option and the underlying asset is above the strike price, the binary is out-of-the-money.

Price Quote   How the value of an asset class is displayed. The bid and offer are shown side by side in a binary option quote. Example: 30 bid/33 offer.

Put   A put option gives the owner the right to sell the underlying instrument at an agreed-upon price (the option's strike price) any time before expiration.

Selling Volatility   Speculating that the underlying asset will remain in a certain range by expiration.

Settlement Fee   Fees charged by a broker if a binary option is held until expiration.

Settlement Value   The price of a binary option contract at expiration.

Short Position   Selling a particular asset class. With binary options trading, taking a short position means speculating that an underlying asset will settle below the binary option's strike price.

Short Volatility   An option strategy that consists of selling a binary option with a strike price above an underlying asset's market price and also buying a binary option with a strike price below the underlying asset's market price. Short volatility strategies are used when an assumption is made that an underlying asset will stay within a range.

Speculation   Attempting to profit from forecasting the movements of an asset.

Spot Forex   The abbreviation for the foreign exchange, or currency, market. The forex market is considered a spot market. A spot market is any market that deals in the current price of a financial instrument. Retail spot forex is traded via forex-dealing firms and banks.

Stock Index   A basket of stocks that is constructed to reflect and track a particular market or sector.

Stock Index Future   Futures contracts based on a variety of global and domestic stock indexes. They can be used to speculate on the price direction of a stock market index or hedge (protect) against a sudden price decrease of a portfolio of stocks.

Strangle   An options strategy involving buying or selling options with different strike prices that will profit if the underlying asset remains in a tight range or moves outside of the range. With binary options, to go long strangle, you would sell a strike price lower than the market price, and you would buy a strike price higher than the market price. To go short strangle, you would buy the strike price lower than the market price and sell the strike price higher than the market price.

Strike Price   The true or false condition relative to the underlying market. More simply put, the strike price is your price target to be achieved or not achieved based on your position (long or short).

Time Decay   The relationship of an options price relative to the amount of time until it expires.

Time Value   The amount of time until expiration. An option with more time until expiration has a higher chance of being settled in-the-money than an option with less time until expiration.

Traditional (Vanilla) Option   Derivative instruments that are exchange traded. An option gives the owner the right to buy or sell the underlying instrument at a particular price. Options are traded on various instruments such as individual stocks, futures, currencies, and indexes.

Underlying Asset   The asset on which a binary option contract is based. Example: US 500 binary option is based on the S&P 500 futures.

Volatility Trading   Speculating on whether the volatility of an underlying market will increase or decrease. Volatility trading means that you are not trying to predict a direction in the market. You are simply speculating whether the market will stay in a certain range or will come out of the range in either direction.

Weekly Expiration   Contracts that expire each trading week. Weekly binary option contracts expire Friday at various times throughout the day, depending on the underlying asset.

Index